THERAPEUTIC
MASTERY

THERAPEUTIC MASTERY

Becoming a More Creative and Effective Psychotherapist

CHARLES H. KRAMER, M.D.

ZEIG, TUCKER & CO., INC.
PHOENIX, ARIZONA

Published by

ZEIG, TUCKER & Co., INC.
3618 North 24th Street
Phoenix, AZ 85016

Manufactured in the United States of America

Library of Congress Cataloging-in-Publication Data

Kramer, Charles H.
  Therapeutic mastery : becoming a more creative and effective
therapist / Charles H. Kramer.
      p. cm.
  Includes bibliographical references and index.
  ISBN 1-891944-42-8
      1. Psychotherapy. 2. Psychotherapist and patient. I. Title.

RC480.5.K69 2000
616.89'14—dc21

                                                              00-024659

                10 9 8 7 6 5 4 3 2

This book is dedicated to Jan—
my very best teacher—
in therapy—
in life.

ACKNOWLEDGMENTS

Several people have been of inestimable help in shaping this book.

Our son Dan, creative writing major, psychotherapist, and philosopher, coached me through every revision during the past ten years. His editing skills, knowledge of therapy dynamics, and wise philosophy of life have been a never-failing support and inspiration.

Since the early 1970s, Sandra Watanabe-Hammond has been a priceless colleague and dear friend. Her workshops and conferences opened my eyes to a new and powerful understanding of the human psyche that transformed both my practice and myself. She helped with Chapter 6.

Bob Shaw, contextual psychiatrist, family therapist, and charismatic teacher, inspired many of the concepts and techniques described in Part V.

Larry Feldman, trusted colleague and friend since the early 1970s, and his wife, Sandy, read the nearly finished manuscript and gave me new insights.

Teaching the idea of use of self has been fine-tuned in many conversations with Michele Baldwin, friend of Virginia Satir and writer about her.

Chip Kramer and Mary Pittman offered a number of helpful suggestions, as did Rev. Ken Phifer and Lucy Bauman of our Unitarian Universalist Church. Several students and patients, who prefer to remain anonymous, provided useful feedback about their experiences with me. Bill Pinsof, my successor at The Family Institute, good-naturedly put up with my insistence on teaching my approach to therapy.

And Suzi Tucker shepherded the book from a rambling, overlong diatribe to the more or less finished product.

Table of Contents

Introduction

Where no counsel is, the people fall; but in the multitude of counselors there is safety.

—Proverbs 11:14*

Q: What is the secret to doing good work?
A: Never to accept anything without question. Never ignore an inner voice that tells you something could be better, even when other people tell you it's okay.

—Frank Sinatra[1]

*Biblical quotations throughout are from the King James version.

T his book is designed to aid you—therapist, counselor, healer—to enhance your natural, already-in-motion creativity that runs like a red thread throughout your life, both inside and outside therapy. Not the quick fix but the enduring change is what this book is about.

I use myself, students, patients, and others as examples, both good and bad. I write about myself as a therapist, as a teacher, and as a person. Real-life illustrations show how techniques of self-improvement can be a path to becoming more effective as a therapist—and a human being. I trust Emerson's,[2] "To believe that what is true for you in your private heart is true for all . . . is genius."

Our humanity is essential for therapeutic chemistry. Being fully present conveys a powerful message to the patient, that of the ability to really listen. Relaxed attentiveness increases the magic and decreases the misery. Shaping therapy so that it works is an art that emanates from our creativity. And art that inspires, as good therapy does, is deeply spiritual, transcendent. I'm sure you have those moments.

Our consulting rooms are sanctuaries where the spirit of the process blossoms, where safety, intimacy, and deep emotion transform lives. The space and time wherein people are exclusively and seriously devoted to the work have the feel of a sacred quest. This book articulates my sense of the surpassing power of psychotherapy.

Competence and success as practitioners grow as we move toward maturity in our personal lives. Life has a strong impact on the nature of professional life, and vice versa. When you are creating a satisfying private life, you are well on the way to a gratifying practice.

The world operates according to tendencies, patterns, and cycles far more profound than anything in books, including this one. It is tempting to call them "laws of life," but they do not function with the rigidity and certainty of laws. Perhaps we can count on them three-fourths of the time. The rest we simply do not grasp at this stage of understanding. This book illustrates many of these "tendencies."

In the slice of life called therapy, the mystery of existence gets played out. There's more to life than psychotherapy—and more to psychotherapy than psychotherapy, to paraphrase famed basketball coach Phil Jackson.[3] Our philosophy of life, our assumptions about mind and spirit, are the foundation upon which we can build unique methods to enhance creativity and personal development.

With steady motivation our innate endowments ripen into self-improvement. Attentive mindfulness, so crucial to effective therapy, can now be learned by anyone using the psychospiritual practices that were not available in my training days. Thus the practitioner models an attitude that engenders beneficial changes. Furthermore, these techniques can be taught to willing patients, thereby accelerating treatment. Training programs do not devote enough time and expertise to the personal development of the aspirant. This book, it is hoped, begins to fill that gap.

This approach can be used by therapists of every persuasion and utilizes any relevant theories and techniques, including those we might invent. My goal is to benefit diverse therapists and patients without such constraints as gender, race, ethnicity, handicap, sexual orientation, religious belief, or clinical syndrome.

I offer this writing in hopes that my evolution toward professional and personal mastery (still beyond reach) might be useful for you. I do not offer *the way*. Rather, I describe my experience as clearly as I can in order to give you images for comparing and contrasting yours. You might decide to try something my way. Or a modification. Or just the opposite. Or ignore it altogether. Or come up with something uniquely yours.

Therapy proceeds simultaneously in two interpenetrating worlds, outer and inner. They are so closely intertwined that we seldom think of them as different. Yet for learning and doing therapy, and for evolving as an ever-more-competent therapist, temporarily separating the two is valuable. The principle is this: differentiate and thoroughly understand the parts, then integration is easier, more meaningful, and more effective. We can use the same principle to facilitate all learning.

The *outer world of therapy* is our everyday domain. Taught and practiced everywhere, it fills our professional journals, makes up the majority of training programs, and dominates our conferences. It is the world of many theories, many methods, many techniques for doing therapy. It has to do with diagnosis, treatment outcome, grants, reimbursement, organizations, standards, credentials, and so on. This is a familiar bread-and-butter world. For some therapists it is the *only* world.

But there is another world, the *inner world of therapy*—the subjective realm: thoughts, feelings, attitudes, behavior, emotions, therapeutic experiences, memories, life history, level of evolution toward maturity, inner cast of characters, style, opinions, personal story, family life, spiritual inclinations, philosophical beliefs. Students get little help with developing their inner world. At most, they are advised to enter therapy, thus sequestering personal growth from teaching and supervision. They are not shown how to integrate their maturation, seasoning, and self-mastery in the consultation room.

I write about your inner world of therapy. There is an abundance of resources about the outer world. The dearth of help in evolving our inner world is my compelling motivation. You can take everything I say with more than a grain of salt, see how it fits with your personality, and what—if anything—is useful in your practice.

For more than 50 years, I have studied, practiced, and taught an array of healing modalities: general practice of medicine and surgery; geriatric medicine; adult and geriatric psychiatry; child psychiatry and therapy; adult and child psychoanalysis; marital, family, group, and milieu therapy. I have attended and conducted numerous classes, workshops, and conferences dealing with relationships, communication, multiple internal selves, body work, Eastern and Western philosophy, morality and spirituality, altered states of consciousness, and more. I have been taught, lectured, scolded, advised, pontificated at, and instructed by dozens of teachers of therapy of all shades from rookie to internationally prestigious. I take bits of each to sculpt a way of my own.

But far more influential is what I learn from life, from practicing, and from therapists. Much transformation grows out of an ever-more-

loving marriage since 1945 with Jan, herself an accomplished therapist, teacher, and author. For decades, in addition to working solo,
we have done cotherapy, cosupervision, coconsultation, coteaching,
coauthoring, coadministration. Vicissitudes of coparenting six psychologically minded children further enrich clinical skills. Two sons,
a daughter, and a daughter-in-law practice a variety of psychothera-
pies, and a granddaughter is majoring in counseling. (Dan, therapist–
philosopher–son, says it takes only one of us to change a light bulb,
but 19 to talk about it!) Your life, however different from mine, offers
many opportunities for nurturing your creative potential.

Self-examination, so characteristic of introverted thinkers, became
habitual during 12 years of psychoanalysis. Then for 25 years Jan and
I explored our relationships in a variety of settings, volunteering for
observed interviews, exercises, and other uncomfortable exposures.
We took our children and their partners—later they took us. We par-
ticipated in individual, couple, and family therapy.

We began doing cotherapy in 1970. Feedback from several hundred
audio- and videotapes of us at work and in our own family discussions
produced perspectives hard to get any other way. Reactions to our
work have been solicited from patients, students, supervisees, consultees, and family members.

I have had in therapy more than 300 therapists: medical specialists;
psychiatrists; psychoanalysts; nurses; clinical, counseling, and educational psychologists; clergy; social workers; counselors. They conduct every form of psychotherapy. Most have been in treatment before. We have spent from a few to hundreds of hours in several formats: individual therapy and analysis, couples, two and three generations, couples groups, family groups, and assorted combinations.

Once I grasped the new family paradigm of self-regulating systems,
I began supervising mental health professionals. By 1960 I had seen
35 supervisees for 300 hours. Now it's hundreds of therapists for several thousand hours. I have done 500 observed family consultations
with therapists having difficulties. Many were taped for study.

Recognizing the clinical significance of a therapist's personality was
intriguing. As a family therapy pioneer (I started doing couple therapy
in 1954), I have known the first-generation family therapists, watched
them work, talked with them professionally and personally, known
them as people when they stayed with us for weekends.

But it was confusing. Each therapist had a unique way of working
and unique explanation. Moreover, there were no one-to-one corre-

lations between techniques and theories. Virginia Satir got everyone hugging and crying. Murray Bowen expounded intellectually about differentiating from each other. Don Jackson made puzzling contradictory suggestions. Fritz Midelfort spoke of religious values. Nat Ackerman plunged into the oedipal triangle. Yet families responded positively regardless of these differences. I gradually realized that each "method" was an accurate expression of each personality. I was hearing *opinions* about the interview facts.

A common denominator jumped out. *They were being themselves, in their own distinctive style.* Passionate commitment to take on the family, a sincere intention of being helpful, offering authentic bits of self—these qualities are irresistible. And exactly what every therapist, including you and me, can give to people.

But our field has emphasized techniques and theories for *doing* therapy and has virtually ignored techniques and theories for *becoming* a better person and therapist. As a result, we teach and learn the less essential while downplaying the heart of therapeutic change: that special quality unfolding between therapist and patient.

I am not against learning techniques and theories. Learn them. Just remember that only what fits for you will be valuable. Become wedded to a method, be fascinated with what others do and say, and you neglect indispensable attention to the evolution of *your* way. Methods give an illusion of confidence, perhaps necessary for beginners. The sooner you give up this confining cage, the sooner you will create your own pioneering way—in each interview, with each person, with each family.

The right tool in the wrong hands leads to wrong results; the wrong tool in the right hands leads to right results. Nowhere is this more true than in our field. Useful techniques backfire in inept hands; "inadequate" ones work beautifully for a gifted therapist. We can develop "right hands" that create with any tool, or create a new tool.

Without teachers, first-generation family therapists took seriously their reactions to families. They intuitively invented methods based on these transactions and on their personalities and backgrounds. I write about them because I know them best. Other modalities— psychoanalysis, transactional analysis, gestalt, client-centered—were also rooted in the founder's personality.

Social revolutions are started by dissenters on the fringes of society. Their mind-boggling ideas attract like-minded followers who are, well, followers. Succeeding generations are less experimentally daring, more "normal," limited to the mainstream by third parties, yet also more comprehensive. If we mimic the appearance of the originators without really "getting" the substance, we mistake personal value judgments—opinions—for scientific truth.

So this book is loaded with opinions. *Anything* you read or hear will be someone's opinion about certain facts. At least, that's my opinion! I agree with Montaigne, who said, "There never were in the world two opinions alike, no more than two hairs or two grains; the most universal quality is diversity." Many opinions in this book can be tested empirically, and I hope they will be.

I risk exaggerating personality and minimizing method for several reasons. We have plenty of therapy technique books. Excessive intellectualization in the whole field needs counterbalancing. Therapists are mechanical and unauthentic when they neglect intuition and feelings. The nonverbal and the nonrational, being harder to express, call for more exposure. Creativity requires synthesis of intellect and intuition.

I write about similarities and contrasts between the beginner and the advanced, neither denigrating the one nor glorifying the other. Recalling what I have learned from both, I often compare myself of years ago with myself now. "Bad and good" is not intended (although sometimes I do preach!). Many differences have more to do with life stages.

I used to do better with some clinical situations: hospital work; couples deciding to live together, get married, have a baby; schizophrenics. Today I prefer work with older folks—retirement, grandparenting, chronic illness, dying, and philosophy of life are my current preoccupations. Different phases of life present different challenges and illuminations. Some ideas I wish I had earlier, some ideas may be useful even if you are more seasoned.

For new learning, we resume beginnership, and beginnings are by no means the same for everyone. Family therapy trainees at the Family Institute often have trouble being students again after serving many years as practitioners. Buddhism recommends "beginner's mind"— wise naivete, open to everything. A good way to meet each day and each session.

Most of us went straight to learning about doing therapy, never paused to build an inner foundation of mind, emotion, body, and spirit. Thus we seldom learned how to learn. So we find it difficult to relearn. From time to time, the most experienced of us must go back to fundamentals—true in every realm of creativity.

I consult regularly with ten therapists who have practiced from a few to twenty-five years. They are fine clinicians. I have referred many people to them without adverse feedback. All are better than I am with specific clinical situations. I respect and care for them a lot. Yet from time to time, we each stumble over fundamentals. Anything that important is worth emphasizing.

Understanding my different states of conscious awareness has been essential to growing wholeness. For example, in January 1990 I underwent four-vessel coronary artery bypass heart surgery. Good friend Joel Lehrfield—Orthodox rabbi, psychologist, family therapist, wise old man—asked how my outlook on life had changed after the operation. "I got a computer to speed up writing because now I know without a doubt that I could die at any moment. I want to get on with it." Gently he said, "That's been true all your life, Chuck, but you didn't really *know* it until now!"

Profound changes in every aspect of life have flowed from my brush with death. Writing is a strong current in this flow. I enter a magical world, lost in putting words to recollections. Hours go by hardly noticed. I am unself-consciously driven by hidden creative forces. I feel an addictive pull. I forget myself. I am in "the Zone." My foot goes to sleep! I write to teach myself, to understand myself, to satisfy myself, to give reality to my experience. I join Montaigne[4] in asserting, "I have not made my book more than my book made me." This exciting and mystifying Zone occurs in every successful therapy.

As a struggling intern at Cook County Hospital, I was advised to: "See one. Do one. Teach one." This cynical comment on the killer 105-hour-per-week workload has a deeper meaning: Observing, doing, and teaching call for three quite different modes of consciousness. We do best when our state of mind matches the task at hand. Some people are limited to one mode; others mix inappropriate modes and tasks.

We readers also learn a lot from reading. We also learn from writing. I encourage you to go against out-of-date inhibitions and write. Anything. All it takes is getting started. You have a lot to say. Follow the advice in Revelations, "Write the things thou hast seen and the things which are." More on journaling later.

It is in your best interest to become comfortable with all these states of consciousness. What we learn in each is different. You become a deeper person and more powerful therapist. And the best way to solidify learning is to supervise and consult. So write and read, as well as see, do, and teach, for optimal learning.

My holistic integration trek culminated in five annual "Creative Use of Self" courses for advanced students where we interweave professional and personal stories to learn the parallels, differences, and mutual influences of the two realms. Evaluation of those techniques and theories that students find most practical is important for this writing.

Conducting therapy requires the courage to act despite our doubts. To begin classes I read this 2,500-year-old statement on the value of doubt.

> —Do not believe in what you have heard.
> —Do not believe in traditions because they have been handed down for many generations.
> —Do not believe in anything because it is rumored and spoken of by many.
> —Do not believe in anything merely because the written statement of some old sage (sic!) is produced.
> —Do not believe in conjectures.
> —Do not believe merely in the authority of your teachers and elders. After observation and analysis, when it agrees with reason, and is conducive to the good and benefit of one and all, then accept it and live up to it.
>
> Buddha[5]

The Buddha also has suggestions we can count on for analyzing and resolving doubt. The Four Buddhist Reliances are[6]:

> —First, rely on principle, not the person.
> —Second, rely on the spirit, not the letter.
> —Third, rely on wisdom, not conditioning.
> —Fourth, rely on complete teaching, not incomplete teaching.

Doubt is a product of the intellect. Like all mental functions, when relied on exclusively, it can be carried to extremes. Doubting every action, every thought, every feeling—everything—becomes analysis paralysis. Decisions must be made and actions taken despite lingering doubt. We act on incomplete information. So how do we move?

There is value in doubt's apparent opposite: *faith, belief.* Doubt needs leavening by intuition, by feelings, by our wish for effective action. Faith, a word seldom used by therapists, complements doubt. To move the enterprise, therapy takes faith. On both sides. We proceed believing that good things will happen. Because faith is nonrational and intuitional, we cannot prove it. Neither can we wait forever to act. Timing is all.

We enter a mess with trepidation born of realistic doubt, but also with faith that somehow things will work out. Intellect and intuition are both essential. Reason without faith is narrow and uncreative, faith without reason is superstitious and foolhardy—trying to fly on one wing. I write about many pairs of seeming opposites that are necessary to each other.

In describing therapy, I compare it to a 90-mile sail across Lake Michigan from Chicago to Saugatuck. We'll be out of sight of land. I can't predict how how long it will take, the weather, the route, the surprises. But the boat is prepared and sound, the crew knowledgeable, I have made it safely before, and I have faith we will get there. *Reasoned*, not blind, faith. Proof is the voyage itself.

As Saint Paul put it, "And what is faith? Faith gives substance to our hopes, and makes us certain of realities we do not see . . . The visible comes forth from the invisible" (*Hebrews*, 11:1–3). To be certain of realities we do not yet see is not only an expression of faith, but faith is a critical element in making the visible come forth from the invisible.

Fascinating research hints at this power. Subjects who believe in psychokinesis are able to influence a random-number generator; skeptics are not. Plants grow faster when prayed over. Heart patients not knowing they are being prayed for heal faster with fewer complications!

Faith is like a toothbrush. Use yours regularly, but don't use someone else's! Trust your inner knowing. Have a clear mind and an open heart. You won't have to search for direction, it will come to you. Have the faith to trust your doubting. Find a creative blend of intellectual doubt and intuitional faith, and go for it!

Now for an overview of this book. Each chapter offers self-development homework to amplify suggestions discussed in the text, to be studied alone or in a group. I encourage reflection and growth that you can build upon for a lifetime. Learn from your daily inner and outer worlds and change whatever might block creativity. Thich Nhat Hanh[7] says, "Our life is the instrument with which we experiment with the truth." I suggest ideas for experimentation that could be a shortcut on your journey. There's no need to go through all my meanderings. Just use what fits for you.

Part I. My therapeutic style. Attitude and stance for approaching every encounter. Framework for the treatment process from beginning to end. Identify essentials. Develop professional standards that serve your needs as well as those of third parties. Know and be yourself. Create your own therapy career path.

Part II. Know your inner selves and how useful they are in therapy. Importance of productive family-of-origin work. Insightful self-analysis for optimal functioning. Qualities and vulnerabilities of a good therapist. Consequences of your own therapy. Your moral and psychospiritual evolution, the forgotten dimensions.

Part III. Enhance your natural creativity. Exercises and procedures for building therapeutic mastery: meditation, journaling, synchronicity, body work, dream work, and more. Learn from your practice. Use everyday life, in and out of the office, to deepen growth and integrity.

Part IV. Modeling and self-disclosure are inevitable. Suggestions for when, what, how, to what purpose, and to whom we should reveal ourselves. Benefits and risks of timely self-disclosure. Handling treatment distractions, especially crises such as your illness. Find your effective and creative style of disclosure.

Part V. We are leaders, whether we like it or not. Discover your own comfortable and powerful leadership style. Significance for therapy outcome. Changing a belief system. Refining a vision. Maturity and mastery.

This book is about becoming effective without straining. It's about doing burnout-resistant therapy and living a burnout-resistant life. Difficult but doable, in our competitive, materialistic culture. And it's too easy for a book to make it sound too easy.

Become a better therapist by becoming a better person by becoming a student of life. Lessons are everywhere. Life is the great teacher. Respect the miracle of life and love the mystery.

We use only a fraction of our ultimate capacity. This guide opens a way toward fulfilling our potential for wholeness—as therapists, as human beings.

THERAPEUTIC
MASTERY

PART

I

The Therapist in Action

The development of general ability for independent thinking and judgment should always be placed foremost, not the acquisition of special knowledge. . . . It is not enough to teach a man a specialty. Through it he may become a kind of useful machine but not a harmoniously developed personality. It is essential that the student acquire an understanding of and a lively feeling for values. He must acquire a vivid sense of the beautiful and of the morally good.

—Albert Einstein[8]

To be nobody but yourself—in a world which is doing its best, night and day, to make you everybody else—means to fight the hardest battle any human being can fight and never stop fighting.

—e. e. cummings[9]

1

Doing Therapy Well

When research subjects are asked, "What was most helpful in the course of your therapy?", they almost never name a specific technique, interpretation, or theory. New therapists are shocked to find that those "important" topics are not mentioned. It turns out that effective therapy is a matter of the personality of the therapist. Former patients typically describe such qualities as these.

—No matter what I did or said, I never got clobbered.
—All was accepted, yet I was led to see where I had gotten on the wrong track, and helped to find a better way.
—It was really great to be able to say anything at all, no matter how shameful, and not be rejected.
—I became more courageous about my life after I heard about hers.
—Sometimes he had more trust and confidence in me than I had in myself. That helped me with confidence in myself. By the time I finally got that confidence, I was ready to quit.

These comments are not proof that people's descriptions are the true reasons for their success. We never know completely the "true" reasons. Good therapy is the outcome of an intricate concatenation of factors, many intangible, a lifelong mystery.

Yet former patients reinforce the notion that certain qualities are beneficial: careful listening, supportive understanding without judgment, compassion, caring, willingness to reveal one's self, respect, forbearance, sensing strengths that have been unavailable. In short, an *attitude* about the work, steadily and powerfully conveyed.

Changes during therapy largely result from a *transformative experience* that is deeply emotional and comes through meaningful connection with the therapist. Intellectual concepts and cognitions are also attained through mutual interchange. As you gain the know-how of theory and technique, you have to throw yourself into the action and put your heart on the line. Time to be brave. Time to be compassionate.

The most common complaints about therapy are the result of poor emotional connectedness.

—I never felt like I was with a real person.
—In three years of therapy, I never heard my analyst make a single comment or express an opinion about me.
—She seemed mechanical, like she was working from a book.
—I received neither encouragement nor criticism for what I did, which was okay at first, but eventually I wanted to know how I came across to him. I never found out, so I quit.

This book is for the practitioner who makes a living doing therapy, who gets satisfaction from being a useful agent in people's lives. I emphasize the fundamentals of making transformative connections, doing therapy well. I risk repeating what may have been pounded into you in graduate school. I risk oversimplification. And I risk sounding as though I have all the right answers for everyone. I'll take those risks.

Truth

Emotional connectedness and truth go together. For patients to feel safe enough to see truth about themselves, the therapist must begin by being truthful.

A woman with 25 years of experience doing individual dynamic therapy comes for consultation because she is unable to make an emotional connection with a female patient. We get nowhere reviewing the interesting history. I ask about the opening of interviews. The patient always comes in and asks, "How are you?" Therapist replies, "Fine," even when she has a splitting headache that muddles thinking. I wonder, "Do you ever tell her the truth?" "No, that would go against what I have been taught." "But she wants an emotional connection as much as you, and sharing how you feel would begin an empathic linkage." "That would be unethical." We didn't have a second consult.

Nothing is more interesting, beautiful, and useful than truth, says William Zinsser[10] in his classic *On Writing Well*, which influenced this writing. The longer I work at this art/craft, the more I see that good therapy requires a persistent and discriminating search for truth. And the older I get, the less certain I am of the truth, or even *a* truth. I am more willing to stand by *my* truth and the *patient's* truth. Finding truth—more accurately, *many* truths—about ourselves really does set us free. But truths are hard to come by. So is freedom.

Great truths can be expressed so simply that they might be dismissed as platitudes. Yet complicated truths—they all are—remain abstract and utopian until fleshed out by clarification. Then we find that all have exceptions and are subject to many, often conflicting, interpretations. Arthur Schopenhauer says that all truths pass through three stages: first, ridicule; second, violent opposition; third, acceptance as self-evident.

Patients complain of what is "ego dystonic": uncomfortable phobias, depression, anxiety, psychosomatic *dis*-ease, obsessions, and compulsions—the meat and potatoes of individual psychotherapy. They also complain about behavior of others. They rarely complain about their ego-syntonic actions: clinging dependence, belligerence, impulsiveness, addictions. These unhealthy and harmful behaviors give some of us satisfaction, not discomfort, but are dystonic for others, making them uncomfortable. Disagreements whirl around what is "really" true, each not seeing as true what is syntonic for one's self, no matter how dystonic for the other. My workaholism, discussed later, is an example.

Treating one person at a time, I hear only partial truth. Sometimes hiding is conscious, particularly by addicts and acter-outers. More often, omissions and distortions are unwitting. Manic-depressives tell about symptoms that bother them, but often omit what bothers others. Family members and friends know about difficult behavior, often dangerous, but I remain uninformed until I include them. An itch for more objective truth motivated me to do so.

But I chase a will-o'-the-wisp—there many truths for each person, and many truths in any group. Often a truth from one perspective seems directly opposed to another, a paradox unfathomable to a logical left-brain thinker. I see A. N. Whitehead's[11] insight that there are no whole truths, only half-truths. Encompassing conflicting perspectives, multiple truths, is a necessity for family and group therapy, and enhances all therapy. Those of you who can hold ambiguity with little discomfort, probably innate yet learnable, are the most natural therapists. We logic-bound ones have to work harder for evenhandedness.

The useful concept of psychic truth has been around for a century. But the assumption that psychic truth equals actuality has led to great misunderstandings, some tragic. Freud got tangled up in this when he first heard women patients tell of sexual seduction by a male relative. He took the stories as true, but later decided that they were preposterous fantasies about what had happened. This view persisted unchallenged until recent years when the thorny problem of true versus false memories of sexual molestation exploded. Unfortunately, therapists who do only individual work do not check their patient's version of reality with others whose psychic truth must also be accounted for.

If truths are relative—are any absolute, short of metaphysical speculations?—how do we sort the likely from the unlikely? My rule-of-thumb: When we are well centered, truth strikes us as real, touches the heart, uplifts. When we are ready, truth gives us pause, sets us pondering, urges us to know more. John Keats puts it, "I never feel certain of any truth but from a clear perspective of its beauty." Learning truths about ourselves, we are well on the way to successful change. And the more insight we have into the truths of others, the more we learn about life. Centered, we can model our truths and reflect back windows of centering and truth in them. Meister Eckhart says, "Whatever I want to express in its truest meaning must emerge from within me and pass through an inner image. It cannot come from the outside to the inside."[12]

But some truths are uncomfortable. We don't want to know them if unflattering. The less centered we are, the less able we are to let in unpleasant realizations. The more deeply we bury a pain, the more we use our favored defenses to resist facing it. The more syntonic a truth, the easier it is to disavow it. Yet if therapy never jars with a painful truth, it has not gone very deep. The truth we need to hear often is the hardest to hear.

Conveying truth is tricky. Raw truth without preparation is a blunt instrument. It must be presented with kind tact, good taste, and right timing. With experience, we have a pretty good idea of what our patients might be in for if they stick with therapy and know themselves deeply. What we know may turn out to be true, but if they are not yet ready to hear it, we do more harm than good—as in all learning. A first grader just grasping addition won't be ready for algebra for many years.

Another drawback to truth: Self learning may set us free, but it does not make life easier. Often it makes things harder. Automatic is easy, certain, unambiguous. No agonizing. But truth about ourselves reveals the opposing opinions of several internal characters. We balance pros and cons, make choices. Many parts shy away from responsibility, clutching stubbornly to their wounds. The problem of finding truth leads to a solution, freedom from neurotic shackles, which becomes a new problem—what to do with freedom. Life truly is recursive.

Still, our task is to lead people to truth about themselves and their effect on others without their getting so upset that they run from therapy or bury truth even deeper. Speaking truths in this way makes euphemisms unnecessary, even counterproductive. I dislike the hypocrisy, the prudery, the deceit of not saying what I mean. Finding a way to tell someone a painful truth is central to our art. Dodging it reinforces evasiveness learned in childhood and makes your task together more difficult. So speak truths, providing you know them, and providing your listeners are ready to hear them. And prepare for the consequences. What we believe to be true about life and the authority for those beliefs passes through many changes (see Chapter 11).

Standards

We must take responsibility for our own standards of excellence. This happened early in general medical practice.

A laborer hobbles in with a knee the size of a grapefruit. The swelling is too big to diagnose without an x-ray. My mind whirls: 18 miles to the hospital, and I'm fresh out of internship with little confidence. Taking a deep breath, I announce that he must have an x-ray. He protests, "Just wrap it up." I flash on appalled instructors. In as firm and friendly a tone as I can muster, I explain why he needs an x-ray and that I will not treat him without it. Angrily, he hobbles out. I can see my small-town practice going down the drain, along with me, my wife, and our child. Later the druggist tells me the man loudly complained to a store full of people that "the no-good new doctor refused to take care of a person in pain," and asked for Ben-Gay to rub on his knee! From that day on, I had more patients than I could handle. It spread like wildfire that the new doc is young but up-to-date and insists on doing things right.

We should be on the side of better mental health for all the family, even when seeing just one member. This means a systems point of view, finding out what works for you, creating a place where you can do your work, and defending your standards until proved wrong.

Sometimes others set higher standards for us than feel right. Don't object. I was encouraged by supervisors and coaches who saw more potential for excellence in me than I did. After weighing the pros and cons, I often adopted their standards. But they should percolate through you until they feel right. Then they are your own.

The situation is more complicated when third-party payers, accreditors, teachers, supervisors try to hold you to standards you believe are not in your patients' best interests. They may strongly believe their yardsticks are "better." Somehow you must practice in accord with your values and still meet their demands by cooperating, or at least by not antagonizing them.

For example, I began family work while in training dominated by the theories and methods of Freud. When teachers heard what I was doing, I got a range of negative reactions from raised eyebrows, to well-intended warnings, to harsh criticism, to veiled threats about my future. Criticsms were many. Family therapy isn't deep. Doesn't produce "structural" change. Has no elegant theory. Is superficial and manipulative, not "psychoanalytic." Seeing husband and wife together, seeing parents with children, and videotaping are inherently unethical.

These fault findings were abstract, hypothetical, not grounded in experience. No critic had ever done one hour of family therapy. Blame came from therapists who nearly panicked at the idea. Twice, psychoanalyst friends got so upset watching a family interview that they left before it was half over! To flourish in this Freudian atmosphere that required great personal and family sacrifice, I downplayed the alarming fact that I interviewed more than one person at a time. Of course, there is a way to avoid criticism—feel nothing, think nothing, do nothing. I can't tell you how always to succeed, but I know a sure way to fail—try to please everyone.

Although some criticisms of family therapy contain kernels of truth, mainly they are simply wrong. They exaggerate its weaknesses and omit its most significant feature: Family system therapy is *effective*. Critics are unsettled when family therapy produces changes not achieved by analysis. My practice is full of such people. So is the practice of Jan, my wife and an accomplished therapist. After a few years, I was gratified that a number of analysts quietly came to me and Jan for marital or child problems. My kids would call it karma at work. I think of it as silent vindication.

Third-party payers also intrude. We must show them the abundant evidence of psychotherapy effectiveness, especially couple and family therapy, that often lowers morbidity, mortality, and costs. Managed care, although difficult and full of faults, has ended interminable therapy, shortened mindless hospitalization, and forced us to validate results. We must influence the larger culture and be sure we do not merely make changes without progress. I am concerned with therapy, not the business or politics of therapy. If we give up ideals—most of us are do-gooders—we are lost. Without hard-fought-for personal, evolving standards, we are ships without rudders.

Be Yourself

The best therapists significantly differ from one another by personality, theory, method, and many other attributes. But they have learned the one lesson that must be learned: how to guide the therapy process. The puzzled beginner can learn it, as well. The best therapists take command using their unique person, their style, their strengths. They imitated others along the way, but found that using anyone else's style comes across as hollow and insincere. It just does not feel right to either therapist or patient.

George Gershwin, 30, on a musical pilgrimage to Paris, sought out Maurice Ravel and asked to study with him. But the great master is said to have responded, "Why would you want to be-

come a second-rate Ravel when you could be a first-rate Gersh-
win?" Gershwin remained himself, composing and orchestrating
a lyrical and rhythmic masterpiece, the tone poem "An American
in Paris."

"Good-enough" therapists, to adapt Winicott's felicitous term, are
true to themselves and what they want to accomplish and how they
want to go about it. There is no "right way" for such personal work.
Whatever helps us do and be what is necessary is right, provided it is
also right for our patients. Can such a principle be taught? Decades of
teaching and supervising have convinced me that willing learners
have the inherent capability to master themselves and their art.

But we are impatient to find a "style," to embellish ourselves so that
patients and colleagues recognize us as special. This may appear so
daunting that we freeze rather than risk blowing it. But style is organic,
as much a part of us as our hair, or lack thereof. The therapist who
either inflates or diminishes self loses uniqueness. We have only ourselves to offer. We are the only species able to interfere with our own
growth. We must divest ourselves of the things we think we know,
things others want of us, somebody else's way. Improvement as a
therapist is inherent in the spontaneous qualities already inside us.

Many therapists spend too much time trying to be someone else—a
losing, unauthentic game. They are more effective when they immerse
themselves in a session, rather than filling their minds with expectations. Rollo May[13] says, "If you do not express your own original ideas,
if you do not listen to your own being, you will have betrayed yourself."

Be yourself. Fundamental and hard to do. Even experienced therapists have trouble with two things that seem incompatible: be relaxed
and be confident. Some days go better than others; some go so badly
we despair of ever doing therapy well. Beginners are tentative, neither
relaxed nor confident. We try not to offend, especially if oversuper-
vised. We disguise insecurity with evasive, soft-pedaling jargon we
think sounds professional, but does not inspire confidence. Where is
the person behind the words? Believe in your identity and opinions.
Therapy is an act of pride, of narcissism—you might as well admit it.
Use its energy to keep going.

Successful therapy is more artistic than scientific. Still, when research buttresses our results, we are more confident. For example,
when partners in a troubled marriage are treated individually, chances
of benefit are about 50-50. Success rises to 70% when they are seen

together. Makes it easier to hold out for both coming. Such facts make a solid base for your artful ways, so keep up with research. Facts are the science. Translation into how-to is the art, blending sparse data with a large dose of intuition. We are toddlers compared with centuries of tradition in medicine, in surgery, in philosophy, in religion, in every enterprise that aspires to help people live better lives.

Know Yourself

Harping on "being yourself" has little value unless you *know* yourself. When we enter this career, few of us really do. The decision to become a therapist has a host of determinants. The more we know about ourselves, the better therapists—and people—we become.

Some graduate schools do emphasize "being yourself." But most students fresh out of school are limited in how well they know themselves. They rely on familiar technique, rather than on an unfamiliar self. Their task is to embark on lifelong self-learning. Older students are farther along that path. Jan became a therapist at 48 after running a nursing home, being in analysis, and raising six children. Son Dan went to graduate school at 40. Married with son and daughter plus 25 years of meditation and Eastern philosophy, he already knew himself well. Not many students are that evolved. Older trainees who may know themselves well still need to learn to know and use themselves in therapy. They too have difficulty when face-to-face with turmoil.

Family therapy training usually does not require students to be in therapy. Many are disadvantaged practicing a method they have not experienced. Not having forged a sense of trust in family therapy for themselves, they will likely shy away from advising it in crisis. But requiring trainees to be engaged in therapy also would have drawbacks. (My bypass surgeon didn't think requiring residents to have heart surgery was a good idea either!) The key then is to persuade people of the value of being on the receiving end of what they are doing.

Knowing oneself is a sure path to maturity, autonomy, authenticity, and full humanness. Freud said, "To be completely honest with oneself is the very best effort a human being can make." To do so means struggling against our capacity for greatness. So how do we go about knowing ourselves? This book is full of suggestions.

Limitations

All therapists, all human beings, have limitations. We are different from one another, we have different limitations. The more we know about ourselves, the more we know those limitations. In addition, many therapists stop evolving once they have built a reasonably satisfying practice that meets external acceptability. They fail to go beyond *doing* their craft to *living* it.

Living in harmony with our therapeutic ideals requires expanded consciousness. It calls for quality of life we promote for others. It means closing the hypocrisy gap between what we say and what we do, who we are and how we live. It means painful self-scrutiny. Personal limitations of the therapist are precise therapeutic limitations. The sooner we appreciate that, the better. Here is an example.

I will never forget my initial exchange with the second of three analysts. She asked what I wanted to accomplish—good question. I said I wanted to be less driven—good answer. She said with a wry smile, "Then you'll have to do as I say, not as I do." I was pleased with her self-effacing humor, an honest statement of comfort with her limitations. She was "being herself," warts and all. But her limitation matched mine; she could not take me farther than she had gone. I got much of value from her, but terminated the analysis even more driven. Sadly, she died a few years later of stress-related disease.

If you *really* want to give up drivenness—or any other behavior— find a therapist who has firmly resolved the same problem. If divorce is an issue, don't go to a therapist in the midst of a messy breakup. They are better divorce therapists *after* they get over their own divorces. This means knowing more about a therapist than credentials and school of thought. It also means you may come up against therapist limitations not evident early in treatment.

Subsequent psychoanalysis also had little impact on my drivenness. (In the 1950s psychoanalysis was the only respected training in Chicago.) Too much secondary gain—raising a large family, a growing practice, grateful patients, professional reputation, building a family institute and a nursing home. Only when life-threatening illness forced me to face frightening and undeniable evidence of my mortality did compulsive workaholism mellow.

Could such a conversion have come sooner, in a less radical and dangerous way? Does every stubborn reader have to wait until threatened by death before changing? Perhaps I could have found a casual and unambitious analyst. But where? I don't know any. The culture of ego-syntonic drivenness continues choosing its counterparts.

Today, there is another possibility. If, when I entered therapy for a crisis in our marriage in 1955, I had taken Jan and our children, the outcome would have been better. Work addiction, comfortable for *me* then, would have become painful after confrontations with the family. My syntonic behavior (irritability, emotional remoteness, inaccessibility, eruptions of demandingness and anger) was having an undesirable impact on my family. But I was oblivious. With family therapy, we would have settled a lot of things earlier, with less unfinished business later. Fortunately, we have done just that as we have gotten older and wiser.

To limit our limitations we need to recognize not only what makes us uncomfortable but to see how we come across to others. This means closing the gap between the person we are with patients and the person we are the rest of the time. It means being our whole selves. My drivenness was a severe limitation to what I could accomplish in doing therapy.

When a solo therapist works at an emotional distance, handling people with tongs like specimens, it is easy to imagine that the gap does not exist. I did it for years. But when the shared experience is the medium of change—and it is, always, even when ignored—you can't get away with that. Perceptive, outspoken patients will blow your cover. The less outspoken will quit first.

Never is this so clear as when Jan and I do cotherapy. Her presence keeps me honest, and vice versa. When a couple brings up a problem *we* have not resolved, we can hardly wait to work on this limitation. Again and again, we appreciate the transformative power of self-disclosure and the safety of the truism that honesty is the best therapeutic policy. Thus honesty, tempered with tact and taste, becomes easier and more natural—not a moral platitude, but a practical guide to professional success.

Reflections

- Early in our work with new patients who have had prior therapy, we should explore the pluses and minuses of their experience. We will learn a great deal about how to proceed, how to accomplish what didn't get done. Do this at the next opportunity.

- How do you handle truth? In therapy? Outside of therapy? Review times when you have been less than honest; compare them with times that brutal honesty backfired. Are you comfortable with your answers?
- How do you tell a person a painful truth that you believe the person is psychologically ready for, but doesn't want to hear?
- Some form of managed care is here to stay. How do you get along with third parties without compromising your moral standards? Are you satisfied with what may have to be a compromise?
- What are some of your strongest ideals? How do you express them in therapy? Elsewhere?
- In one sentence describe your strengths and limitations. How do they play out in the therapy you do?
- Who have been your heroes, the people who have influenced you most? What are their strengths and weaknesses?
- Dialogue with someone you trust and spell out your ego-syntonic issues. How do these affect your therapy?

2

Creating Your Framework

From the time we first think about becoming a therapist, we create and recreate an inner structure, a deeply felt framework, yet often we do so without much forethought. It behooves us to study what goes into that structure and how it evolves. Yours is different from mine, yet knowing about my evolution, motivations, and transitions may be useful as you craft yours. Let's start with a basic question.

What is Therapy?

"Racquetball is my therapy." Or gardening. Or taking a nap. Or being with a lover. We naturally find ways to feel better and solve problems. Seeking help is characteristic of the human condition. Usually such efforts are beneficial—therapists say "therapeutic"—and family sages, clergy, neighbors, friends, and shamans have always been sought out by those in need. Today we have available a variety of ways to change ourselves: self-help and support groups, training workshops, spiritual practices and quests, wilderness adventures, alternative healing. These too can be therapeutic, often bringing benefits comparable to those of good psychotherapy.

Therapy is a special piece of this general effort to improve our

15

lives—an artificial, clumsy, expensive invention of the twentieth century, a new and different way of organizing the therapeutic experience, the institutionalization of a generic process. Therapists are oddities in a conventional world, and therapy is also, and not incidentally, our way to make a living. To paraphrase George Bernard Shaw: You must not suppose that just because we are therapists, we never tried to earn an honest living!

Therapy is a metaphor for life. Good therapy promotes a good life, and vice versa. Ideally, therapy functions as a starter-upper, getting people to the point of taking charge of their own evolution. The amount of time spent in therapy is a miniscule bit of a lifetime. Yet it often is the catalyst for precious growth.

When I worked in public clinics with the poorly functioning chronically ill (schizophrenics, addicts, brain-damaged), the goal was to "develop common sense." Better-functioning people (phobics, parents of acting-out adolescents, those in unhealthy relationships) have usually exhausted common-sense solutions. They need deeper dynamic therapy wherein mutual collaboration with a therapist defines the work.

So what is *therapy?* Therapy is a relationship between two or more persons who identify themselves as therapists and one or more persons who want some kind of change. The relationship is therapy when the parties agree it is therapy—a contract. Equivalent definitions apply to diagnostic evaluation, supervision, consultation, psychological testing, experiential teaching—*any* contractual relationship between professionals holding themselves out as available for specific purposes and those seeking their services. These services are often therapeutic without being defined as therapy. Conversations outside of therapy may be similar to those inside therapy. The critical factor is *mutual agreement on the intent of the relationship.*

This raises the question: What is *required* for results in therapy? Early in his week-long workshop, Bob Shaw, contextual psychiatrist and family therapist, asks what the group considers necessary to do therapy. The blackboard quickly fills up. The *patient* must not have brain damage, be chemically impaired, or psychotic. The patient must be able to communicate; be able to define a result; be willing to be a patient and commit to putting in the time; break down denial; be sensitive, honest, and able to trust. The *therapist* must believe in self, make a diagnosis, have strategies, be reliable, listen, be in command, have insight and understanding, be willing to take a risk, and have empathy for the patient.

When we run out of "requirements," we go back and find that someone had good results without the so-called requirement. All the various items are helpful but none are absolutely necessary. And you can *help* someone, that is, be therapeutic, without a contract, but until there is mutual agreement on the intent, it does not deserve to be called therapy.

A Glimpse Into My Therapy Framework

Family interview over, I join students watching behind the mirror and we review the session. Then the focus turns to me, my techniques, what I was thinking and feeling at various points. A lively discussion ensues, the observers vying for my "correct" label. To my amazement, each offers a different opinion.

The first thinks I studied transactional analysis with Eric Berne because I do what Berne did, but without his language. Another says I'm a behavior modification therapist and don't know it! A third watched Nathan Ackerman, grandfather of family therapy, and my way is like this. To another, I'm like Virginia Satir, grandmother of family therapy, conducting communication. Another says that I may not be doing psychoanalysis any more, but I sure work analytically.

Competition to please the instructor was probably a coloring factor. Still, I felt complimented by their conjectures. Who wouldn't enjoy comparison to those greats? And in a sense, each comment was correct. Yet I was not aware of *any* therapist or method during the interview, no preconceived approach at all. I was responding—or *thought* I was—to this family, to the sort of people they are, to the trouble they are having, and, most significant, out of the sort of person I am.

So, what *is* my correct label? There is truth in each assertion, different sides of me, like blind men feeling elephant parts. I have read most of Berne and done workshops with his followers. I studied behavior modification in its heyday, and found it useful in coaching these parents of an acting-out adolescent. I have spent five decades searching for better ways to help people modify their behavior! Nat Ackerman and I came to the family field via child psychiatry and psychoanalysis. He stayed in our home, and we had much in common. I watched him work, read his books. He gave the keynote at the inaugural of the Family Institute, which I founded in 1968. Virginia Satir was an early influence. We got to know each other when she spent a weekend with us and conducted a workshop with the staff and the board. I have been involved in psychoanalysis since 1953: personal analysis for 12 years, graduated from the Chicago Institute for Psychoanalysis, and have practiced for a dozen years. It would be strange if I did *not* think and sound like an analyst.

Still, these explanations are incomplete. I was not merely imitating idols, although I did for a while after first knowing them. I was not just using a crazy quilt of patched-together techniques from differing, possibly conflicting, ideologies. I was being myself, with my background, at that moment, with that family, being observed by those students.

My therapy is hard to label. A student ventured, "*Smorgasbord!*" Not having a buzzword identity to sweep through the field as others have is a distinct disadvantage. But it is an advantage to not be beholden to a method—makes for freedom to try anything, even fall on my face. Teaching an "experiential" course, Jan, Michele Baldwin, Sandra Watanabe-Hammond, and I had the same problem—we were dissatisfied with labels. Terms that come close—humanistic, therapist-centered, interface, family of origin, cast of characters—that identify parts, but not the whole. My meandering career also could be called comprehensive, holistic, inclusive, integrative, unifying, human-relationship-systems-with-a-heart, outside and inside people. I'm still not satisfied.

I suspect my dilemma is not so rare. Most therapists build an amalgam of approaches. They learn a technique, but find that it is not applicable in all situations. So they try something different. Or they go to a workshop and learn another technique. Gradually the practice evolves into its present form. Dissatisfaction with results is a powerful motivator. You may learn something about the evolution of a career from an overview of my search.

A Kaleidoscope of Frameworks

Every class in medical school was compelling. In dermatology, I wanted to be a dermatologist; in thoracic surgery, a chest surgeon. So I took an internship that rotated through various specialities, and then went into solo general practice. Responsible at last for actual patients,

I was ecstatic. I loved the work: on call around the clock, charging heroically into the night, three or four house calls and hospital rounds every day, seeing tangible results. But after a year, my nurse stormed into my office, slammed the door, and with tears streaming down her face yelled, "Chuck Kramer, if you don't take a vacation, I quit. You're driving me crazy."

I took a vacation and also a surgeon partner. This eased the overload, but not for long. Next came a pediatrician, then another general practioner. I had more family time and concentrated on diagnostic and treatment problems. Patients were either organic (with physical disease, treated by medicine and surgery) or functional (no disease, treated with reassurance and placebos). The former were mainstays of medical school, colleagues, and hospitals. The latter, far more numerous, I knew least about. Bored with common medical problems, I read up on psychology, went to state hospital meetings and psychiatric conferences. Filling in for my partner, I found myself at 9 P.M. repeating in a monotone for the tenth time that day what a mother should do for her child's diarrhea, and wondering whether I could stand doing this for the rest of my life.

But what to do? I was supporting a growing family and I dared not leave for a low-paying residency. Besides, I wasn't ready to give up the secure illusion of certainty that materialistic medicine offers. Then came good news disguised as bad. I had part of my medical education in the Army during World War II, so I was obligated to serve two years during the Korean war. I would use the time to find out whether psychiatry was for me. I grabbed the opportunity, breaking "never volunteer" advice, and spent two years practicing basic military psychiatry.

Then for a broader education, I went to Elgin State Hospital, a rich museum of psychopathology. But the likelihood of treatment was slight: Patients' troubles started early in life. So I took a two-year fellowship in child psychiatry at the Institute for Juvenile Research, the first child guidance clinic. At Elgin and IJR the most useful and intriguing understanding of psychological matters was the psychodynamic ideas of Freud proposed by psychoanalysis consultants. I went through the Chicago Institute for Psychoanalysis and began practicing adult and child analysis.

Once again, my ambitions were thwarted. Most distressing was the power of analysis to form a transference neurosis intensely focused on me at the expense of the analysand's intimate partner. I think the divorce epidemic was aided by psychoanalysis. And the fall in the divorce rate in the 1990s parallels its decline. (The average Chicago analyst has only two patients in analysis.)

Child therapy was also frustrating, with good results for many kids, but often not lasting. Some improved quickly but were removed before gains were solid. Others improved, therapy ended, and a sibling developed symptoms. Most disturbing were nine kids who improved, and then their parents divorced. "I entered medicine to help people, not harm them. What am I doing if fixing a child helps split up the parents the child depends on? Sometimes the child's symptoms are the glue keeping the parents together." Colleagues were no help. "You are only responsible for the patient, not everyone in the family. Some couples *should* get divorced." This glib rationalization seemed irresponsible and unethical. But I didn't have the tools to do anything else.

Thus began my foray into family therapy.[14] Seeing two or more people together, I suffered beginner's anxiety all over again—I *was* a beginner. My attention jumped erratically from person to person. Starting to understand one, I had to focus on another, then another. I wanted to go farther with one—familiar territory—yet was pulled into the orbit of others. The linear, one-track, logical thinking that served so well in medicine and psychoanalysis kept falling behind a multidirectional bombardment. Occasionally a dramatic shift in dynamics precipitated remarkable and lasting beneficial changes. The conviction that what I was doing was better in the long run for all the members kept me going.

Family work opens a whole new world of action. I get on my feet, move people around, exchange comments with little reflection, get into family reconstructions, do empty-chair work, enact dreams, *participate* in the activity I ask others to do. I don't ask people to do something I have not done. Such liveliness demands being fully present in the moment with little on my mind, free of concepts and premature diagnoses. I learn how much of the present I miss by wallowing in the past and agonizing over the future. What was or might be is easily included by extending the work, so long as "what is" is firmly established.

This engagement brings me into unfamiliar territory, quite different from drives and defense mechanisms. I am struck by the beauty of people doing the best they can, struggling to fulfill ideals by freeing themselves from self-perpetuated family bondage. My identity as a therapist and as a person has been assaulted, stretched, humiliated, enlivened, expanded, and eventually integrated into a new, more holistic cooperation among my interior selves. I befriend parts untouched in analysis. We playfully look at life's predicaments and stop taking everything so somberly. I get down off my perch. It's growthful because it's so risky and error prone. It's scary, and I love it!

We humans are the most interesting, inspiring phenomenon in all creation. We need not be imprisoned by psychopathology, physical handicaps, traumatic history, family dysfunction, or existential puzzles. We are capable of choices, of freedom, of strongly held ideals—ideals that, in harmony with our native endowments, draw us toward a self-selected future. We are okay just the way we are, and paradoxically, we are capable of reaching our greatest potentials.

Because the most influential element in therapy is the therapist, our presence, attitude, attention, peace of mind, self-acceptance, level of consciousness, and stage of personality evolution are what count. In the therapy I do and teach, personal and professional development interpenetrate. Attention is given to interface: the lively boundaries between student and patients (conventionally, countertransference), student and current family, student and original family, student and teacher, along with colleagues. Methods are taught in the context of the student's personal functioning. What fits is encouraged. So is inventing creative responses. The rote mimicking of someone else is identified, the underlying dynamics of that method are made understandable, and the student is helped to find a congenial way to use the substance.

The heart of using self-oriented practice and teaching is creating harmony among the therapist's cast of characters, an idea more precise, detailed, and practical than psychoanalytic internal objects. Therapists work on their internal characters and teach patients and students to do the same, watching for places where parts interact and clash. Self-understanding is extended to all relationships. Key to this approach is the teacher's demonstration of mastering inner selves (see Chapter 6).

I am more in need of direction and synthesis than analysis, of inspiration than moralizing. I inspect my vision of the future, my philosophy. Years of meditation and other psychospiritual searches reveal how often both I and the people coming to me have lost touch with a spiritual gyroscope. We need to recreate a guiding moral and ethical center for whatever we might accomplish.

These developments do not negate earlier interests. With practice I move from a relationship view to a deep interior view to a surgical view to a spiritual view—whatever is needed. I honor the strengths of people who somehow manage their lives no matter the disarray.

Giving up loyalty to one modality to move to the next necessitates major changes in thinking and feeling, yet bit by bit such shifts seem almost inconsequential.

In adopting a new view, I am tempted to disparage former views. This is a mistake, the rabid convert syndrome. Don't confuse the still valuable with the outmoded. All approaches have a place, even when the new is more effective. Eventually, I hold all of them in harmony; each contributes to an integrated whole. Truly, the combination is different from, larger than, and more powerful than the sum of its parts. And what is true for a part is not necessarily true for the whole. Don't demonize, harmonize!

Moving from one approach to another is not a matter of simply adding gimmicks. You cannot truly grasp a new way without realizing profound changes in *yourself* and everything you believe. Some students of family systems may expect merely to learn a trendy technique. Surprise! Becoming a systems thinker forces alterations in outlook that reverberate throughout all relationships.

At every step, the future looks risky. I often don't know where I'm going. But looking back is remarkable. The whole path seems logical, understandable, coherent, almost inevitable. Professional and personal evolve together, nurturing and propelling each other. I feel more my whole self, wherever and whenever—having moved from spontaneous to deliberate, back to spontaneous-with-insight. From uncomplicated to complicated to wisely simple. From naive to sophisticated to empty-minded. From anxious beginner to confident expert to calm beginner's mind.[15]

It helps to follow Albert Einstein's rules for work: (1) Out of clutter, find simplicity. Everything should be made as simple as possible, but not simpler. (2) From diversity, find harmony. (3) In the midst of difficulty lies opportunity.[16]

Release the attachment to control, not control itself. Stay composed when everything seems hopelessly out of control. We don't need to know *what* to do so much as we need to learn how to behave effectively when we *don't* know what to do.

No one has exactly my background. Each person has a unique life course. The Family Institute's founding philosophy was to create a place for many minds to work, each one on its own path, yet sharing ideas. Emerson said, "I have been writing and speaking what were once called novelties for thirty years, and have not now one disciple . . . no school of followers. I should account it a measure of impurity of insight, if it did not create independence."[2]

22

For centuries, physicians, philosophers, and theologians viewed humans in three domains—body, mind, and spirit—and yet understood them to be one, interdependent and unified. Interest in one domain did not exclude the others. But for the past few hundred years, materialistic science has dominated the medical healing arts with nearly exclusive emphasis on the body. Historically, mental and emotional life have been minimized, and spirit ignored. Still true today. But perhaps changing.

Patient care has been parceled out among disparate professionals—physicians, social workers, clergy, healers—all avidly defending their turfs. Care is often lacking because it is as fragmented as the personalities and families being treated, even in psychotherapy where we might expect collaboration among professionals. Too often a family goes to a hodgepodge of medical specialists, individual therapists, religious advisors, and healers—none of whom communicate with each other.

What most people actually need is hard to find: a trusted health coordinator with the ability to offer medical know-how, compassionate insight, and spiritual guidance. Few exist. It's a challenge for our society to reward those who offer truly comprehensive care. More likely, we are subject to criticism of our ethics, inaccurate professional identification, and uncertain reimbursement. One ambitious goal of this book is to propose what we must *do* and *be* to become the kind of practitioner who is able to truly address the whole person.

Reflections

- What is your "therapy?" Are you satisfied? Does it give you what you need? What are some of the things you want to do but "never seem to have the time to do?"
- Fill in the gaps in your medical knowledge (we all have them) and notice the relevance to your therapy.
- Few therapists adhere to a "pure" method. Write out your present framework for therapy, its kaleidoscope of ingredients, and the path you took to get here.
- Consider your style of risk taking. Did you ever take too great a risk in your career and regret it? Were there times when you shied away from taking risks only to regret that? What's the next thing on the horizon that entails a risk and how will you go about taking action?

3

Getting Started

The personal transaction is the essence, the heart, of good therapy. The patient who engages, however tentatively, is the one who feels more safe than not. Trust comes with sensing that the therapist has a beginning grasp of the presenting dilemma, is able to relate to it with knowledge, directness, and compassion, and is ready to learn more. Feeling understood is feeling loved, and our patients—as ourselves—need love above all else. Out of love come some of the most important qualities: humanity and warmth and honesty.

Like all beginners, I felt vulnerable and tense. We want to put ourselves into the arena, yet find it difficult to do so, caught between doing and not doing. Minds are cluttered with bits of information we cling to for safety, but which we are unable to sort out and use with priority and confidence: What I read in a book, heard from a lecture or supervisor, how a patient makes me uneasy, how my uneasiness might affect that person, am I doing it right, on and on. Mind clutter interferes. When I first sat down to commit an act of therapy, I was far stiffer and more awkward than when I was about to walk into the room. The task is to find the human being behind the tension. Ultimately, what we have to offer is not a technique, not a theory, but who we are.

Although therapy requires some review of what happened before

24

the first meeting, some therapy, unfortunately, focuses almost entirely on the past, both remote and recent. Beginners may be unaware that the therapeutic process itself contains useful information. Reworking what has happened in therapy may be unimportant for symptom reduction, which is all some people want, but it is valuable for achieving lasting results, and can begin in the first two sessions.

As analysis and reanalysis of the moving process unfolds, everyone should be learning more about themselves—patients to enhance their present and future, therapists to be able to create an appropriate approach for each particular patient in each particular situation. Through trail and error, and in small steps, the expression of what we learn about ourselves becomes our unique method, to be shaped and reshaped for other contexts. A dialectic emerges between spontaneity and planning, a loop: spontaneously being one's self, observing the effect, evaluating the short- and long-term outcomes, fine-tuning, being spontaneous in the same or slightly different ways, and so on.

> *According to Lao-tzu[17]:*
> *A good traveler has no fixed plans*
> *and is not intent upon arriving.*
> *A good artist lets his intuition*
> *lead him wherever it wants.*
> *A good scientist has freed himself of concepts*
> *and keeps his mind open to what is.*

The art is further complicated when interviewing two or more people together. What makes one feel safe may frighten another. And, beyond the scare engendered by meeting with a stranger in a strange place for a strange purpose, are the uneasiness and mistrust many feel with other family members. Bringing them together takes sensitive handling for *all* to feel safe, *all* to feel understood. They need to know that the therapist is on everyone's side, even when the sides appear to be in opposition. This is sometimes misunderstood to mean that the therapist must *approve* of everyone's behavior. Not so. Once each person knows that the therapist is on his or her side, behavior can be confronted when it is detrimental to others. It is just as detrimental, although perhaps less obviously, to self. Here is another place where the use of internal parts (see Chapter 6) has great value.

Each patient wishes to be favored. A mark of excellence is the ability to be special to each, while respecting and relating to the whole system. Even-handed concern makes possible wise decisions that may solve several problems at once, a result in which win–win system thinkers specialize and that win–lose linear thinkers have trouble comprehending. What we must do is make an *arrangement* (of each session and of the whole therapy) that hangs together from beginning to end and moves with economy and warmth. Such a structure is achieved through repeated trail–error–correction.

Many therapists are naturally "feelingful" and intuitive. Logic and order are not strong points. Yet logic and order turn out to be fun and useful and anyone with an inner part that can think logically can speak, write, and do therapy well. In the course of integrating feeling and intuition with logic, the blend is even more fun as we become skillful at using our whole selves.

We learn whatever we truly believe we need to learn for survival. The way to survive and thrive in this profession is to take the plunge. Learn from direct experience. You can also learn from other therapists. You can even learn from bad therapists what *not* to do. How to recognize good from bad? Simple. If watching or reading or hearing about a therapist makes you wish you could be in therapy with him or her, that would be a person to learn from.

Good therapy has aliveness that keeps all parties working from session to session. Technical gimmicks do not "personalize" a therapist. It is a question of using ourselves skillfully in order to achieve the greatest understanding and the least confusion. Mark Epstein describes Buddhism's "skillful means." Make decisions and deal with problems in a way that is appropriate to the situation and that causes no harm. Such skill arises out of compassion when we address problems without disaffirming a person's humanity. The parent who offers a sponge after a child has spilled milk is using skillful means. The one who sends the child to bed is not.

As beginners, we worry about what to do with new responsibility. Such worry is counterproductive. Compassion comes effortlessly when we are fully present and paying close attention with *nothing else on our mind*. When we listen devotedly (like a Quaker) with a beginner's mind (like a Buddhist) useful ideas emerge in the moment. Read the situation as accurately as possible and respond to whatever is happening. Trying to apply someone else's method keeps us from tuning in and discovering a fresh, original solution, the most skillful means.

The only way to learn therapy is to *do* therapy. Push yourself to do a certain number of hours a week of whatever method you are learning. Put in the time, gain experience and confidence, identify your best way of working with common problems. The Family Institute requires students to have at least four families in treatment. When too few are being seen—four are barely enough—there is too much opportunity to obsess about irrelevancies. Therapists with only one or two cases hold conferences that ramble on beyond the point of diminishing returns.

Sometimes, even after you have learned all you can from your mistakes and have done your best to correct them, there are a few that cannot be fixed. Therapy founders. So terminate, start another case, get on with it. Patients can learn a valuable lesson.

> *A woman is looking for therapy. I ask about previous treatment. Embarrassed, she tells of going to a respected colleague. He seemed impatient and finally said, "You're not motivated for therapy. You don't realize the seriousness of your problems. I don't want to take the time to work with you." Recovering from the shock of this confrontation, she pondered hard and decided to try again. In our therapy she takes her problems seriously, works well, and has productive results. We both benefit from my colleague's honesty, brutal at first, but helpful in the long run.*

Ours is a field in which beginners expect to do it perfectly the first time. No one else learning a difficult skill—athlete, musician, painter, juggler—has such an unrealistic and grandiose expectation. If they do, they soon learn painfully. Some of my early cases should never have been started, let alone struggled with. Often patients had enough sense to quit before I did. My practice review of 1964–1974 (following) shows that I turned down more requests for treatment than in the ten years before 1964, and the number who withdrew decreased by the same number.

Brief Therapy

You should have a firm grasp of brief, problem-centered, solution-oriented methods. You will use them daily, no matter how or where you practice. Much of therapy, and much of life, requires problem solving. However, I spend little time on this subject as it has been written about at length and is taught everywhere. Unfortunately, the often-ignored drawback of such exclusive training is the limit on what can be accomplished. Doing nothing but solution-seeking eventually becomes a narrow philosophy of life.

Problem-oriented advocates often put down long-term therapy, and sometimes with good reason—we should avoid the pitfalls of endless treatment. But there is value in developing both perpectives. Most therapists who define themselves as brief therapists have little experience with longer cases. However, those doing growth-oriented, education-for-life, long-term therapy must also be expert in problem solving or they can't take people beyond a crisis.

In 1964 I reviewed all 140 of my families and couples treated during the previous ten years. The most common number of sessions was six. The number of patients dropped rapidly between 12 and 15 sessions. Brief, symptom-oriented, I call this category "first phase" therapy. Between 15% and 20% of patients continued for from six months to several years. Largely educational, relationship-oriented, potential-seeking, I call this category "middle phase."

I repeated the study in 1974. I had been developing the approach described in this book. I seldom had a time limit in mind when first meeting with people. Nearly all my appointments during a week were middle-phase cases, and I had a reputation for advocating long-term therapy. So it was a distinct surprise to find that the curve of number of sessions over time was exactly the same as before: modal average of six sessions, sharply diminished numbers after a dozen, and 15% to 20% continuing for varying periods up to several years.

In discussions with students and consultees they found similar patterns. Those in private practice had curves like mine. Others, serving a more dysfunctional population, also most commonly had six sessions with a smaller percentage going beyond 12 to 15 sessions. Conclusion: The unfolding process ends naturally without control by the therapist—or by insurance companies. Trust it.

There is a crucial difference between individual and couple/family therapy. Needy individuals with poor intimate relationships easily devolve into never-ending dependency on the therapist in lieu of a partner. Before I learned about systems, I had many of these patients. We slipped into unresolvable transference–countertransference jams. But in treating and supervising thousands of families, I have *never* seen this. Sooner or later, someone complains about lack of progress. Many things can happen at this point, but interminable dependency-supporting therapy is not one of them.

Even if you do only brief therapy, expand your horizon to include the tribulations of becoming and being a better therapist in order to be fully available to those seeking help. This means becoming a whole person. And it means guiding others to become whole. There is more to life than solving problems. Life is less a problem to be solved and more an experience to be lived and savored. The same is true of therapy.

Nowadays, when I finally help solve a problem, whether my own, a supervisee's, or a patient's, it is usually because I have done tens of thousands of hours of therapy. I have been there before, or somewhere in the vicinity, and have a surer hunch how to fix what has gone wrong than I did as a beginner. Thus the recommendation to do more therapy.

Sometimes we despair of finding solutions. All of us get stuck and sometimes the outlook appears hopeless. That is when we have to remain compassionately present with our patients (or students, or spouses, or children, or anyone we care about) until we can see what is coming next. There are many times when people are less in need of solutions and more in need of a trusted companion as we stumble through the uncharted wilderness. And we may need more people in the room, not fewer.

Therapeutic Paths

When patients become lost, it is generally because we have not helped them create and stick to a path. Most likely, we do not have a clear idea of what the best path would be. Early in our careers this is because we are uncertain of how to go about therapy. With more experience, confusion is more traceable to interface problems. At times we all get lost. Acknowledging that we are in fact lost cements the therapeutic alliance and when we are patient enough, we find what we need to get back on track.

> *A seasoned therapist brings a case to class for consultation. The story is complex: tumultuous marriage, messy divorce, conflictual second and third marriages, court custody battles, and disturbed children, stepchildren, half-siblings. The atmosphere is tense, uneasy, a bit frightening. Pausing for breath, he sighs, "I'm lost!" I look at him sympathetically, "I am too!" Stunned silence. I turn to the group and ask plaintively, "If anyone has any ideas, please come up and join us." Three women pull up chairs. One speaks of her child welfare agency where families like this are typical.*

Another recounts a similar case with which she is struggling. A third speaks movingly of growing up in such a family. The anxious confusion melts as we relax, taking in the new data and making plans. Anonymous evaluations give this class top score for the year.

Occasionally, we should ask ourselves, "What are we trying to accomplish?" Often, we are not sure. It helps to know objectively what we say and do. Therapists who have not studied their own audio- and videotapes have missed opportunities for greater self-awareness. They are puzzled by questions such as, "Have I done or said what I meant to? Are my ideas and feelings clear? Do patients understand my ideas, even though hearing them for the first time? Have we an emotional, empathic connection that moves us toward where we should be going? Can we sit tight in the face of ambiguities?" Surprisingly, what we see and hear doesn't necessarily match our memory.

If we don't know where we are going, we had better find out. The vacillation between clarity and confusion that is inevitable can be monitored with patients from moment to moment and whenever needed. When that does not do it, there are many ways to go. I deal with "hang-ups" in Part III of *Becoming a Family Therapist*.[18]

Thinking clearly about therapy is a conscious act. Good therapy doesn't come about automatically or without thought. If you find therapy hard work, it's because it *is* hard, one of the hardest things people do. By "hardest" I mean that becoming a good therapist demands a long period of learning, examining and appreciating mistakes, finding correctives, making new ones, and evolving our own style. We are exhausted at day's end, more so by the end of the week, even more so by vacation. We need to take time off more frequently. The average therapist works entirely too hard and too long without a break.

We sometimes see no tangible results. Some 15% to 25% or more of our patients (depending on the clinical population) do not improve. A few get worse despite our best efforts. We are constantly on the alert. People we have helped turn against us. Some of us get sued. We go for long stretches receiving little or no appreciation. We tread a narrow path: Care too little, we won't have much of a practice. Care too much, they will break our heart. These are some of the high prices we pay.

With all these pressures, it is not surprising that it is difficult for the beginner to be himself or herself. Good therapists are born *and* made. Being a good therapist takes more than naturalness, it takes discipline.

(Ever hear of a concert violinist who did not have *both* native talent and years of lessons?)

The appeal of our field is the delicate balance and interplay of intangibles. Look for these values: links between past and present, tug of the future. Observe closely. Hold the hype. Hang around the old-timers, the best; get to know them. Ponder the changes. Speak and write well.

As you get your priorities in order, learn about blind alleys, and gain confidence, you see that there is no patient, no family, no clinical situation you cannot understand in your framework. Your personality will be intact and your approach will hold together. The very act of meeting with people in trouble summons out of you some relevant cluster of unanticipated thought or memory or feeling. Every encounter activates a different level of consciousness, brings forth an aspect of yourself that may be surprising. Don't fight this current. If it feels right in a particular context, it is valuable. Building each awareness into your practice will gradually fit all of you and your style into an edifice that will never come tumbling down.

This is not to say you should treat everyone; no therapist can or should. Just fit the presenting situation into your frame so you understand it reasonably well and have some idea of what might be done. You don't have to be the one to do it. You will learn what kinds of problems you are good with and with what kinds you are not so good. Build a cadre of trusted professionals you can refer to. The more personally you know them, the better. Get opinions from whomever your patients and you could benefit: senior therapists, psychological testers, medical and surgical specialists, biofeedback practitioners, massage therapists, 12-step groups, alternative medicine, clergy of every faith, divorce and estate lawyers—resources grow daily. Match patients with the best person for them. First-rate therapists make first-rate referrals. Therapists who never make a referral are so averse to exposure that they are willing to compromise their results and their patients.

Each new therapist starts from a different place and heads for a different destination, yet acts as though competing with teachers, colleagues, and every therapist out there "marketing." Beginners are awed by publications, university appointments, credentials, conference presentations. Even experts are easily impressed.

My friend, a renowned therapist, saw an equally famous "expert"
in the hope of saving the marriage. My friend now realizes that

therapy never got going because fame was the wrong criterion for selection.

Fame simplifies reality so people take it as reality. Fame is proof that people are gullible. Sometimes beginners observe "master therapists" and conclude that such therapy is beyond them. These fears can inhibit learning for years. Forget the competition. Go at your own pace. Do what you can do, the best you can, and get on with it. The only real contest is with yourself—and someday that will mellow, too.

I write so confidently without knowing you, the reader, because I am convinced that effective therapy springs from unconscious roots. Although each therapist is a unique individual, it is also true that, as therapists, the more deeply we explore ourselves, the more we find in common with the rest of humanity. One goal of this book is to help us trust and use our unconscious to become better therapists and better people.

The therapy we do reverberates within us twenty-four hours a day. Our minds are always at work. Even asleep, the unconscious is busy problem solving, warning, exulting, clarifying, showing a path. These are presented in the gift of dreams that can be understood with a little practice and help. Our job is to get out of the way of those powerful, wiser, less familiar parts and let them work for us. In the long run, they have our best interests at heart. And this means patients' best interests. Therapy also resonates within them. Much of the power of system therapy is because those present in interviews usually live together, so the impact of sessions richly percolates both interiorly and among family members. Parallel processes make us aware at a deep level of some of their dynamics, as well as ours.

A seemingly effortless style is achieved after years of strenuous effort, repetition, and fine-tuning. Good therapy, like good dance or good music or good springboard diving, is a thing of beauty. Inspiration plus perspiration. Very little is accidental, and yet there is always plenty of room for the unexpected and the spontaneous. And when we know what we are doing and have confidence in ourselves, at bottom we are working to please ourselves.

Reflections

- With one of your next referrals, arrange to have the session videotaped. (Audiotaping is easier, but less revealing.) Make sure you are in the picture. Are you fully present to all? How awkward are you? How big is the gap between yourself being in the room and being out of it? Ask someone you trust to watch the tape with you and play it with these questions in order to see yourself as another sees you.

- Check your last few referrals to other practitioners. What were your criteria for referral? Was each a good match? How did it work out? What have been the long-term results? When we don't get feedback, we lose valuable learning.
- Think of a recent patient or family where good chemistry flowed from the beginning. Why do you think it happened? How have you felt about it? How can more therapy go like this?
- Review a case that just never got off the ground. Why not? Is there anything in how it played out you can learn about yourself?
- You're in the middle of a session, confused and lost, unable to figure out what is happening or what to do. List as many ways to deal with this as you can think of. Experiment with these tactics next time you are lost. Better yet, rehearse with an empty chair *before* you get lost. Call in each of your characters (see Chapter 6) for consultation.

4

The Process Moves Along

T rust the therapy process. Sometimes it is so rich that analyzing it risks belittling it and destroying its essence. Don't try to explain the inexplicable. You may get in the way of patients making their own connections, bringing their emotions into focus, robbing them of the chance to access disowned corners of consciousness.

Dialectic between content and process is inevitable. We learn to balance both. What makes therapy touching is content. Life generates its own emotions. Patients are experts on the facts of their lives—the content. Let them take care of content; your responsibility is for the process. Don't get lost in content. When you forget facts of their lives, they can remind you. *They* haven't forgotten.

> *A psychiatry resident bemoans, "When the family gets to bickering over who said and did what, I get fuzzy, lost. I try to keep track, but eventually give up. This also happens in group therapy, and even in some staff meetings!" Which reminds me of an old psychoanalyst joke he has not yet heard. Question: How can you stand listening to that stuff all day? Answer: Who listens?*

Like all good jokes, this both disguises and expresses truth. We must stay aware of the process, the theme, the red thread that connects and makes the facts understandable. We listen with our "third ear," an intuitive sense of the less obvious flow. Getting caught up in details of content so obscures process that we lose leverage for change. I tell the resident he is experiencing what we struggle with as long as we practice. The family, like most, is all too knowledgeable about facts. What they can't see, and what creates problems, is the complex flow of the process they are engulfed in—the fish that knows nothing about water.

You need, I say, to take a mental step back to get a wider view. You might comment on the process, "You go round and round repeating yourselves, not hearing each other, not finding solutions or anything new." You must get out of the content trap and shift attention to the process they need to change. This will not cure them, but it will move them in the right direction. I imagine a zoom lens in my head. When too close to see the forest for the trees, I zoom back until I can encompass the whole picture. At other times, I zoom *in* for a more intimate close-up, depending on what we are trying to accomplish.

Therapists trained in individual methods, and often in individual therapy themselves, are awkward at zooming back. If they make a sincere effort and still have trouble with group process, they might be wise to treat only individuals. Others find that they do not like zooming in. They might be better off doing groups. Or administration. We can find a way compatible with our natural inclinations by using ourselves as finely tuned instruments. Experiment with many therapies, clinical syndromes, age groups, and constellations of people. You will gravitate toward those that work for you and your patients. And practice zooming. But don't expect the "natural inclination" cluster that is right today to hold forever. Interests change, we move through life, suffer traumas, perhaps marry, have children. Our preoccupations shift.

Different situations call for different approaches. Your task is to present yourself in a way that serves best. Find the right voice, the right language, the right structure. See how much of what you say does not need to be said. "A great tailor does little cutting." It's annoying to patients and students to be inundated with words. A master can move us with few words, few brush strokes, few musical notes.

Attention to the details tells people, even if unconsciously, that they are in the hands of a careful person. Take pride in organizing therapy. Organizing is more often neglected that you might expect. Tension and pace are essential. Every component should do good work, and transitions pull the therapy along from phase to phase. Trust the process—it is stronger than you think. But it is only as strong as the structure you build for it and the control you maintain over it from beginning to end.

Tact, Taste, and Timing

Webster's *Unabridged Dictionary* gives us clues to understanding these elusive, yet essential, topics. Although each has its distinct definition, in therapy they usually fail or succeed together.

Tact is a keen sense of what to say or do to avoid giving offense; a discriminating feel for what is appropriate, tasteful, or esthetically pleasing; skill in dealing with difficult or delicate situations. A better statement of the art of good therapy can hardly be found.

Taste overlaps with tact. It is a sense of what is fitting, harmonious, beautiful; the perception and enjoyment of esthetic excellence; what is seemly, polite, or tactful to say or do in a given situation. Good therapy is a thing of beauty.

Timing is more than tact and taste, yet includes both. It is central to being effective. Good timing is synchronization: adjusting movement so as to select the best tempo and time for doing something in order to achieve the desired, maximal effect. The good therapist presents a new idea just as the patient becomes ready to assimilate it. And the good patient lets the therapist know when ready to take in a new idea.

One distinction between a beginner and that same therapist years later is a quality so intangible as to be almost impossible to define. Yet, like love, we know it when we see it. Asked late in life how his trumpet playing changed over the years, jazz great Louis Armstrong rasped, "Now, I play fewer notes." He was too modest to say "fewer and better." Tact, taste, and timing are knowing what will and won't work, then doing what works and avoiding what doesn't, all at the right time. Wisdom!.

Tact encompasses economy, precision, sure-footedness that cannot be imitated. It comes from the free expression of ourselves that has been honed by facing up to the painful results of poor taste. When it is right it is powerful; when wrong, disastrous. Lack of tact, bad taste, and bad timing are humiliating and can wreck therapy. Here are examples.

I learn a lesson I will never forget. In a first couple interview, I inappropriately and thoughtlessly tease a patient with a hearing aid to "tune us in" when she doesn't hear something. She's humiliated. Despite my awkward and embarrassed apology, after a few sessions, they quit prematurely and never return.

An interface mistake—tactless, tasteless, and poorly timed. I had anxiously rushed to establish rapport. I was the one who needed to tune in to what she was ready for. Her husband was an orthopedic surgeon who had successfully operated on my hand years earlier. I was eager to show him I was as good in my field as he in his. Narcissistic!

Now I can tell about exquisite timing. I do a two-day workshop on "Dying and the Family" with Elisabeth Kubler-Ross. In opening remarks, I list what I hope to accomplish in a first interview, including having a good laugh.

Elisabeth and I interview a couple whose son is dying of cancer. There is nothing funny about such a tragic predicament, so I drop any though of laughing with them. For forty minutes this distraught mother keeps up a steady stream of anxious talk, while the stepfather sits by quietly. Neither Elisabeth nor I can get him to join in as he repeats that it is her son they are here for.

Most of her anguish and eye contact are directed to me, so when she pauses for breath, I ask gently if is there anything that might help. She blurts out, "If he would just say something once in a while, it would be a big help." I lean toward her and murmur, "My dear, if you would just shut your big mouth once in a while, maybe he would." The four of us explode with laughter. The tension in the room subsides, the stepfather talks and the mother listens. They have a warm, tender, equal-time talk during the remaining 20 minutes and leave with upbeat plans for their newly found harmony on behalf of the boy.

Her intense eye contact told me we were simpatico. She trusted me, knew I cared, and wanted help. Moreover, she wanted caring and help from her husband, but had been asking for it in an oblique and counterproductive way.

Tact and taste are currents that run all through therapy. The most difficult learning for a beginner—or even veteran—is confronting that will cause little resistance and significant change. Support must accompany confrontation. I hold up a palm to represent a mirror for confronting and the other hand at right angles underneath for supporting.

Perfect tact and taste are a gift—and probably do not even exist. But they can be acquired. The trick is to study and absorb them. Listen to good music, commune with nature, read good authors, practice an art form. Hang around therapists who impress you as most able to influence others through good taste, tact, and fine timing. And notice what works.

Imitation and Identity

We find ourselves imitating others. I recall using the same words and tone my therapist used with me. The more we respect and envy them, the more we imitate, often unwittingly. I remember first hearing myself speak to our toddler the way dad spoke to me—in words and a tone that I hated! We are shocked when we first notice, but should not be. We need models, in therapy and in life, both positive and negative. You will find your voice, and the identities of your models will be indistinguishable. Imitation is a temporary and necessary step as we put together what is right for us, our identity.

Look for the best models. Find therapists who do well the kind of therapy to which you aspire. Learn their taste, their tact, their timing. The ones who are right for you make great mentors. And you can always discard what doesn't fit. Read the best, going back to Freud. Jung's ideas make a rich complement. Dip into our tradition. Steep yourself in the literature and find out what the best have said and done. Learn about the greats and compare their methods and personalities. Then you can evaluate every fad against a solid framework. Recognize genius. Distinguish the true innovator from the mere imitator. It's a lesson in humility to find that the brilliant insight that seems so original was articulated years earlier by someone else.

Beyond taste, beyond simplicity, beyond clear thinking, the great ones resonate with realms within us that we may not have yet defined. They reverberate with truths we know in our bones. As we touch into deeper parts of ourselves, we find, without making a deliberate effort, that we are doing the same with patients. And although they may not realize it, a deep experience is what they really come for.

Important Things

Snow is falling in clumps, cars clog the street. My 9:00 A.M. patient is late, so I ponder on how slow her therapy is going. What have I missed? Do I have an interface problem? What is she doing to hold things back? The phone rings and my 10:00 A.M. patient says he will be on time, but needs to leave early because of the weather.

When she arrives with just ten minutes left, I fear the delay will slow us down even more. I describe the call and say, as supportively as I can, "We only have ten minutes." She asserts, "Then I guess I only have time to talk about important things." She summarizes her life and the therapy so far, then lays out the changes she plans to make.

In subsequent months, therapy moves forward as never before. When the conversation veers off unproductively, one of us recalls that snowy day and we get back to work. During a good ending we agree that those were the best ten minutes of her life, and that before then, we did a lot of talking about unimportant things.

Those ten minutes weren't the entire therapy. They worked because of hours of preparation and follow-up. But who knows how long we would have meandered without the snowstorm? An unfortunate by-product of the psychodynamic tradition is assuming that since the fundamental rule of free association connects everything, then everything is equally important. But free association is scarcely "free" when it fails to connect with ego-syntonic material. As I noted earlier, 12 years of analysis did nothing for my destructive drivenness. Experiential work with Jan and the family did. Some things in life are inherently more important than others.

A similar misapprehension hinders family therapy. Because every process in the family is connected to every other, everything and everyone is believed to have equal importance and power. Distinctions are erased, leaving a murky muddle. Nothing stands out, no fulcrum for change. A crucial concept in General System Theory is missing, the leading part. This is the part that exerts the most control over the entire system. An illustration: A boat under sail, weighing many tons, is a system of opposing forces—wind, water, hull going in a certain direction, trim of sails. All parts are important, but one is most important. When everything is balanced, a fingertip on the tiller—the leading part—will change direction. Pressure anywhere else makes little difference.

Clinical situations have a leading part where a small influence can leverage a large change despite conflicting pressures. The most evident pathology, where attention is focused, where people are hurting, is often the least able to change. Example: mother and son locked in mutual destructive hostile dependency. Easy to diagnose, hard to change, especially when the unavailable father is not considered important. We are trained to identify the pathology, the noisy problem, not the change agent. Such stuck patterns improve when it is realized that working with the father is crucial. He is the one most able to change. The reverse, father–daughter symbiosis, calls for a similar strategy of helping the mother change her part in the family dynamics.

> *Many sessions are spent coaching the parents to improve their parenting. Week after week, they agree to try a new tactic, and week after week, they fail. Inadvertently, they mention that the mother's mother lives upstairs, a fact the hurried brief therapist had failed to learn. Grandma has the leading part in raising the children. Nothing changes until she joins the interviews.*

Therapists become consultants and carry along this encumbrance of thinking everything is important.

> *It's a complicated hospital consultation. We struggle for two hours to understand. Fragmented patient and family, multiple impairments, many hospitalizations and misfiring attempts at therapy. All accompanied by fragmented treatment teams. And now, fragmented, misfiring consultation! Exhausted, it's time to go. I head for home, but a nurse catches my arm and pleads for just one minute about another desperate case. Frustrated and eager to move on, I snap, "What's the most important thing you want to do?" She tells me. I rattle off, "Do this . . . and this . . . and this" and beat it. One-minute consultation. Two weeks later, the mess that took two hours has not budged. The nurse who stopped me at the door is ecstatic about the good changes that occurred in her case.*

Find the decisive leading part and work with that. When it changes, the rest will follow. If not, then keep searching for the leading part. Keep your focus on what will be most transformative. When you do not have that leverage, you just grind along. Einstein speaks for me, "I soon learned to scent out that which was able to lead to fundamentals and to turn aside from everything else, from the multitude of things that clutter up the mind and divert it from the essential."[8]

Do Therapy as Well as You Can

Psychotherapy is an art/science to be practiced with imagination and skill, using the best "materials." It calls for a passion for quality, impatience with the second rate, a deep belief that excellence is its own reward, for therapist and patient alike. Liberate yourself from having to fulfill expectations of others that are not right for you. Succeed or fail on your own terms. This may mean changing jobs, locations, fields. Students in family training often make career changes. Individually oriented agencies lose interest in family therapy when reality hits: Does a family of seven need a larger room, seven charts, seven diagnoses, seven insurance billings?

We will always come up with new technologies. The valuable aspects of new approaches can be integrated into our style. Yet on the whole we have enough techniques and principles to be helpful. Where, then, is the edge? Ninety percent of the answer lies in the hard work of mastering the tools discussed here. Add a few points for natural gifts, such as a good ear, a sense of rhythm, a feeling for people and their language, a sense of the fitness of things. But the final advantage is the same as in every other venture. You have to *want* to do therapy better. You need commitment. You must really care.

Defend your work against intermediaries who have other fish to fry. Too many therapists let themselves be brow-beaten into settling for less than their best. I believe that "my style"—the expression of who I am—is my most marketable asset, the one that sets me apart from colleagues. I don't want anyone but me fiddling with it. I stick stubbornly to the way I am evolving until convinced otherwise. I have spent so many years experimenting that I have faith my style is right for me—but perhaps for no one else. But I have changed, and will again when life requires it.

Defending what we do shows we are alive. Patients put up with our idiosyncrasies because we are serious—and effective. Be serious about your work, but don't take *yourself* too seriously. Standing my ground has brought more patients and teaching requests than it has driven away. People know I work with care, and that I am reliable.

This attitude has served well. For instance, knowing from painful experience when a systems approach is a better choice than treating one person, it is easy to stick to it. When a spouse, say, wants therapy for the marriage and the partner refuses to come, that says more about the marriage than it does about me or about couple therapy. It usually means that deepening their intimacy is not likely.

What you do should be an expression of you, not the supervisor. If you let your distinctiveness be supervised away, you lose your main strength, you betray yourself. It's a sin to tamper with a therapist's style. But supervisors sometimes come on strong and do what supervisees let them get away with. Students acquiesce in their own embarrassment when they blindly follow advice, only to have it boomerang.

Students with teachers of the structural-strategic, Bowenian, and problem/solution-centered persuasions are often taught by formula. So their patients may be treated by formula. Such teachers feel secure in their method and want no deviation. A student trying a fresh approach is at odds with those serving their own purposes. My objection is not to teaching any particular approach, but rather to being locked into one way. These methods are prone to formula promoting. Narrow pursuit of a technique is a greater block than is no technique. An open mind is necessary for an expanded mind, for the fullest expression of our untapped potential.

Your style of therapy—and of supervising and teaching—is yours and nobody else's. Take your talent as far as you can and guard it with your life. Only you know how far that is. Doing therapy well means believing in your work and yourself, taking risks, daring to be different, pushing yourself to excel. You only do as well as you make yourself do.

Reflections

- Sharpen your skill at discerning process from content in a videotaped interview of an experienced therapist. Note the contrasting responses to comments on process and on content. Do the same with one of your interviews.
- Find examples in your cases of both good and bad timing. How can you predict that an intervention will be more helpful than harmful?

- Who did you imitate as a teenager? As a student? As an adult? How have these imitations become a part of you?
- Identify the leading part in two current cases. How do you know it's the leading part? How does working with that theme compare with time spent on peripherals? See how quickly you can spot the leading part in your next several cases and whether dealing with it affects the flow.

5

Ending

We don't like endings. Not only are they unpalatable, but they remind us of separations in the past, of the future loss of loved ones, and (less consciously) of our own demise. Lest you assume our profession has escaped this universal human frailty, consider there facts.

- Freud practiced psychoanalysis for more than 40 years before writing about termination.
- A 1971 annotated bibliography of 2,000 books and articles on family therapy written in the 1950s and 1960s contained not one reference to ending.
- Journals are full of advice on how to start therapy, but very little on how to *end* therapy. (The same number of cases end as start!)
- Training programs generally pay little attention to endings.
- Therapists are far more savvy about engaging than about terminating.

My experience sheds light. The first time I taught termination was the most difficult class I ever had to prepare for; I stalled, forgot, mislaid notes—classic ambivalence. Many agency consultations had ambiguous or white-lie endings; of several dozen only a few were wrapped up forthrightly and amiably on both sides. I even feel uneasy as I write, after teaching endings for 30 years. Nothing about ending is easy.

The Institute studied Jan's and my closed cases. Looking at the names, I am flooded with memories, anxiety, sadness, and an urge to avoid the subject. Even a family with good outcome and toward whom I have positive feelings is unsettling, although the fear of finding bad results is negligible. Recalling sessions held as long as 40 years ago brings back discomfort. How much pain I absorbed working in an emotionally charged atmosphere! I'm sensitive to separation, been told I'm hard to leave. But I am not alone. The lack of follow-up studies is undoubtedly related to similar aversions. The "reasons" given for not checking results smack of thinly veiled rationalizations, if not projections.

Ironically, not writing about ending contradicts its value. A good ending is as important as a good beginning. Effective therapists know when and how to stop. A good termination may accomplish more than all the preceding sessions. Even in only one meeting, how loose ends are pulled together, the quality of rapport, the clarity of understanding, have an impact. We are nonplussed when the most salient fact appears on the way out the door! Many recall our last therapy session. The most significant feature of an entire therapy may be found in its termination, sometimes near the end of the last interview. Only in stopping can we truly see.

Ending is implicit in starting; engagement assumes disengagement. "How long will I be coming?" is on every patient's mind. And the therapist's. Asked in a waiting room how many sessions people expect, the most common answer: one! As we need a framework for starting and sustaining, we need a framework for ending. How therapy is conducted influences the way it ends, and its management should be consistent with the basic strategy.

Withdrawal from Therapy

Withdrawal occurs during the first few sessions when patients are dissatisfied. Polarization may develop with an eager therapist trying to engage foot-draggers. Sometimes the most influential person (who may not be present) takes a dislike to the therapist or perceives a threat to his or her influence, engendering a counterreaction and setting off an upsetting escalating power struggle over who is in charge. A therapeutic alliance is not established. The course is downhill from the first.

Beginners are understandably occupied with starting, having made a heavy educational investment in time and energy. We struggle with anxiety, from healthy anticipation to near-panic, relieved by getting under way. Action overcomes stage fright. What a shock when patients quit without warning, mysteriously. Such endings are embarrassing, irritating, damaging to self-esteem. And sloppy. Andy Ferber, pioneer family therapist, complained, "The first eight families chewed me up and spit me out!" We get into this work to help, and our very motivation is questioned. Strong reactions are not well integrated in the face of anxiety to start another case.

The high failure rate of beginners can be attributed to lack of experience and confidence, incompetent supervisors, unfortunate choice of patients, and unresolved attachment/separation issues. I made mistakes, such as missing appointments, coming late, ending early, billing errors, forgetting a vacation, overeager attempts to get people involved. I made them all! Futile. Frustrating. Forced me to look in the mirror and ask myself why I'm so invested in their doing what *I* think is best. Or keeping them dependent. Or vainly attempting to achieve unrealistic perfectionistic goals. The rescuing missionary syndrome.

Not all abrupt endings are instigated by the patients. Therapists also stop unexpectedly and traumatically. This happens in programs when a trainee fails to inform people of a transfer. And some managers see therapists as easily and painlessly replaced. The manual of a Preferred Provider Organization cautions therapists, "Do not let the patient get attached to you." This makes it easier to switch to a cheaper therapist if therapy threatens to go on "too long." The importance of the therapeutic bond is denigrated, much to the distress of patients and therapists. *Involuntary* interruption by the therapist is addressed in Chapter 18.

Some patients enter treatment, then decide not to continue for any number of reasons. A working alliance is tentative, not solid. Trying to convince them to continue won't work. Better to acknowledge that they aren't getting what they want. They need to save face to try again.

I make it clear whether I will be available should they decide to return. Their declaration of health is accepted at face value. For some people, it would be most welcome.

With the help of others, we sort out two different questions. How much discord is due to inexperience? How much is due to personal issues? Training is needed for the former; resolution for the latter. Misdiagnosis of the distinction aggravates things. Th unskilled rookie, labeled by a supervisor with countertransference, searches for non-existent personal problems and loses out on training. The advanced practitioner, offered skill suggestions, feels misunderstood and over-looks interfering personal issues. Occasionally, both occur. *Becoming a Family Therapist* speaks to these matters in greater detail, using examples.

Negative Therapeutic Reaction

I focus mainly on therapists and less on techniques. However, some endings and the effect they have on us are so intertwined that attention must be given to the interaction. The negative therapeutic reaction is illustrated in the following composite case of five men early in my practice.

Therapy goes well for a few weeks or months: symptoms subside, alliance develops, good response to interpretations, growing self-observation and insight. Then, without plausible reason, I am puzzled by a paradox. Symptoms worsen following interviews when I expect progress. In each case, the patient regresses, snow-balling session after session, and whatever I do makes things worse. Catastrophic! With the patient agitated and suicidal, dis-ruption in family life makes hospitalization inevitable. All were hospitalized where I could not see them. Stays were long and stormy, and one man killed himself three months after admission.

This turn of events was devastating; I could not fathom it. "I'm doing the same things that worked before, only now the patient is getting worse. How could this be?" Traumatic for a professional who has vowed to "First do no harm." I racked my brain, talked to colleagues, lay awake at night, felt miserable.

Every therapist should know how to handle this negative reaction because it is much easier to prevent than treat. After I figured it out, I never had another in 25 years. The key is recognizing and interpreting *mini*negative therapeutic reactions. A good hour with new insight and effective work is followed by one where symptoms are reignited, mo-tivation is diminished, and it feels like the step forward is canceled by a step back. When recognized and interpreted, the swings become less extreme and progress resumes. One man said, "I don't mind if the pendulum swings back and forth, just so the clock moves on."

Do not assume therapy is not working. On the contrary, mininegative reactions are a sign that therapy *is* working. Take courage to take action. Unconsciously, these patients feel guilty and ashamed by progress and threatened by success, as though it is bad to feel good, dangerous to grow up, scary to be responsible and stop therapy. "If I grow up, I can no longer indulge myself in symptoms."

These common miniregressions call for reanalyzing the symptom dynamics. Be alert and keep them from escalating by timely and accurate interpretation. An effective approach is identifying the patient's personality parts that cooperate and the opposing parts that sabotage. The internal battle rages between characters wanting to get well versus ones maintaining status quo. Resolution harmonizes the personality and frees energy for more productive use.

The key to clear understanding and calm management was work I did on myself. I was dumbfounded that a part motivated to be effective was being undercut by a part that wanted people to stay sick. The convoluted "logic" of this very young part was, "If patients are sick, Chuck will have plenty of work. But if they get well, he will be out of business." Work this out and save yourself the agony (see next chapter).

Mutual Ending of Brief, First-Phase Therapy

First-phase therapy, lasting one to about 12 sessions, is variously known as Ericksonian, strategic, structural, problem-oriented, solution-oriented, psychodynamic. The presenting situation alleviated, it's time to stop. Uncomfortable symptoms are reduced. Patients have more confidence and function better, pleased with improvement, perhaps disappointed if changes are more modest than hoped for. Giving up therapy is a bit of a loss, but regret is slight. Anxiety about the future is dealt with. Offsetting these concerns are relief from expending time, energy, and money; release from dependency; and new plans. Ending is simple, conscious, rational, often planned from the start. Managed care makes it cumbersome to go farther, and for many, this is all that is needed. Therapists interested only in brief therapy settle for ending. First-phase therapy is vulnerable to interruptions and plateaus. Illness and vacations break continuity, and the resumed therapy may not have the same quality. There may be an unexpected ending. This is far more likely than in middle-phase therapy where momentum survives interruption. Brief therapy is based on "Are we getting any help?" rather than on a therapeutic alliance.

But some patients vaguely sense that the subsiding problems have deep roots. Awareness of underlying conflicts varies across a spectrum. Some are glad that their troubles are relieved, and that's all there is to it. Others fear difficult self-exploration. Still others are aware of lifelong problems, but have been unwilling to dig into them. I raise the pros and cons of going farther, then abide by their decision. Sometimes scheduling appointments farther apart is useful.

But about one-fourth of patients will be shortchanged if not encouraged to enter a growthful middle phase. I point out relationship problems and how future complications can be prevented through more work now. Example: an acute school phobia vanishes in brief therapy. Underlying problems (covert phobias in parents, marital conflicts) are better resolved now with a strong relation to the therapist, rather than waiting until the family explodes. Some 10% to 15% can be nudged over a hump of resistance into the middle phase. But this takes a therapist who is committed to long-range work, and cooperation from whoever pays.

Those who terminate need to know that no matter what happens, they need not be ashamed of returning. I say, "We have done good work together and are familiar with each other. Not hearing from you will be good news that you are getting along okay. It will also be good news if I *do* hear from you because you are wise enough to realize you need help again." Some need several brief rounds, and a few move into long-term therapy.

Reaching a mutual ending is easy for therapists. The job is done. No big decisions. No mess. Personal reactions to saying goodbye are lesser versions of those at the end of long-term therapy, and easily handled.

Mutual Termination of Long-Term, Middle-Phase Therapy

When therapy goes beyond first phase, the focus steadily shifts from symptoms to relationships, from "how-we-are-doing-now to how-we-are-doing-in-life, from treatment to psychoeducation. My middle-phase cases had from 25 to 300 sessions over a half to seven years. It takes over a year of practice before we are skilled enough to bring a family through the first phase into the middle phase. It's worth it, for both family and therapist.

Your job: hold a view of where you are and keep the process flowing. The pitfall: let the habit of meeting bog down without clear mutual goals. The most common negative of my 500 observed family sessions with referring therapists was lack of aliveness. Therapy is dead; participants have slipped into a stalemate, neither progressing nor quitting. I am a rescuer for therapy-in-progress, bringing fresh interest to get moving or stop.

Compared with first-phase therapy, the middle phase is more organized, predictable, relaxed, fun—for patients *and* therapist. Trust builds: there's less concern over whether patients will show up, pay the bill, work between appointments. They are more responsible for themselves. They come in ready to work and to take a risk, to share feelings of working together, to look at ego-syntonic behavior that makes trouble for others and see the need for growth in their relationships. The alliance is strong and getting stronger. Optimism and positive feelings are palpable. Silence is comfortable.

Periodically, the turmoil of earlier material intrudes, presenting an opportunity to reexamine those dynamics and solidify resolutions. Gradually, these disruptions are less frequent, deepen the work and eventually mellow to a shadow. Not only are the presenting problems gone or much improved, but areas not considered a problem have come forth and have been well handled.

This is a wonderful time to use any techniques you have learned. With a firm alliance, people have tasted the satisfactions of progress and are willing to try whatever keeps progress going, whatever makes good life better. What you suggest they do depends on their inclinations and your resourcefulness. Creditable recommendations come from a therapist who has done them. An incomplete list: gestalt; drawing and painting; transactional analysis; dream work; sex therapy; audio- and videotape playback; couples group, and longer sessions; meditation and biofeedback; self-improvement workshops; 12-step and support groups; spiritual retreats and quests; men's and women's groups. What comes out in these is grist for the mill in the ongoing middle phase.

Throughout therapy I mention the importance of a good ending, especially if there is a history of painful separations, losses, or impulsive endings. I remind patients of their goal of independence and self-sufficiency, which confirms the idea that our relationship paradoxically is both connected and temporary. Therapy is a stage in life, I am a coach/teacher; along the way, we value steps toward self-reliance and autonomy (like parenting). "How will we know when we're done?" arises naturally. Since we start with a vision of what people want to accomplish, we have a built-in marker for when we will be finished. "Graduation" becomes a part of our private lexicon, so progress checks are informative. Internalization of the process gradually transforms inner characters into inner therapists who will always be there.

From time to time, patients wonder if they are ready to stop, more tentative than planful. When the *therapist* recommends stopping, there is usually an intense recurrence of the dysfunctions that brought them into treatment, and a temporary weakening of the alliance. Until the therapist has been through this a few times, he or she often feels discouraged and ineffectual, as though the first phase has to be repeated. Typically, the family sees no connection between the regression and the suggestion of termination. The therapist may also have trouble seeing that they are caught up in a temporary setback.

In a sense, things start over. Old conflicts are reworked; recovery is faster than the first time. Eventually, termination is suggested again and another regression occurs, this time less severe, shorter, and easier to reverse. Oscillation between progression and regression is an expectable and desirable working through, and firmly embeds healthy changes into the internal characters. When termination can be discussed realistically without regression, it's time to set a date and then stop. Patients mourn the loss of the therapist as well as their symptoms and harmful interactions. They often connect their leaving the therapist with the loss of people in the past and the anticipated future loss.

Therapist Reactions

We all have some unresolved separation anxiety, so it behooves therapists to identify our reactions to it, reactions that may range from transient nostalgia to painful depression. The more psychic energy that is taken up by unfinished business, the more prone we are to mismanagement: stop prematurely to avoid threatening material, or discourage ending to perpetuate dependency. Other problems: over- or underresponsivity, irritability, sympathy, being placating, ignoring strengths, rescuing, feeling guilty about not helping enough. Some develop psychosomatic headaches or indigestion.

Fantasies and dreams may parallel those of our patients. Uncharacteristic errors, often when patients regress, contrast with previous smooth functioning. If you have difficulty with separations, you will have difficulty with patients' regression. Changing style—suddenly becoming more talkative, unnecessarily reassuring—makes you suspicious of having a counterreaction. A common blind spot is failing to see that reactions of the patient are related to anxiety about ending, and acting as though there is a brand-new problem.

Compared with individual work, counterreactions to families are often more noticeable. After a long complicated middle phase, accumulated transferences onto the therapist by all the members are both burdensome and enriching. The last session of a long therapy is moving. All of us are touched by a shared experience we will never forget.

Posttherapy Relationships

Sessions stop, but therapy never ends. We are internalized in people for the rest of their lives, becoming members of the family. Even 20 years after ending, we have been told by former patients that when trouble comes, they ask themselves, "How would Jan feel now? What would Chuck say?" We become whatever they need us to be—arbitrators, catalyzers of conflict resolution, atmosphere setters, consolers, role models. How accurately they predict our responses is striking. *And they become a part of us.*

Resolution of termination, transference, and countertransference gradually lessens, but never ends—that's okay. When therapist and patient socialize beyond termination, it helps to consolidate therapeutic changes with a break between therapy and socializing, even for a few months. Often great benefits occur after ending, especially if there is a strong need to "do my own thing." Phone calls, holiday greetings, and personal contacts revive feelings on both sides, more working through. Ultimately, the end stage resembles a successful solution to disharmony in the family: direct, person-to-person, healthy relating undistorted by negative or positive emotion.

The ending of treatment of a married couple by a married couple can be unique, because this form of therapy has power and depth that's hard to explain. It has balance and equality found in no other format. It's not about patients or friendship or family or lovers, yet partakes of these and more. We know a great deal about each other.

We would do anything for each other, yet know we would not ask. Trust and respect and love are profound. For example:

> *Knowing we have four social workers in the family, a woman calls for advice about social work schools for her son, born while she and her husband were in therapy. After talking "business," we reminisce about shared memories, families, and current lives—23 years after termination! We speak warmly of our time together and fondness for each other. Intimacy within limits. Gratifying. Had I only practiced short-term therapy, I could not savor this rich realm of life. Felt great all day.*

Jan and I see several terminated couples socially. Four joined the Family Institute board, and offered unique counsel. We agreed on ground rules: not expecting a return to therapy; fairly long interval before joining; agreeing on how to avoid role confusion; agreeing to leave the board should regular sessions be needed. One couple did return twice when a child had problems in college. Our knowledge of each other led to quick and successful solutions, without disrupting board membership.

Pivotal is the idea of "hats" that I learned in small town general practice where a person might be patient, neighbor, friend, and bowling buddy. "Now we have our patient and doctor hats on" sets the boundaries for that particular time together. Our tie to each other is not so much severed as transformed and enriched.

Reflections

- Jot down different ways you have seen people handle endings. How many apply to you? Identify good and bad ones.
- Review the last ten patient endings (even for patients seen only once or twice). Which would you change? Play with how to do so next time.
- Describe your earliest memory of separation, loss, or ending. How did you feel? What did you think? What did you do? How did that work out? Describe a decision you made then. How is that decision operating today? Is it still appropriate?

- Starting with that early memory, track your reactions to painful losses up to the present. Is there a pattern? Are you satisfied? If not, what are you going to change that would be healthier? If it's easier, start with a recent loss and trace it back to the earliest memory.
- Death is the ultimate ending to life as we know it. Death conditions all endings. What is your view of death? Is it final? A transition? Meaningful? Is it a topic you can discuss with your intimate partner and others? With patients? Is there a connection between your view of death and how you handle treatment endings?

II

The Therapist as Human Being

The ideal therapist . . . ought to be at least a fairly healthy human being. This explains why training in aesthetic perceiving and creating could be a very desirable aspect of clinical training.

—Abraham Maslow[19]

The older you get, the stranger your earlier selves seem, until you can hardly remember having made their acquaintance at all.

—John Updike

To strengthen what is right in a fool is a holy task.

—The I Ching, or Book of Changes[20]

6

Internal Cast of Characters

The idea of "hats" mentioned half humorously in chapter 5 actually represents a fundamental aspect of what it means to be human, which is the focus of Part II: the therapist as a human being.

Consider this. In the heat of a crisis or an intense emotional onslaught, we sometimes say or do something uncharacteristic. John McEnroe, famous for tennis tantrums, once said that he was two different people, reacting to situations in an inexplicable way. He went on to say that he didn't have control in these instances and later couldn't work out why his emotions ran away.

Like John McEnroe, most of us view ourselves as a unit, an entity, a person solid through and through, predictable, consistent. But faced with an array of choices, how often we think, "A part of me wants this. But another part of me wants that. And yet another wants something else." We are vaguely aware that we are divided, but usually make a choice and move on, thinking we have resolved the dilemma. We assume that these are just our reactions and opinions, the various reactions and opinions of one person. But we are not a single person. We are many.

Looking at others, we are even more likely to see them as unitary with fixed qualities. As a result, observations can be baffling. We read of a serial killer whose neighbor cannot believe he's the same mild, harmless man who does kind things for people. One book describes President John Kennedy as a heroic and charismatic leader, another details his vicious manipulations and philandering. Princess Diana was widely hailed as dedicated and charming and yet seen by others as self-centered and extravagant. How can such things be?

In recent decades, a few therapists and students of personality have taken these puzzlements seriously. Let's examine the possibility that multiplicity is an inherent feature of mind. This is not a new idea; it dates back at least to the early Greeks in Western culture and to philosophers in the ancient Orient. In this century, we have Freud's ego, id, ego ideal, superego; Jung's animus/anima, shadow, archetypes; Berne's Parent–Adult–Child; Perls' top dog/underdog. More recently, we have the inner child, abused child, divine child, inner critic, hidden observer, thin-woman-trying-to-get-out, and other demons and angels.

Various approaches to the many facets of personality that prove more useful and true to the actual state of the internal world have also been developed, such as Assagioli's subpersonalities, Voice Dialogue, Inner Family System, and inner parts work. In my view, these efforts to describe our inner mental landscape suffer from an "anatomical fallacy." The assumption has been that the mind is made up of components, structures, levels, and so on, that are basically the same in everyone, with only quantitative variations to account for qualitative differences among people. How we are internally is prejudged by theories, concepts, and assumptions. Everyone has an ego, a critic, a shadow, just as everyone has a heart, lungs, and liver.

What if some intuitive, curious, not-so-rule-bound maverick says, "Let's turn our study of people inside out and start with what *they* say about their internal world. What if each of us is actually unique, that there are no two inner worlds exactly alike, and that each person is a better authority on what goes on inside than anyone else, with or without credentials? What if an effective creative method for identifying and harmonizing our multiple inner selves can flow from this insight?"

Well, my dear friend and colleague Sandra Watanabe-Hammond[21–23] has done just that. She convinced me of her view through persuasion and clinical stories, and by helping me make big changes in my own inner world. This, after all those years in analysis! She calls her method "Cast of Characters," or simply character work, and I am immensely grateful for her help with this chapter. (See References and Suggested Reading.)

Once I gained some mastery of my characters, I applied the ideas to patients and our interplay. The approach is more powerful than any other modalities I have practiced. I am privileged to be part of a breakthrough that heralds a new era in understanding people, their problems, their capacity to change, and how to facilitate change. I feel once again the excitement I lived through at the birth of family therapy in the 1950s.

Underlying Principles and Basic Techniques

The notion of an inner world peopled by distinct characters is constantly evolving and deepening. Still, we can be guided by a core of principles—not prescriptions—but ways of working without imposing our ideas about how someone *should* be.

1. Our personality is not a monolith. It is a coalition of five to ten competing and cooperating selves who differ in age and gender, size and appearance, perhaps not speaking the same language. With different memories, histories, and stories of the same events. With their own habits, energy levels, opinions, emotions, perceptions. Holding different attitudes toward themselves, each other, and outside life. With unique abilities, priorities, beliefs, and survival mechanisms. Often they are at cross-purposes, forming countless alliances and collusions, plots, ploys, and plans within the group. Characters embody and energize a person and determine the course of his or her life. They constitute an intricate relationship system. They cannot be adequately described with an IQ number or a single adjective. Some are rigid; others flexible. Some have easy access to awareness; others have none. Some are innate; others are learned. No wonder we are so confused!

2. People who come to therapy, not to mention the masses who do not, usually are overusing one or a few characters. We grow up in a society, in families, and in an educational system that overvalues verbal ability and linear analysis. Individual characters are not capable of a full life; those nourished by a particular culture are overdeveloped, while others are undeveloped or hidden from awareness, sometimes for decades. These latter roughly correspond with Jung's "shadow" and Freud's "unconscious." The unavailable strength, energy, creativity, and talent of little-used characters rob us of assets. Robert Ornstein[24] puts it, "The idea

that we have one rational mind seriously undersells our diverse abilities. It oversells our consistency, and it emphasizes the very small, rational islands in the mind at the expense of the vast archipelago of talents, opportunities, and abilities surrounding them."

3. Under right conditions of safety and compassion, characters are identified, talked with, and induced to reveal themselves by finding their own voice and the parts they play in life. Each is fully dimensioned and real, not the same as tangible. Each chooses a name, rather than a label, a unique feature. A name serves as a magnet, drawing to it the character's identity and history, knowledge and wisdom, ideals and inspiration—the power of truth itself. The question, "Do characters actually exist?" is ultimately irrelevant. What is important, in contrast to material objects, is not whether they exist, but whether their use is beneficial.

4. Speaking directly with each character is the most reliable way to know about his or her life. We learn their problems and pleasures, and how the system works from everyone's viewpoint. The direction and course of therapy flow from this information.

5. Until one is sufficiently aware, inner life is such a complex mix that misrepresentations, misconceptions, and conflicts are inevitable. We function according to which character is dominant at the moment. (Multiple personality disorder is a pathological variant and beyond the scope of this book.) As this state of affairs becomes increasingly comprehensible, there is more compassion, trust, harmony, flexibility, and accountability in the internal world. Characters grow in their ability to function creatively in the best interest of the whole, once their survival is not dependent on dominating or subverting others.

6. Each character is important. Each contributes to the makeup of the whole: texture and shape, resilience and humor, intelligence and emotion, body and spirit. Our laudable parts have dark sides; seemingly negative ones have hidden strengths that need to be recognized, appreciated, and utilized. Each contributed to survival at the time of their emergence, and each survival strategy is crucial to understanding the nature and quality of our current life. Valuing and living with all characters is possible and desirable.

7. There are seminal experiences in each character's life that form knots of pain, fear, and anger that inhibit the ability to "live right," as well as produce the strategies to ensure survival (early decisions in TA; fixation points in psychoanalysis). Until knots are untan-

gled, characters are likely to recapitulate their past, applying inappropriately to the present situation the tactics that worked in the past. *Now* is the same as *then* without awareness of the passage of time.

8. Unraveling knots of pain and fear is important. Much time is spent on the past as it still operates today: family of origin, sociocultural context, peer and sibling relationships, and so on. Compassionate, supportive, attentive direct work with kid characters makes a huge difference, marked by changes in appearance and energy patterns, attitudes and behaviors, better boundaries, less fear and anger, more joy and laughter, and responsivity (rather than reactivity) to life. Working with kid characters shifts how the past informs today; the past is no longer so special.

9. Bringing into focused awareness the full scope of our multiple realities heals in ways unlike conceptual and strategic forms of therapy. Once we are familiar with the full range of our inner lives, we can trust our intrinsic ability to correct and heal ourselves.

10. Other than these guiding principles, we do not lock into any preconceptions about what we will find when exploring each person's inner world. There is no urgency to get the person in line with a preset agenda or template. Each character is approached as the expert on itself, able to describe and embody its unique life.

11. Profound transformation is possible and lasting. Simply let it happen naturally with the least interference possible. The process takes off without preprinted maps. Much change happens after sessions when precise work done with characters moves through the whole system.

12. Therapists need several virtues. Mindful awareness of what is happening in the present without grasping, condemning, or forgetting. Curiosity without preconceptions. Fearlessness without aggressiveness to work with raw, unsanitized inner life. Noninterventionist without passivity. Ability to converse in ordinary language without talking down to characters. Respectfulness and appreciation for whatever is.

13. Character work externalizes what is internal. Then we deal with components, just as with any system: individually, in dyads, triads, and as a group. Once a safe relationship is established, we are free to use a wide assortment of techniques, from conversation to movement, to active graphics such as drawing, painting, photography, and videotaping. Characters write journals, stories, and po-

ems in their own handwriting and colors, invent rituals to finish unfinished business, and more. They grow into mutual awareness, acceptance, and accountability.

14. The goal of therapy is to mellow the overactive and build up the weak ones, getting them into balance so as to use all assets in harmony. Eventually, characters mesh smoothly without conscious attention, like a well-tuned engine. When stresses trigger the start of old dysfunctional patterns, creative problem solving, not panic, flows more naturally.

15. The beauty of this work is that people identify their own characters, do 95% of the work, and harmonize them like a fine symphony orchestra. Some do well with once-a-month or irregular visits; others need intense, detailed therapy of variable duration. It is unnecessary to be in therapy; some achieve remarkable results working on their characters after a class or workshop or reading about the method.

16. Jan and I find this work rewarding for couples. They may not want to expose themselves in front of their partner, so we work individually, then come together and share internal casts. They agree that this knowledge will not be used against the other. Knowing each other's inner landscape, they usually recognize some, but not all, of the selves. Typically, each has a few characters that get along well with a few of the partner's, and some that do not get along at all. This permits conflict resolution to be more specific and less personalized. Blame is diminished, less toxic, easier to minimize, and eventually given up. Once internal life is manifested, the techniques in item 13 can be used jointly.

17. I suggest the approach with everyone I see. Some find it more compatible than others. Early on I note hints of a divided self. Women usually catch on quickly, yet men become fully involved because they feel safe as the experts on their own lives. With some who can't do full-fledged exploration, modifying characters who make trouble for them and others is sufficient. Rarely, a person refuses to get into it. People gain a handle on themselves they never had before, even after years of therapy. They like being in charge of studying their characters and their therapy—and their lives. They like doing the work outside of sessions and not being dependent on the therapist, who is primarily coach and catalyst. Because their achievements are self-described and self-correcting, they own them.

An Example of Character Work

The internal cast I know best is my own. They introduce themselves just as I discovered them in 1982 in Sandra's workshop. They are real and accountable, as they speak of their origins, likes and dislikes, place in interactions, and changes as a result of character work.

"I am *President Frank*, the intensely active part that occupies most of Chuck's waking life. I am *Frank* after a friend of my folks who enlivened parties by tearing phone books in half, and *President* because I have taken him from president in medical school to six corporations to the Family Institute. I have been dominant since he decided on medicine at age 13, and I am responsible in large part for the 'success' of music, athletics, medicine, and psychiatry. I do not easily share my feelings because I play my cards close to the vest, and because I do not have a good handle on feelings. If it cannot be reduced to logical words, it is foreign to me. I am Chuck's child-eye view of his father, who was seen as having these traits. I am convinced by experience that a little selective self-disclosure is a good when it helps therapy. But when revealing personal things, I speak of thoughts, facts, theories, concrete instances, the literature, and logical conclusions. Emotion, compassion, nurturing are expressed indirectly by doing, achieving and providing.

"I am achievement oriented. Powerful. Meticulous. Interested in others less for themselves, and more for whether they can help me reach my goals, which I want them to accept as theirs. Critical, but more so of myself. Compulsively organized. Hard driving. Successful, but I pay a heavy toll in stress diseases like high blood pressure, diabetes, and coronary arteriosclerosis. I'm a 'hot reactor.' Because I take everything too seriously, I seethe with anger that bursts forth with frightening intensity when I reach the boiling point. I intimidate and silence other characters, and get into real trouble with Jan and the kids."

At this point *Doctor Softy* speaks up. "I'm also prominent in Chuck's life. I'm often in conflict with *Frank* and occasionally overwhelmed by him. I look and act very different: overweight, careless dresser. Laid back, a bit depressed. I relate easily to feelings and people of all ages, all cultures, all personalities—because I'm not critical or judgmental. I'm easy going, get along great with Jan and the kids. I'm like Chuck's mom. Some of her favorite lectures to him: 'You think too much, too moody. You'll be the wealthiest man in the graveyard. I never worked a day for pay in my whole life and I turned out all right. You work too hard, don't know how to have fun.' Now I say those things to *Frank*."

The next image is a stereotype of myself at 17, a free-spirited jock. After trying on several names, *Duke* feels right. "I don't know what I wanna be when I grow up. I don't think about it much. Clothes are big. Guess I'm girl crazy. I love anything that moves—athletics, driving, sailing. Can't wait to be out from under my parents—when I can do anything I want to without worrying about what they think. *Frank* says that's impossible, but he's a stuffed shirt. I hate being told what to do, but don't rebel for fear of getting caught. What really counts is what I see and hear right now. I don't care if my body hurts, just so I get back in the game. I'm cool, with it, clever. *Softy* and *Frank* are nuts, too serious about everything, always fighting. I tell them to lighten up, but they don't listen.

"I tell my pals anything, maybe brag a little, but don't show how I really feel. *Softy* says that's because I don't even know I don't know. I only tell parents and teachers what I think they want to know, and keep it upbeat. I hide stuff I do; maybe I'm a little sneaky, because I know they don't approve. Also, I pretend I'm not hiding the fact that I'm hiding. I say: Be cool. Casual. Off-hand. Relaxed. Don't think too much, unless it's about sports or girls or jazz. Don't be anything like *Frank* or *Softy*. Be a smooth boy. Looks are important, especially to my friends."

After playing these three I'm blank. Sandra suggests that during the month before the next workshop I work on these by writing down everything I can think about them. I do this, having a separate section for each, getting the feel for them, and using whatever writing style feels right. By the next time, I'm quite clear about *Frank, Softy,* and *Duke*, and ready to see if any more images come up. I had the notion that these are my major parts, anyone else is minor. Was I wrong!

A memory flashes of my mother's ageless mother who lived with us until I was a teenager. She was—and is within me—a very important good-parent figure, a "lady" in the old-fashioned sense. My character's voice represents and blends with my actual grandmother's. They feel inseparable. "Everyone in the family calls me *Nannie Ball*. I believe in doing things right, not making trouble, minding my own business. I do not approve of *Duke*, but keep it to myself. He's funny, but I don't let on. Proper. I get along fine because I never pry. I stay young, never tell my age, and keep Chuck young. I stay calm and live with little fuss. I believe in self-sufficiency and not being a burden. I only tell about myself to a few trusted friends, and then I keep it positive. I don't look back, but am willing to when Chuck asks. I never criticize him or the family, think nearly everything they do is great. I watched five-year-old Danny's misbehavior without comment, later congratulated Jan and Chuck on how he had improved. My father was the only physician in the two families, a factor in Chuck's choice of profession and our closeness.

"I am a private person. Appearances are important. I made my way in the world with dignity, respect, and care. Shame is dreadful. I concealed my divorce in 1905 after just a few years of marriage. I cut ten years off my age to get a job, then when they thought I was 65 I was too proud to admit I was only 55 and worked ten more to retire. Chuck and I admire each other so much it is easy to be a part of him."

As my image of *Nannie Ball* fades, I sob. Sandra wonders if another character has come forward. I feel very young and cry inconsolably. "I'm *Chuckie*. I'm five. I'm always moving. I cry easy, but sometimes I laugh a lot. I'm nosey. I get scared. What's going on with the grown-ups? I love candy, comics, games, playing tricks. I tease a lot. *Duke* is the greatest. When I feel bad, I crawl up on *Nannie Ball's* lap at night and on *Edith's* in the day. They tell me to be good and do what *Frank* says. I made Chuck get sick because I ate too much candy and ice cream. [heavy sobbing] I'm scared of *Frank*, not *Softy*. When I wear hats and clothes I really am a cowboy, police officer, soldier, firefighter. I like attention."

Edith is modeled after the black housekeeper I was close to as a preschooler and in early grades. She was soft, warm, fat, good natured, and dressed for comfort. Ageless and loving. Superstitious, she was spiritual without a lot of words. She also speaks with the same voice I heard as a child. "Ah looks afta *Chuckie*, make sure he's happy. Nothing he do be wrong. He lissens to me, 'cause he knows ahm tough underneath. Ah taught *Chuckie* that Gawd made some black an' some white, but we's all the same inside an' we should all love each other." Edith helped me be at ease with all people, taught me to be congenial, even when tense. These qualities are important to me.

Several years later, *Chris* emerged. He does not like to be quoted, so I simply describe him. I don't know his origin. He seems to have been with me from the beginning, and is felt as a profound connection to universal consciousness, God, Life Force, Essence, Overself. He is ageless, with no beginning and no ending, and yet keenly present. He is world weary, has seen and done it all, while removed from the fray.

Chris was active in childhood and adolescence, but banished by **President Frank** in medical school. However, his anonymous influence continued indirectly, hardly noticeable to me and to other characters, yet people say—to my surprise—I have a spiritual quality. It is *Chris* they sense. He is tall, gaunt, with a long white beard, cloaked in a hooded gown reaching his sandals. I only get glimpses of his face. He speaks in deep, measured tones. Until I "saw" and "heard" him, I wasn't sure whether this figure was male or female, and assumed it was androgynous.

Chris is gentle and soft, yet a firm dreamer, philosopher, idealist, and vegetarian. He is not someone you can laugh with over a beer, but you can chuckle with him at life's ironies. He influences by pushing for adherence to principles, a stereotypical religious figure, a mystic in touch with other worlds. He reminds me of my oldest son, Dan, philosopher, meditator, mediator—a quiet leader. If *Chris* must be categorized, which he abhors, he is Taoist, Buddhist, Hebrew, Christian (thus his name).

For 40 years, I was not aware of him, and am touched and grateful he has come forth. His reentry is enhanced by aging, giving up work decisions, brushes with death, and many spiritual practices. This is *Chris'* time. He is now our powerful internal leader. Other characters respect him, trust him, and are in awe of him. Now that I have found him—perhaps we found each other—I will never again lose him.

My Characters Doing Therapy

Frank is the force behind my professional evolution, and *Softy* makes my work more human. *Frank* was dominant from general practice through analysis, with *Softy* smoothing the path. But they were often at odds—hawk and dove. Only since family and experiential therapy has *Frank* dulled his edge and become no longer dominant. He was brought out by frustration, challenge, criticism. When the only character out front, he was angrily aloof, intimidating, controlled, and controlling, with a mind like a steel trap. He's likely to lock horns with people who don't see things his way, even after his best rational explanations. He has little patience with whiners, which gets him into trouble in and out of therapy.

Softy says, "I love medicine and psychiatry because I'm truly interested in my patients, who in turn love and feel comfortable with me. *Frank* they admire, respect, and fear. I'm badly organized because I react intuitively and emotionally. Have a hard time saying No (thus my name), especially to those I'm fond of; I don't want to hurt their feelings, which would hurt me. I have trouble setting limits, for others and myself, so I can be taken advantage of and not realize it. I know better than *Frank* does how to have fun. I reveal stuff about myself without discomfort and don't see what the big deal is about self-disclosure. I'm lazy at times and not as ambitious as *Frank.*"

Duke seldom came into therapy until recently. If he popped up with a wisecrack, it was only with patients he knew well, and even then he quickly ducked back inside, knowing that *Frank* didn't approve. Now he is more active, both in and out of therapy. People who come back after therapy years ago say I talk more, am more fun to be with, laugh more, tell more jokes on myself, and have lightened up. They like it, and so do I.

Chuckie hid when I worked, only came out when other kids were there. He likes to goof around with them, but only after he knows them. He, like *Duke*, has come out more in recent years. In cotherapy he gets silly with Jan's eight-year-old *Barbara*. Now he's just himself all the time. Whatever is going on with *Chuckie* is what you get.

Nannie Ball is a quiet stabilizer, has great endurance, patience, and equanimity. She sees that things are done properly and in good taste. Seldom taking an active leadership role, she nevertheless is a firm foundation for all relationships, inner and outer. She gets along with all characters and is a good mediator when tempers flare because she wants everyone to be the best they can be.

Edith's natural nurturing comes through in my work and people experience me as more caring and supportive. She is shy with the other characters, but also is a good mediator as she gains confidence. She only discloses what is safe and conventional, keeping her opinions and personal life to herself. Although she has had hardships, she doesn't mention them. *Edith* keeps a polite, respectful distance from all parts, except for *Chuckie*, whom she mothers. Her wisdom and belief in spirit that others hardly know about bring her more fully into my life.

Chris listens, comes up with epigrams, metaphors, parables, philosophy, unique perspectives, and quaint *non sequiturs* that sink in later, conveying timeless wisdom. Has a deep respect for the power and flow of life. His motto: "Accept. Let it be. Be your best self. Trust the universe. But cut the cards!" *Chris* reveals self indirectly. Patients report I am more serene, more open to bringing up religious and spiritual topics, more caring, loving, compassionate. He does not speak about self, shows depth through oblique wise comments that are on target and startling. He speaks from experience of the heart without saying so.

When things get confusing and direction uncertain, *Chris* has a calm, sensible, principled suggestion—always suggests, never lectures. Content to let therapy (and life) unfold with a minimum of tinkering on the part of feeble humans. Although ethereal and otherworldly, he is also practical. He convinced me to get back to writing, thinking it important to share whatever wisdom I have gained from training, from patients and students, from friends and colleagues, from family. He sees spiritual and psychological flow as following an inclusive law of life: you and me, back and forth, circles and cycles, giving and receiving, mutuality, reciprocity, taking in and giving out. His philosophy has been quietly guiding my transformation away from the one-way street of doctor to patient.

I internalized these images from the important people in my early life and have been trying, with slow but increasing success, to accept all parts comfortably. For years, *President Frank* and *Doctor Softy* were the main actors and in frequent conflict, whether in work, in the family, or in my view of how life ought to be. It has been difficult for each to accept the other's assets and limitations.

As *Frank, Softy,* and *Duke* mellow, and *Edith, Nannie Ball, Chuckie,* and *Chris* take their rightful places, I'm feeling unfamiliar serenity. The inner orchestra is harmonious—I'm conducting it, not vice versa. Although I realize that personal experience is easily convincing, I can't help but wish that all therapists, all people, could have this transformation, and at a younger age. But this idealistic fantasy is just that. Still, I believe a new paradigm is in the offing. The deception that we are monolithic will yield to a truer understanding of ourselves as naturally multiple.

This insight and the methods that flow from it give us the possibility of therapeutic mastery far beyond the methods in vogue today. When we are clear about our own internal worlds, we can be clear about which specific parts are interacting with specific parts of another patient or person. When the other also has command of his or her parts, the way is open for dialogue that can be precise, objective, and mutually healing. We both evolve toward greater, more complete, more whole humanness. Maybe *Chuckie's* hats are more profound than merely a little kid's game.

Once again—know thyself. Examine your inner life, along with your outer world.

Reflections

- See how far you can go in identifying your internal cast of characters. Watch for upsurges of emotion—these come from a character who is pressing front and center, momentarily taking you over. Get to know it well, using whatever will reveal it: give it a name, write its autobiography, draw it, put it in an empty chair and converse with it—be creative. Sandra suggests having the curiosity of a detective and the patience of a puzzle solver.
- You will pick up a hint of another character close to the first. Do the same with it, and with as many more as come to mind. Then get them to talk with each other. Setting out a chair for each and moving from chair to chair is an effective way to differentiate one from another.
- For an enriching perspective, bring in a trusted colleague—ideally, one also doing character work—to witness and facilitate what you are doing. Jan and I were immensely helpful to each other. Or form a peer group of like-minded colleagues. Or take a workshop or seminar; there are many today. Use the material in "Suggested Readings."

7

The Good Therapist

Studies of how good therapists come to be are rare, and generalizations are risky. Still, we can identify some of the complex qualities of a good therapist. And impressions are worth mentioning in the hope that researchers will shape guidelines for trainers.

Some General Qualities

The therapist who knows his or her internal characters, the many facets of personality, is able to use them flexibly and effectively in therapy. Therapists come in many flavors, via many paths. They can be said to have a favorable genetic endowment. That does not mean that therapists are born, not made. The old nature/nurture battle has given way to synthesis: inborn capacities require transaction with enhancing nurture for full flowering. True, some may succeed in painting, music, writing, dance, athletics by talent and self-learning alone. But therapists are more accurately compared to concert violinists: None are self-taught. Native talent must be there, but guiding, shaping, and encouraging it are also essential. Genetic endowment is *necessary* but not *sufficient*. Once education gate keepers have selected prospects with "good-enough" endowments, nurturing nature becomes the task. A favorable environment is necessary, but is not by itself sufficient either.

Effective therapists are realistic optimists. They know the worst that can happen, yet believe that things will get better or they wouldn't be in this business. They have a solid conviction that if they patiently endure, good things will happen. They like people, and arouse hope in the worst of circumstances. They see strength, where others see only weakness, pathology, or immorality, and have a deep respect for health—physical, mental, spiritual. They are effective despite naysaying internal parts. They are nonthreatening persons who create a safe place where patients feel cared for and protected, knowing they will not be exploited. Honesty and reliability are evident, as are warmth and generosity and a sense of humor. In truly listening, empathy is obvious. Right listening is crucial to therapy of every school: active, not passive; receptive, not grabby; accepts what is actually heard, not what is expected; hears each person without pigeonholing.

Successful therapists—people—have wholeness, uniqueness, aliveness, openness, compassion, integrity, and full humanity, born of a healthy balance among inner selves. On some days I am filled with these wonderful qualities; on others, am not! I am speaking of what I aspire to, how I am at my best, my ideal. I also know that *any* quality, however noble, becomes problematic if overdone. So monitoring ourselves should be built in.

Some therapists are *known* to be effective. *Why* they are is intangible, but therapists recognize intuitive brilliance. Lionel Blitszen was such a man, hardly known now. Following Franz Alexander to Chicago, he attracted many patients and supervisees. Today his influence lives on in admirers' quotes, such as, "If a therapist and patient are in a room, it helps if the therapist is not anxious!" He didn't write, join academia, or administrate. He moved people with grunts, body language, facial expression, compassion, and exquisite timing—not preachments.

Training cannot make a gifted therapist. But when combined with inner work, it can make us ordinary mortals effective. With persistence, we take strides toward our potential. A good therapist is well along in personal evolution, moving toward Maslow's ideal of self-actualization, authenticity, autonomy. The more integrated and fully functioning as a person, the more these qualities perfuse therapy. Maslow says[19]:

The good parent, or therapist, or educator practices as if he understood that gentleness, sweetness, respect for fear, understanding the naturalness of defensive and regressive forces are necessary if growth is not to look like an overwhelming danger instead of a delightful prospect.

Some Specific Qualities

Intelligence

Many in the average, borderline, and even retarded ranges have natural healing abilities: loving empathy, patience, healing touch. Some make fine nursing home aides, affectionately appreciated by patients and staff, natural helpers who have a simple, down-to-earth spirituality. In various groups—Daybreak is an example—retarded persons provide devoted care for the massively physically and mentally disabled, care not given well by academic types. There is something about an overdeveloped, overeducated intellect that interferes with human-to-human contact.

At the other extreme are the gifted. Two supervisees who had been told their IQs were over 150 hid this because it burdened relationships. Rapid learners and eager questioners of life, the gifted hunger to know. The smartest in any group, they wonder, "Should I use my smarts and risk being called a wise guy, a threat to an insecure leader? Should I expose myself to envy and scapegoating? Or should I play dumb and stultify my best feature?" They need complex challenges, or difficult teaching, or original research. The brightest students don't necessarily make the best clinicians. Schools set great store on intellectual achievement. But training for an art is incomplete when thinking brains are valued above intuitive hearts.

A high-school psychology teacher is in analysis. Bright and well informed, we get into profitless competition over who is right about nearly everything! After a lot of frustration for both of us, I step back mentally. It dawns on me this guy is smarter than I am. I can never win. Moreover, he opens my eyes to the futility of "winning" with patients. If we don't both win, we both lose. After I quit arguing, he does too and the analysis moves. More comfortable, I tell my realization. He already knew it. We agree that being smart is no protection against being neurotic, and I don't have to be smarter to help him. Years after a good termination, he writes warmly about his new position, satisfying marriage, emotional freedom, and appreciation for our work.

Sensitivity

This is also necessary, but not sufficient, and is found across a spectrum. Like so many crucial psychological matters (love, for example) sensitivity is hard to put into words. Yet we know a sensitive person when we see one.

Sensitivity, like other qualities, has drawbacks at both ends of the spectrum. The too-sensitive therapist is often drawn to psychodynamic and humanistic styles. She or he may be unprotective of self, vulnerable to being sucked into a family, too identified with victims, overwhelmed by responsibility, headed for burnout. Enthusiastic for the sensitive student, teachers may act as though sensitivity is linear—the more, the better—hardly aware of pitfalls. We may not see oversensitivity camouflaging insecurity. Caring too much is the way the oversensitive person knows to be valued. And being valued is important. Not usually thought rigid, they can be as inflexible as an obsessive-compulsive. Detrimental to their wish to be good therapists, they may be more sensitive to slights *from* others, less empathic to the pain *of* others.

At the other end is the undersensitive therapist, who has gotten through by strong "left-brain" skills: goal-oriented, good grades, conformity, one-track-mindedness, overpreparation, attention to detail and completion of assignments. He or she is shocked to discover these skills not only count for little in therapy, but sometimes interfere with systems work. The cognitive, logical, controlled personality fits brief methods. Unless the personality becomes more balanced, he or she is headed for a rigid, boring, rote style that also has burnout written all over it.

Distinguish between *capacity* and *function*. People at both ends may have equal sensitivity capacity. But the undersensitive is not as sensitive as he or she appears, and the undersensitive is not as insensitive. Function is incongruent with capacity. Childhood socialization can exaggerate traits until they are dysfunctional. Both fail in *optimal* sensitivity. Both need to move from the extreme. This could be done in therapy. But they typically are drawn to therapists with similar traits, so may not change unless therapy tones down overfunctioning intellectual or sensitive parts. And if training seldom focuses on the person, optimal sensitivity may be missed.

Because of the misconception that sensitivity is an unadulterated good, a supervisor may try to "pull" sensitivity out of seemingly undersensitive group members. This not only fails, but compounds the problem. Instead, the supervisor needs to entice out underused characters. Furthermore, a tug-of-war with the undersensitive leaves oversensitive members without help in taming and optimizing their overreactive characters. Similarly, therapists who overprize sensitivity have trouble with the ostensibly loving, sensitive partner stuck with this ostensibly unloving, insensitive blob. When they set out to fix the undersensitive they are in for a rude awakening when the balance shifts, as it must if therapy is to succeed.

Energy

Most therapists are high-energy people. Physical and psychic energy are thought of separately, yet usually found together. Severely paralyzed by polio, Milton Erickson's motor expression was limited, so physical energy was sublimated into psychological energy. His staying power for creative work is legendary.

The mental health field has a range of physicality. Some therapists sit quietly, talking and listening. Others are restless, get to their feet, move people around, write on the flip charts, sit on the floor. Some are hesitant about "acting out." Still others enjoy teaching and directing activity in groups. Only doing psychoanalysis is not for me—sitting behind the couch, unable to see faces, stuck in the same chair, fine-tuning the same technique year after year. Still, some friends do fine with this sedentary style and cannot function with more than one person in the room. They rightly just treat individuals. Students presented with a smorgasbord of practice possibilities invent a style congruent with their inborn energy.

Psychological Mindedness and Systemic Thinking

We need psychological mindedness, and patients should develop it too. Family therapists need a special kind not considered necessary for work with individuals: thinking and acting systemically, relationally, taking into account all facets of life, the lives of significant others, and the multiple interconnections. We need a wide field of vision. My peripheral vision happens to be very good, a help in team sports, a hinderance in bowling. Does the field of vision differ between individual and family therapists?

The family therapist also needs to be aware of *internal* systems of self and patients. In the therapy I and my supervisees do, both the inner and outer worlds are important. We shift from one to the other as required. This shift becomes easier and more automatic the more we do it. Tough task, not entered into lightly without guidance. While family sessions are more energy-draining than individual sessions, the nondisclosing person who sees only individuals ends up exhausted.

Hedgehog and Fox[25]

To catch a chicken, the hedgehog (porcupine) advances slowly, carefully, quietly, in a direct line, pausing, creeping forward. The fox jumps around, distracts, confuses, surprises by grabbing from an unexpected angle. Both get the chicken.

Hedgehogs know one big thing. Foxes know many little things. Hedgehogs know separation and compartments. Foxes make connections and consensus. In my experience, men are more likely to be hedgehogs, and women to be foxes. Each has strengths and weaknesses. And the genders have many exceptions. To be whole, we need the strengths of both.

The hedgehog focuses intense stubborn intellectual tunnel vision for power, like a train on a track, not much affected by its surroundings. Switching tracks is awkward, disorienting. Gets him through law, medicine, business, engineering. Men have dominated these fields, but women are making inroads as they strengthen their hedgehoggy selves.

The fox skips from interest to interest, keeping many things in mind, is good at coordinating interactions, has a wide field of vision. She or he is reactive to what is interesting and influenceable. Fox distracts self, may have difficulty maintaining focus, can lose power when spread too thin.

Definitions are revealing. *Hedgehog*: military defensive position capable of maintaining itself for a long period when encircled by an enemy; made of crossed logs or steel bars embedded in concrete; designed to damage and impede the boats and tanks of a landing force. *Fox*: clever, cunning, or crafty person who tricks another. Or braid made by twisting two or more strands of yarn together. Or a painting with excessively warm tones, containing too much red.

Call them "levelers" and "sharpeners." Levelers minimize everything, including their reactions, especially unfamiliar things. They use bland approval, "All right, not bad, could be worse, okay." They emphasize commonality, have seen it all, done it all. Hard to excite. Sharpeners maximize everything, "Terrific! gorgeous! Fantastic!" They emphasize uniqueness, importance, and brilliance. Easy to excite. These "opposites" attract, marry, and fight. An exasperated wife whines, "I rush around fixing dinner, doing laundry, helping with homework, answering the phone. He can't even watch the baby while he reads the paper." They latch onto the leveler–sharpener idea, finding it handy to understand parts of themselves that both fight and keep them together.

For half a century, psychotherapy was dominated by hedgehoggy men who considered their style "normal," and women's foxy, emotional, flexible style "hysterical." Women gained prominence when they used their hedgehoggy parts, and were praised because "they think like men." What a putdown! This is changing for the better. People are deeper and more complex than their stereotypes. As we aspire to integration with access to every part, we resist categorization. Men are undergoing "feminization," women "masculinization." Each is bringing forth aspects of self that have always been there, and now are more freely emerging.

It is no accident that family therapy arose in the second half of the century and that women are in the majority in practice, teaching, and research. Good family therapists are natural people persons and able to relate to more than one person at a time, even a roomful. They respect the individuality of each, can be firm yet fair to each, and never make one feel inferior, even when praising another.

Both leveler hedgehogs and sharpener foxes can make effective therapists. Each needs to enhance the less natural style: become hedgehoggy sharpeners and foxy levelers when needed by allowing less dominant characters to have the floor. Inner harmony, effective therapy.

Family therapists are a gregarious lot. For many years, I attended conventions and private parties of both family therapists and analysts. The differences are striking. Family people are outgoing, talky, effervescent, self-revealing, emotional, noisy, active, foxy. Analysts are guarded, intellectual, somber, withholding, avoiding their analysts and analysands, poker-faced, straight-laced, hedgehoggy. I must be doing something right when analysts tell me, confidentially, I am too family oriented and family people say I am too analytical.

There is magnetism between method and personality. I gave a talk on family therapy with adolescents. Then George Klumpner, old friend and fellow candidate at the analytic institute, and later president of the Chicago Psychoanalytic Society, spoke of individual therapy with teens. The talks were *very* different, and I listened uneasily to discussant James Anthony, our child analysis teacher. He noted the differences and said, "If you are a Chuck sort of person, you like what he says. If you are a George sort of person, you like what *he* says." This book in a nutshell!

The difference between tunnel and wide-angle vision is both in-born and learned. We can unlearn and relearn, fine-tuning our assets for wholeness. Takes a lifetime. Anyone looking for a purpose in life has a ready-made opportunity right inside. And today there is more help than ever. We use what life brings to achieve what we really need. We have assets, and liabilities that can turn into assets. For example, many therapists wear glasses or contact lenses. Is near-sightedness an influence for our field? Perhaps a child with visual weakness remains close to the mother. This need for closeness in order to see people better persists through life as both a vocational and personal need. It has been true for me and for Jan.

> *On a college basketball date I point out a friend Jan couldn't recognize. I hand her my glasses. She can see! We goodnaturedly tussle over the glasses. True to our hedgehog and fox preferences, I want to watch the game and she wants to look for friends. Our personal and professional lives bear out a need to be close to others and to each other, physically, emotionally, spiritually. And nei-ther is still so hedgehoggy or foxy.*

Therapeutic effectiveness has improved, and I have come to believe that we all can achieve far more than we think. Envisioning possibility creates pathways to results. We have hardly touched potentials for growth, for creativity—the evolving therapist and the patient in trouble. And the therapist in trouble and the evolving patient. To believe that people are fragile, empty, sick victims is to encourage those very characteristics—what poor therapists do. But to believe in possibility encourages actualization—what good therapists do.

Reflections

- Put yourself and each character on a sensitivity scale from one to ten. Do you change with different patients? With different situations? In or out of the office? With your partner? Are you satisfied?
- Ask yourself and your characters similar questions about hedgehog/fox and sharpener/leveler. See if the next

couple you treat can use these ideas and note how they play out between them.

- Reconstruct a time in therapy when you were over-sensitive. How did you recognize it? What did you do? Do the same for an undersensitive moment.

- Describe yourself in those moments when you are a good therapist. Contrast that with moments when you're not at your best. See if you can identify how your characters are functioning in those two moments. During the bad times, are one or a few parts dominant and others in the background? Where do you need to work to gain more internal balance?

- What childhood wounds continue today? How do they interfere with—and how do they enhance—your current life? Will you still be a therapist if you pretty fully resolve them?

8

Vulnerabilities

The Therapist-To-Be

As kids we survive an array of family crises: physical illness, cultural and geographic displacement, accident, surgery, death, abuse, financial disaster, divorce, substance misuse, family disharmony, mental illness,—any of life's predicaments.

Sometimes the matchups are startling. In child welfare, the history of a couple placing a child in a foster home is often similar to that of a couple becoming foster parents; some families try to solve problems by getting rid of a child, others by taking in a child. Many workers are effective precisely because they, too, have lived through family turmoil, are savvy about the ins and outs of placement. Experience is not what happens to us, it is *what we do about what happens*. A to-be therapist shapes traumas into a career. The poet Novalis puts it succinctly, "All the hazards of life are the elements out of which we can fashion whatever we like."

We forget how narcissistic children are. Narcissism is our birth mode and is never fully outgrown. We assume we are the center of family events, to our benefit or harm, especially harm. Ingredients for the life script of a character as *victim* are in place. Another character identifies with the *persecutor*. When family members experience a tragedy, a *rescuer* character comes forth. And rescuers are easily victimized. The victim sends out alarms for help. The rescuer attempts to protect the victim from the persecutor, and all three are polarized, personalized, and intensified. When rescue fails, the victim turns on the rescuer, who then feels victimized and betrayed. The victim becomes the persecutor, the rescuer becomes the victim and the original victim is at odds with both rescuer and prosecutor. If we have not resolved conflicts among our victimized, rescuing, and persecuting characters, we easily slip into such roles as therapists.

Some therapists start out as scapegoats and take on the role of spokesperson and therapist in the family.

> *Jimmy, nine years old, has a school phobia. After he returns to class, carried screaming and kicking out of the family session by the principal, we continue weekly meetings to prevent a recurrence. By the fourth session the phobia is gone. Two younger siblings gossip about a drunken neighbor. Jimmy interrupts, saying they are here to work on their problems, not the neighbor's. During several months of family work, he is an active leader. The mother is thinking of leaving the family, but is terrified at the idea. When Jimmy, her oldest, closest child hears this, he asserts he will stay in school; he likes talking about problems, and isn't so scared. After productive couple therapy, they agree on divorce without the children becoming symptomatic. This vignette also illustrates unconscious therapeutic alliance, when Jimmy says what the therapist has been saying.*

A child stressed by family pressures develops a rescuing character who feels impelled to do something. A strong obligation to help becomes the motivation for a helping career, and a potential for stress and strain. This analogy is useful. In a testing lab, experiments are conducted with construction materials. Wood frames, cement blocks, steel beams are subjected to increasing pressure. Before they break, there are microscopic changes in structure, but the load is still upheld. The break is the threshold beyond which a load cannot be safely carried. *Stress* is the internal change before the break. *Strain* is the break. People have similar internal sturdiness that handles everyday stress without breaking, plus the resiliency to recoup if they do.

When a family difficulty is seen as primarily physical, the child observer may be drawn to a field that deals with the body: medicine, nursing, physical therapy. True for me, not necessarily for others.

At nine, I carelessly throw a ball into the roof gutter. Dad gets a ladder to retrieve it, while I lounge listening to a radio wrapup of the Cubs' baseball game. I know I should help, but steal minutes to hear the statistics. Suddenly I hear a scream and a crash. Dad has fallen. Devastated, I rush to him in a haze of anxiety and guilt. Three lumbar vertebrae and the right (dominant) wrist are crushed. He spends three months on a traction frame and three more in a steel brace. In the midst of the Depression.

Fast forward four years. I am called to get up for school, but still snooze, half awake and guilty. I hear another scream and crush. Dashing into the bathroom, I find Dad on the floor, arms and legs thrashing, eyes rolled back, blue face, chomping bloody foam. It is the first of the grand mal convulsions that plague him, and us, for the rest of his life. Three weeks later, I melodramatically announce, "I've decided to become a doctor." Fantasies of finding a cure for epilepsy were vivid from the age of 13 until I was far enough along in medical school to see that my bent was practice, not research. I have wondered if my motivation, reinforced by Mayo's opinion that his epilepsy was caused by the fall, would wear off, but after 50 years it hasn't! For decades, I was sure it was my fault. More leftover childish narcissism.

When catastrophe is seen as psychological, the child may gravitate toward a field involving people: social work, ministry, psychology, therapy—true for Jan.

When Jan was nine years old (interesting age concordance!), her mother delivered premature twins. One died, the other struggled for months. Her mother was depressed. Shortly after, her mother-in-law died while Jan's father was pressing to finish his Ph.D. Down to 80 pounds, Jan's mother went into a sanitarium for a six-month rest cure with no visitors. She recovered, returned home, and Jan developed tics, which was misdiagnosed as St Vitus' Dance. Jan was confined to bed for five months and was not permitted to receive visitors, read, or even walk to the bathroom.

A child is distraught when a parent she or he depends on for survival might die. Trying to understand, the child is a good observer, but a poor diagnostician. This psychologically minded, bright, sensitive, energetic person, often affected more severely than others, is impelled to do something, even fall ill, in the hope of rescuing the parent. Inner characters muster their distinctive, often opposing, survival strategies. The child takes on attitudes, feelings, and behaviors designed to help. A life decision is made. The younger the child, the more inappropriate, frustrated, and persistent the efforts. Kid characters become therapists of sorts, attempting to help others and thereby vicariously trying to help themselves.

The young helper takes on an impossible task. Yet helping is seen as necessary for survival—of the self and of the rest of the family. But the child is poorly prepared for the job. Intelligence and judgment are still immature; life is just beginning. And as surgeons tell you, it is a bad idea to operate on family members. Plus the job is taken on without training, supervision, literature, or previous experience as patient or therapist! No wonder our first case turns out badly. Nevertheless, we charge ahead, doing the best we can, and making a reactive decision that will both benefit and bedevil us for a lifetime.

Some children stop trying and turn elsewhere—schoolwork, reading, activities, sports, friends, anything outside the home. Some kid characters create walls, fogs, amnesias that keep much of childhood out of awareness. Withdrawal, too, will both serve and pester them later and is no protection against internalized conflicts and unfinished business. Trauma coalesces dynamic forces into energy patterns that remain potent.

Early Decisions

Therapy, training, and personal development loosen energies from old dysfunctional attachments, and healthy endowments are partly freed for doing therapy. Yet early patterns remain, to be reactivated under stress. Kid character decisions are strikingly early, clear, precise, and longlasting. You should have a working knowledge of early decisions and later redecisions as developed by the Gouldings.[26,27] How these concepts are utilized is the essence of character work.

I presented these ideas in a seminar. One member said very young children aren't capable of making decisions. An excellent, experienced social worker whom I respected for years spoke up.

> At 18 months—*I checked the dates*—*my parents decided to take a three-month trip and leave me with a relative. They explained*

this and said they wanted me to be a good girl, get out of diapers, and take care of myself. When they returned, they lavished praise for my success. This set a compulsive lifelong pattern of top grades, self-sufficiency, and the need to take care of others. At 55 I regret not having fun. Without husband or children, I've taken on too much responsibility. Cutting down and enjoying myself is the hardest thing I've ever done. I am convinced that at one and a half I made a survival decision that I remember so clearly and have been living out for my whole life, especially since it is no longer appropriate.

The Inner World

A future therapist is adept at tuning in to subtle clues and signs of trouble. The "right-brain-dominant" girl is often a psychological detective, thinking and talking about her feelings about people. The "left-brain-dominant" boy takes on a healing role, but is not necessarily aware of the nuances to which he responds. Both are avid readers, imaginative fantasizers and constant observers of life.

Our potential therapist is thoughtful about inner events, vulnerable to hurts, cares what happens to self and others. Some have reactions they can put aside; others brood, growing overly responsible and self-critical. All this promotes feeling different from peers, whose opinions are very important. Loneliness is a prevailing tone, even in a crowd. Overreacting to presumed slights fosters a sense of rejection. The young person feels not-good-enough. For me, music and sports were life-saving ways to deal with these feelings. For Jan, it was top grades and extracurricular activities. Years later, the segue into therapy came naturally for us both.

A character may present a false persona to the world. Depression and psychosomatic illness increase self-preoccupation. Comfort is often sought through reading: novels for escape, psychology to understand, philosophy for ultimate answers. Families advise self-effacement: "Don't be pushy," may chide the introspecter for being too serious. Mom teased, "You think too much. You'll be the smartest man in the graveyard." The child bonds with the nurturer, usually the mother, who shares many of these qualities. This narcissistic parent draws on the child's ability to intuit needs of others. Often marital stress is detoured through a parentified child. An entry in Jan's diary at the age of 12 tells of being trapped in family anxiety.

Why is it that sometimes I wake up tense? All day I have been kind of worked up. Betsy [14] and I had a fight this morning. Why is it that sometimes the sight of her makes my blood boil and I just can't get along with her? Others can. And Mother, with her cool, calm hardness, with a surface it's hard to get through. What makes her so I-want-to-be-loved and yet so unfeeling? And yes, I love her so much, but I guess she sometimes strikes the devil in me. And Daddy follows her lead in everything. My only real friend in the household is Bobby [three], though everyone is kind.

A character evolves who embodies the qualities of the nurturing parent. *Doctor Softy* has many of the attributes of my mother, and was central in my becoming a physician and family therapist. Along with the necessities for these nurturing professions, he has Mom's soft heart and soft head. Jan has a corresponding character, *Simone*, who has many nurturing qualities, so important for therapists. Peers in late childhood and adolescence see us as nice people, considerate and responsive. We become trusted confidants to friends; our practice moves beyond the family. We may be seen as soft, nonmacho—okay for girls, still not okay for boys.

The Later Years

Thus we move toward therapy as an ego-syntonic career despite, or because of, modest material rewards. Hyperconscientious, we go into therapy and training where everything is psychological. Isolation fades as we enter the exciting world of like-minded, parentified ex-children. We do well as patients, and as we do therapy. Some enjoy people like ourselves: professionals facing gender issues, living arrangements, separating from family of origin—themes of young adulthood. Others gravitate to a practice mirroring their family of origin: abuse, alcoholism, divorce, eating disorders, child placement. After character work, they have valuable inside knowledge. But if poorly resolved, they are strained by people with similar problems.

Others prefer to work with people perceived as different from themselves: inpatient psychotics, the aged, homosexuals. The gulf between therapist and patient feeds an illusion of protection from "contamination." For example, Jan and I bought a nursing home as young adults, ran it for 30 years, only to lose interest as we neared the age when we might need one ourselves!

Immersion in the world of therapy is valuable for learning. But we may alienate those not sharing our giddiness. Characters can get out of balance. We are a minority, weird. As we fine-tune our therapeutic selves, we risk "therapizing" ourselves out of suitability for the ordinary world. It helps to be called on ivory-tower smugness and confronted with the pragmatics of everyday life. Bowling works for me.

I write a lot of reference letters. Comments about strengths are monotonously familiar: bright, compassionate, sensitive, responsible, energetic, persistent, well liked—qualities selection committees seek. I also mention limitations. Most are exaggerated positives: overly sensitive, too involved with patients, resents criticism and direction, can be stubborn, tries too hard to please, takes on too much, struggles to carry out unrealistic goals. The very wounds that impel us into the field also make us vulnerable. As psychological mindedness grows, so do its hazards. And few professions are more fraught with emotional hazards than therapy.

Caring and Confidentiality

Wishing to help is ubiquitous. Yet the greater our need to make things right, the more vulnerable we are to those who make us impotent when our helpful efforts don't help. Eric Berne[28] and transactional analysis are no longer trendy; parts work is closer to reality, richer, more effective. Still, Berne's analysis of what can go wrong is on target. "Why Don't You—Yes, But" is the most common game help requesters play. Their complaints invite us to give advice. Typically, they have tried proposed solutions and have failed. Or they reject a suggestion with rationalizations. Or they try in a way that doesn't work. The rescuer therapist playing "I'm Only Trying to Help You" eventually catches on. Social workers and nurses are prone to playing this game.

The patient's kid character frustrates the therapist's parental character. The kid gets symbolic revenge against the parent, and collects another grievance against an unhelpful world. We all have kid and parental parts, set up for games. "Yes, but" is ego-syntonic. Spot it early, don't take offense, don't be set on helping, and don't tie self-esteem to the notion that patients should be helped in the way *we* want to help.

Intuitives turn inward when expectations do not work out, feeling guilty, ashamed, powerless. These feelings are strong when seeing just one patient, stronger still when working with a couple/family. We are sensitive to attacks and frightening possibilities, necessary as they

85

may be to deep therapy. We care too much. When I see an over-committed practitioner, often doing individual work, I suggest ways that patients can break our hearts despite our best efforts: quit unexpectedly, fail to develop potentials, switch to a rival therapist, continue on a destructive path, commit suicide. The traditional cocoon of confidentiality around patient and therapist distorts perspective and harms both. Systemic therapy requires *comprehensive* confidentiality.

> *An elderly man asks a student nurse for confidentiality. Eager to build the rapport that she was taught is a cornerstone in the helping relationship, she assures him that whatever he says is just between them. He confesses plans to commit suicide and elicits a promise not to tell his daughter. After a sleepless night (I gave my word, can I break it? What about rapport? What if he goes through with it tonight?), she is relieved to find him alive in the morning, and owns up to her supervisor who coaches her to discuss her mistake with the patient. All of us learn something, including the patient's daughter, and he never makes a suicide attempt.*

Assuring exclusive confidentiality is a beginner's error, drummed into students when systems are ignored. Some confidentiality issues, however, are more subtle, complicated, and difficult to manage. Therapists perceive violence as alien, incomprehensible. The real possibility of violence paralyzes common sense.

> *A woman is known to be homicidal by her parents, three psychiatrists, and her friends, yet no one takes action to control her. She poisons food intended for schoolchildren and opens gunfire on a playground, killing one child and seriously wounding others.*

A lethal combination of exaggerated need to help one person, to understand, hesitation to act, and false notions of confidentiality linked with failures of communication among professionals set the stage for this possibly preventable tragedy.

Understanding

Understanding is a bedrock value for therapists of all schools. We are devoted to more understanding. Comprehending something, we feel solid, oriented. When we are understood, we feel acknowledged, loved. Not understanding, we feel anxious, disoriented. And when we are not understood, we feel lost, unloved. Understanding is seen as linear; more is better and certainly couldn't hurt. Another virtue carried to a fault.

Therapists with an intense desire to understand muse, "I'll take action when I understand, and not before." Thinkers more easily engage in thinking, feelers in feeling, than in taking action. Not quickly understanding a cross-firing family, we pause while casting about for understanding. Meanwhile, more poorly understood material pours forth, giving further reason to hesitate. The wish to be perfect, launched in the family of origin and augmented by education, impairs spontaneity and flexibility with injunctions: be careful, do it right, use proper techniques properly, don't fail, don't look bad, don't embarrass anyone. Intuitive therapists with a heavy dose of psychodynamic therapy and training are particularly susceptible.

My dad, a taciturn introvert, urged, "If you don't know what to say, don't say anything. At least you won't make a fool of yourself. People assume you know and choose to be silent." So I became a psychoanalyst! I have struggled ever since to overcome this pretense. The understanding-dependent therapist is overwhelmed by an overload of feelings and hints of violence. Analysis paralysis sets in. Patients wonder why they come; they could squabble at home and avoid the trouble and expense.

Brugh Joy[29] enjoins: Delete your need to understand. He does not ask us to delete understanding, only the *need* to understand. Understanding simply *is* and has nothing to do with actual need. Need interferes, is a way to control and live by the idea rather than by the flow of reality. Without need, we are without encumbrance to experience what is.

Action

At the other extreme, therapists uncomfortable with not understanding act without waiting. They enter turmoil so fast that patients feel they have not been connected with, not understood, not cared about. Therapists doing brief therapy or with little insight must watch for this trap.

Both the overly patient and the impatient therapist lack confidence. The first eventually learns that enough can be known in a few minutes for effective action and finds that more is understood *after* taking action. We realize there is no complete understanding; we always have unknowns. The impatient one learns to keep quiet long enough to gain solid knowledge for action. I do not object to action, only the *need* to act.

I made both mistakes many times before finding the right timing. Waiting longer than people can tolerate causes dissatisfaction, a stalemate. Reacting before they are ready does so as well. We must artfully combine understanding with action in a way congruent with our personality. Then understanding leads to action that leads to understanding, ad infinitum. "I understand, and I'm taking action to help."

Resistance

A misused and maligned term! Resistance is often used when reluctance is more accurate. Hesitation to make an appointment may or may not be resistance. Some say resistance doesn't exist, only poor therapists. Unfair.

Resistances are both a mark of progress and an impediment, appearing often in therapy and supervision—when, how persistent, how handled, how caused are significant. Something crucial is approached. The system reveals structure and function. Our gift is helping people bring their characters into balance in order to diminish their power. We mainly analyze resistances.

When therapist and patient decide on action, resistance shows up: The patient doesn't act, acts badly, misunderstands, is upset over the outcome, fails to report, decides to quit. Instead of charging ahead, understand the dynamics. Don't ignore resistance, don't attack it. Identify a game, stay out of it, and use it therapeutically.

Our coalition of characters sustains our psyche; without them we would be psychotic. When they live harmoniously, we are calm. When action promises change, some parts want change. Resistance is the result of other parts working to continue the status quo. All sides have sound reasons for doing things their way, so they battle for and against change. Character work is the answer to resolving resistance, which takes repeated action and fine-tuning. We learn, slip back, relearn, slip back again. The ultimate test is to integrate learning into life; what was effective by plan becomes automatic. We take charge of our selves and become our own therapist. Time for termination.

Treatment is complicated when another person accompanies the patient. This partner is not hurting in the same way, may oppose "unnecessary" therapy, and might sabotage progress. Couple therapists know partners who come only to "try counseling" and disprove it. The unconscious parts of the patient that resist change are harder to get at when the partner is expressing them. It is easy to say the partner is "resistant" to therapy and thus fail to find the parts of the patient that resist change. Sorting these levels out with two people is taxing, and even more so when children and grandparents are included.

Circumstantial Stories

We love stories so much that narrative methods have sprung up, a welcome innovation. But problems arise when stories are misused. Therapists are poor lie detectors, have more trouble detecting lies than resistance. People who think it is in their best interest to falsify succeed. Our wish to help makes us gullible to manipulative stories. A man phones a therapist and they have this conversation.

> Is this Dr. _____?
> Yes.
> I'm suicidal and I don't think I can control myself.
> (*Pause.*) Yes?
> I'm gay and my lover just left me and I'm so depressed.
> (*Longer pause. In a nonblaming tone.*) What do you want from me?
> (*Even longer pause.*) I want an appointment.
> He arrives, enthusiastic. "That call was the greatest. I'm not suicidal or gay, but that's a good way to get to see a therapist. You're the fifth one and the first who didn't fall for my story. They made appointments without finding out what I want. They were interested in stories, so I gave them plenty, and got nowhere. Talking to you shook me up, realizing I've told stories all my life to get away with things—and conning myself to keep from facing unpleasant things." They do productive work together.

We are suckers for stories, love to hear them and tell them. Good therapists convey powerful messages by storytelling. Resurgence of this tradition is a wonderful development, but here I am talking about a misuse of stories: the circumstantial manipulative tale. I used to listen to long stories about "way back then." Not knowing where the story was leading, I would struggle to remember everything. Not sure what it had to do with now, I sometimes missed the point. Now, if I am not clear about what the person wants, I interrupt gently and firmly early on and say something like:

- I can listen better if I know what I'm listening for. We should be certain the story is relevant to our purpose.
- I'll get confused if you tell me too much before I know the point.
- Before you tell the whole story, tell the bottom line in one sentence.
  I'm getting lost. Maybe you're telling me more than we need.
- Later we can explore what telling complicated stories does for you. For now, let's get to the point.

I have a similar problem with referrers who launch into interesting dynamics, juicy history, and debilitating pathology. Omitted or lost is a concise statement of what is wanted. Plus, each family member wants something different. The dynamically oriented person is over-involved. I don't say so, but as soon and kindly as possible I say that it's better if I take a fresh approach without preconceptions. Tell me what the patient/family wants, what you want, how this has been handled, and how we will collaborate. I can always ask for details. Usually the referrer accepts taking a new look. I risk frustrating the caller and giving a false impression that I don't care about psycho-dynamics—a small price to pay for starting out right. If we try to help before having a mutually agreeable contract, we are in for trouble. Sometimes the caller does not know what is wanted and wants help to find out, which frees me to listen unencumbered. The point is finding the point. Then I am free to let the story wash over me, not straining to remember, and trusting intuition to alert me to the significant. This also applies to supervision and consultation. Hearing the point before the story eases getting to what is important. Therapists are so in the habit of rambling on about a familiar case that listeners are swamped. The ability to state a concise objective is a needed discipline.

Our background and training make us susceptible to human-interest stories. We know that details are important, and sometimes an entire case hinges on the correct understanding of a detail. Unfortunately, early in our career, the combination of taking a neutral stand on data, along with the lack of experience, convinces us that all details are equally important. So we must hear them all. When we know the point, we listen more intelligently for relevant details.

Vulnerabilities of the Disciplines

Having several disciplines represented in the same group and with a range of family backgrounds is richly rewarding, sometimes tumultuous. Diversity challenges the leader and brings multiple perspectives to the work. Each field has strengths and weaknesses. And many do not fit the stereotypes.

Family physicians and psychiatrists are useful to other students. But they are indoctrinated to be leaders of the team, often believing that they are better educated, better qualified. It's not easy for them to listen to "lesser" types whose ideas might be better. They must modify a decade of focus on one patient, straining to encompass a whole person, let alone a whole social system. They value linear thinking, logic, protocols, solving problems, rote memory. Thinking laterally or metaphorically is not easy. If they are not materialists when they enter medical school, they are when they leave. It's a leap from cause-and-effect to mutuality.

Nurses have useful medical know-how, and are excellent observers. But they suffer from being servants to physicians and from working in hospital hierarchies. They do not feel secure working independently, and there is controversy as to whether they should. They are vulnerable to helping too soon, too much. The motivational appeal of the floundering person can backfire.

Social workers, who make up the majority of the therapeutic profession, are mainstays of the field—people people, doers, feelers, compassionate, caring, and impatient with theory. "Tell us what to do." They have little training in medicine and may miss organic factors. They fall for the victim's hard luck story. The openness that makes them accessible, may also make them vulnerable.

Members of the clergy are natural therapists. Caring attracts people, especially of the same faith. They struggle over telling others what to do, a problem in moral dilemmas. "Do unto others as you would have them do unto you" doesn't work in a family conflict. Many begin doing therapy with people from their congregation. There are several ways to do this, as long as the therapist and clergy roles are clear. Some function as both, others refer.

Psychologists are often bright and well informed. Trained in research, they think of themselves as scientists. They have trouble integrating intellectual and intuitive selves. They will pursue a "theoretically correct" path whether or not it works. I asked Sylvia Schmidt, colleague and cofounder of the Institute, how come in the holy trinity of child guidance—child psychiatrist, psychologist, social worker—the psychologist is always the smartest. With a wicked grin she said, "They just *think* they are!" They are least interested in religion, belief systems, and spiritual matters, although that is changing.

Family therapists coming directly into the field know about families. But when trained only in family and group process, some are uneasy with just one person. They also lack experience with major mental and physical disabilities.

These vulnerabilities can be overcome. Physicians can get down off their perches and learn to think systemically. Nurses can gain confidence and independence. Social workers can rein in their rescuing efforts and educate themselves about medical matters. Members of the clergy can temper moralistic judgments. Psychologists can become more holistic, compassionate, and down-to-earth. Family therapists can learn to integrate individual and systems work, and enhance their understanding of mental and physical illness. We all have vulnerabilities. It behooves us to recognize them and to keep them from interfering, releasing attachment to professional identity with all its trappings, and relating as one human to another.

Reflections

- Identify early decisions fueling your entry into this field.
- How are those decisions affecting you today? Are you satisfied that they will hold good tomorrow as a foundation for achieving life goals?
- Study Consultation Room Games in *Games People Play* by Eric Berne.[30]
- Have you found disadvantages in your wish to help, to be caring and confidential, to understand, to take action, to deal with resistance and stories? What are you doing about them?
- Think of a time when were you victimized. How did you contribute? Which characters were involved? How are you lowering your vulnerability?

9

Empathy and Limits

Developing and maintaining effective empathy involves our most skillful and creative artistry. Yet it is given short shrift in training programs dominated by short-term and problem-solving philosophies.

Empathy is ordinarily defined as the therapist's benevolent understanding of the patient's experience. The emphasis is on the patient. In contrast, the masterful therapist, positioned at the therapist–patient interface, looks into both systems, tastes both, is empathic with both— and just as benevolently appreciative of his or her own subjective reverberations as of the patients'.

Being gentle, supportive, and empathic with self doesn't come easily to therapists—"Easy on patients, hard on self." Living by this motto does an injustice to both parties.

Why is it an injustice to be easy on patients? While a supportive working alliance is being established—empathy is a necessity— patients need to hear what you honestly think. They need gentle but firm confrontations. They need to know truths they may have avoided for a lifetime. A frequent complaint about previous therapy is, "The therapist was too easy on me." People are more resilient than therapists imagine.

An injustice to therapists? Absolutely. The vast majority of us are harder on ourselves than on our patients. The notion that the welfare of the patient comes before the welfare of the therapist is a destructive fallacy. (See Chapter 18.)

Empathy that includes the therapist is not as easy as focusing exclusively on patients, but it is essential for full functioning when our goal is lasting change. It is possible to be empathic simultaneously in both directions. More often, empathic awareness alternates, now with the other, now with the self. Keep a balanced awareness of both. Empathic experience in therapy is powerfully moving and shapes us as surely as anything in life.

We are best prepared for empathy when there is nothing at all going on with us, when we are free of mental clutter with no strong feelings, no expectations, no concepts to validate, no restlessness, no aim other than simply to be present. Bare attention: the beginner's mind to Buddhists; devout listening to Quakers. Observe phenomena just as they manifest. Without baggage, ready to be surprised. What you already know is pushed to a far corner of the mind, clearing the way for an empty foreground. This is why I want little or no background before meeting a new family—it is easier to be receptive without preconceptions. Seeing a new family in this state of mind may seem impossible at first. Meeting strangers is always anxiety provoking. Theories and techniques press upon us when we are casting about for a life preserver. But each time you achieve an empty mind, remember that the next time will be easier, even as your knowledge of patients accumulates.

Empathy, as I use it, is the ability to participate in the sensations, feelings, thoughts, and movements of another while making similar introspective observations. We use all our selves, body and mind, as sensitive diagnostic and treatment instruments. We become a measuring stick of psychological closeness/distance and of whether we are accurately attuned. When we identify an experience of another, we check to see how well our experience matches theirs. Such a connection establishes empathy, and the therapeutic alliance is built on repeated linkings.

Most empathy is passive. We listen expectantly, wait attentively, and are ready to sense a connection. When it comes, we are interested, supportive, and let our awareness be known. Sometimes what others are experiencing is not obvious. I let imagination, based on my whole life, make tentative educated guesses, introduced as such. I'm willing to be corrected.

Active empathy is riskier than passive; we are more likely to be wrong. But it works well when expressed with a sincere desire to understand in order to help. When people are not forthcoming, they need aid in identifying what is happening. Encouraging patients to fine-tune both their and our perceptions further cements the alliance—people fully cooperating on a shared project of great importance.

Affective empathy is the most common and best known. Because affects are contagious, we can compare our sensations and feelings with theirs. Depressed patients induce a little depression in us; anxious patients, anxiety; manic patients, excitement; seductive patients, sexual feelings. A bit of contagion is necessary for accurate empathy—a taste, neither gulping it in, nor spitting it out. We turn this taste to advantage.

Kinesthetic empathy has been shown experimentally. Observers, unable to hear, can tell that two people are in tune when their postures and movements are in synch. Shared movements, usually unconscious, are accompanied by feelings of being on the same wavelength. Even brain waves synchronize! We can deliberately mimic the posture and movement of another to get a sense of what the other is feeling. Empathy between cotherapists is essential.

> *Jan and I interview a family sitting in a semicircle with one of us at each end. We both lean forward as we explain who we are and our purpose. When ready to hear from the family, we simultaneously lean back and cross our arms and legs. We have no idea we are doing this until we see the videotape. It looks like a choreographed dance. We were well attuned that day.*

Cognitive empathy is interesting. The longer we work with someone, the easier it becomes to complete their sentences mentally, which is another way to monitor empathic growth. The more accurate our predictions, the stronger is the connection. To be more active, choose a pause to take a stab at what might be coming next—like old marrieds!

Empathy should build as therapy proceeds, and it is most powerful at the end. But it does not rise smoothly upward, rather, it moves faster, now slower, now not at all. Most important is a break in empathy, a time when we hope we are on target, but are not. If we have built a solid collaboration, we will probably hear about it. Or we sense that something has gone wrong when connection slips. Or we are unaware of the break and can only infer it by the patient's acting out.

Breaks in empathy are inevitable in long-term therapy. They are both therapeutic emergencies and golden opportunities. A break must be recognized and repaired as quickly and solidly as possible. We apologize, correct our perceptions, and reestablish connection. The interacting psychodynamics of both parties are analyzed, then more self-understanding. In the long run, a well-handled empathy break is a live demonstration that mistakes are human, not fatal, and can be a source of new learning.

We probably have an innate capacity for empathy that can be enhanced by training and life experience. It can be taught by senior clinicians and learned by students. One of the best things we do in therapy is teach empathy between family members. If nothing else is accomplished, developing empathy for each other makes a huge difference. A daunting challenge is being empathic with all members, even those not present. Achieving good empathy with one person is difficult enough. The more people in the treatment system, the more difficult it is. We are most effective when keeping these multilateral connections in approximate balance. Therapists committed to individual therapy find it difficult. So do therapists who work primarily with individuals who have been severely traumatized or have serious psychopathology. Overidentification impairs empathy with others in the system.

> *A social worker has long experience in working with sexual abuse. She is an advocate for her patients, whom she sees as innocent victims. For the first time, she is assigned to treat a male adult accused of abusing a little girl. She enters the session on the verge of panic. Her wish to help is paralyzed by disgust, rage, blame, and impulses to attack him. She struggles to keep from blurting out, "You evil perpetrator!" In the course of many weeks of supervision, controlling herself gradually pays off. In the long run, she achieves empathy that is actually therapeutic.*

Skillful empathy with everyone in the system is the sine qua non for family work. Perfectly balanced empathy is aimed for, yet rarely achieved, and is not really necessary. Therapists keep a mental tab on empathy with each member. When an imbalance is noted, attention can be given to rebuilding empathy with the one who needs it. The therapist who cannot do this would be better off doing individual work—and so would the patients.

We all have overly empathic days, and others when we lack empathy. Swinging between them is unavoidable and only a concern if swings become frequent or extreme. A few therapists are habitually off target.

Being Overempathic

When we are overempathic we are weak on setting limits, letting treatment structure deteriorate—usually by not setting clear boundaries early on. We have trouble saying No *(Doctor Softy)* or taking decisive action, such as restraining a child when necessary. The action the too-good empathizer is reluctant to take is precisely what the patient needs. A childhood pattern is being repeated. The patient needs external controls to compensate for faulty internal controls, to replace what was missed in being parented. Time for character work.

External controls, whether by a parent or therapist, come first—loving, consistent. Then the child or patient internalizes these qualities for a lifetime. Advice from a management consultant on how to treat people: The three Fs—be friendly, be fair, be firm. Overempathizers are good with the first, agonize over the second, and are hesitant about the third. Common examples of sloppy limit setting include:

—Patient regularly comes late and presses to stay beyond
   the time limit.
—Unpaid fee balance grows larger and larger.
—Agreed-upon homework is done poorly, if at all.
—Patient fails to keep appointments without notice or good
   reason.
—Frequent phone calls about trivialities.
—Excessive, nonproductive chitchat.
—Requests for unnecessary help in reaching avowed goals.

I am not suggesting strict rules that permit no deviation. Rather, it is useful to define early how you work best regarding appointments, fees, and so on and then see how those limits are tested. One break may be insignificant, two make you wonder, three are a pattern. The more experience the therapist has, the sooner he or she intervenes.

Testing limits gives insight into dysfunctional areas that need attention, an opportunity for both the therapist and patient to deepen understanding. This is particularly true of behaviors that are syntonic for the person but drive others crazy, such as chronic lateness, careless bill paying, constant complaining, manipulation, and belligerence.

Some patients never test limits. Therapists who like an orderly life are pleased, failing to see that blind "compliance"—overvalued by physicians—is a sign of rigidity, a need to placate, a fear of authority, or an unwillingness to take risks. Although these traits do not make people uncomfortable, they are as much in need of change as defiance. Conventional therapists, themselves compliant, do dull therapy that accomplishes little, if they are unwilling to stir up trouble.

Overempathic therapists typically have similar problems with parenting. Sensitively aware of children's frustrations, unhappiness, and needs, they are overly permissive. The child creates trouble to elicit limits. Similarly, the too-compliant child makes life easy for parents and teachers, as well as for child therapists. Yet this child may have unrecognized internal stalemates that limit flexibility and creativity.

> On the news during the Vietnam war, we see a graduating high school senior ceremoniously offered an American Legion award as the outstanding student. He says he does not believe in competition or the American Legion, and refuses the award. I have three patients who received that award. They cheer, wishing they had had the guts to do the same. They are exhausted by efforts to be perfect.

When we see patterns in adults, we should watch for parallel problems in child rearing, which is true of *any* difficulties that show up in therapy. And conversely, we can expect that people who have trouble with parenting will eventually bring those problems into relationship with us.

The overempathic has so much difficulty with limit testers that it deserves elaboration. Here are my guidelines for curing severe acting outers.

Step 1. *Get them to fall in love with you.*
Step 2. *Steadily apply clearer, firmer limits.*
Step 3. *Handle your reactions to their reactions.*

Dynamic, client-centered, and humanistic therapists have little difficulty with step 1. Eager to please and hoping that a positive relationship will be followed by less acting out and more emotional growth, they are supportive, caring, empathic. Isn't that what therapy is all about? The needy lap it up and become proficient at eliciting these goodies. The therapist makes small accommodations: a more convenient hour, a little extra time, handing over tissues, phone calls. Minor transgressions of structure are overlooked, possibly silently condoned.

These gestures of goodwill are defended as necessary to establish rapport, to meet the needs of the patient, and so on. Nothing wrong with that—interest and concern are essential to bonding. When a therapist appears distant or uncaring, patients won't stick around. But sooner or later, therapists err on the side of being too available. Or, realizing what is happening, they swing to being arbitrary and rigid.

Sure signs that step 1 is reaching the point of dwindling returns: the therapist feels irritated by demands; feels taken advantage of; discovers that certain patients have run up big bills or phone repeatedly, and so on. Time to move on.

Step 2 gives the overempathic a workout. The more solid the rapport is, the more abrupt and unsympathetic limit setting feels—to both. What is needed is the affirmation of limits in a way that is constructive and supportive—and the setting of new limits (with agreement, if possible) without damaging the relationship or driving the patient away. Different therapists set limits in different ways:

> *Early on it was desirable for us to talk on the phone as often as you felt you needed to. Now things are different. You have tapped inner resources for taking better care of yourself. It's time to cut down and eventually cut out phone calls.*
>
> *It's not good for either of us to let your bill get any higher. You must figure out a way to do that, and I will help.*
>
> *You ask for things to do between sessions, I suggest some, and you don't do them. I'm not helping you by participating in that dance. What shall we do? Not make an appointment until the homework is done? Not give homework? You not ask for it? Stop therapy? Let's use this to understand something important about us.*

Step 2 is much harder than step 1 for the overempathic. If step 1 is done well, then step 2 triggers hostile objections. Impact is greater: The longer step 1 has lasted, the deeper is the attachment, the looser the limits, the more narcissistic the patient, the more irrational the transference. "Hostile objections" may be pale a term for the flagrant acting out and vengefulness of the hurt "victim." Therapists are so intimidated that they believe their worst fears are true: Therapy is failing and the patient is psychotic. And the "betrayed" patient's worst fears seem to be true: "Once again, the world is unsafe. I can't trust anyone. I thought you'd be all-giving. Now you've turned on me." Hurt and rage may be handled by suppression, withdrawal, suicidal gestures, abrupt quitting, impulsive decisions, bitter complaining, psychosomatic ills, flirting with therapy elsewhere.

Be prepared. They will throw the book at you. Catastrophes are far easier to *prevent* than to correct. Your job is to empathize while standing firm, to minimize guilt and shame, to compassionately help the patient to see what he or she contributed to this situation. As the patient becomes calmer and more rational, the present can be connected with the past. The time is ripe for character and family work.

Step 3 is hardest for the overempathic person who wishes to please, wants things nice, shuns conflict and violence. These people are natural creators of loving bonds, narrowly defined as showing support, caring, affection. They are not good at fostering independence and autonomy, which are equally loving and necessary. Our goal is to promote emancipation from therapy, to put ourselves out of business. Therapy that drags on out of bilateral dependency robs the patient—and therapist—of a most valuable and growthful aspect, namely, dealing constructively with ending.

Success may require that we engage in the sequence many times: renewed attachment, more limits, patient's response, handling our reaction. Each sequence gets easier, shorter, more expectable and understandable. Each is an opportunity to gain insight into the strengths and weakness of internal characters. This opens up alternate options, under more conscious control, that make for a better life—for the patient and therapist alike.

These steps are basic in raising children. Parents' natural love makes bonding easy. But limits are overdone, underdone, or both. When offspring protest, resolve and confidence are strained. To stand by while a young adult takes risks and makes mistakes is anguishing. Yet this is precisely what parents must do for a child—therapists for patients.

Being Underempathic

The overempathic depends on feelings and experience, hoping to understand without taking risky action. The underempathic depends on cognition and technique, hoping to take action without feelings or impactful encounters, relying on structure and strategies—essential for therapy, but not the end-all. Two prominent methods of therapy are structural and strategic, often lumped together. Highly technique oriented, they feature standard procedures to relieve symptoms in just a few sessions. They are easy to teach and learn, easy to write about and research, and attractive to those who seek certainty, control, and recipes for change, the darlings of managed care. Many structural and strategic therapists are scornful of insight, impatient with delving into the past, little interested in empathy, and critical if strong action is not taken in the first minutes of a first interview. Their biggest drawback is the structure on which they rely: Patients feel in a box, not understood. The dynamics that fortify problems are untouched.

> *A woman phones for therapy; her kids are wild. As is my hard-won custom, I see the parents without the children. They describe 16 weekly meetings at a clinic publicized as structural-strategic. The problem: chaos every morning getting three ornery sons up, dressed, fed, and off to school. Family therapy focused on what the parents might do. After many failed tactics, there was no change and the parents were frustrated. They asked if they could come in without the boys, and were told that it was against clinic policy. So they quit. I ask if they have any idea about the chaos. Long pause, then the husband stammers, "We didn't get to the real problem." "Which is?" More embarrassment. "I have trouble with impotence. It's been a long time since we had sex. After trying nearly every night, we're both crabby. But I would never talk about it in front of the boys."*

I am grateful for structural-strategic therapists. They supply me and my students with families looking for someone who really listens and understands empathically. Many therapists, limited to brief methods by training, are capable of going deeper. They do so when disillusioned by temporary results, or when their own family needs empathy as well as action.

The therapy taught influences more than patients. It creates an atmosphere that pervades the professional community.

> *A colleague, a mainstay for more than a decade at a renowned structural-strategic clinic, feels isolated after his child is killed. Few coworkers express condolences and support. There are no meetings where his pain might be ventilated and alleviated, no*

human contact to show that anyone cares Not surprisingly, he soon leaves.

The good news is that many years later, the clinic staff decided their earlier work excluded affect, meaning, and spirituality. Therapy must begin with relationship and emphasize empowerment, not technique. Therapists preoccupied with a method are not present to anxieties, hurts, and longings of patients—or colleagues—as though it is better not to know about these "softer" sides; might interfere with the method. Better to think of patients as black boxes with only inputs and outputs. Such therapists approach parenting similarly.

The underempathic has no opportunity to implement step 2 (setting limits) and step 3 (dealing with reactivity) because step 1 is never established. Patients never develop a loving attachment, and the possibility of caring too much doesn't exist; therapy won't last that long. What therapists drawn to behavioral and problem-oriented methods want is to stay away from feelings, dependency, and the past—quicksands that delay results. Difficulty with limits or hostility is preempted by controlling structure before step 1. The current cost-containment climate rewards them: mandated time limits, focus on symptoms, and the rest.

Synthesis

I'm against neither empathy nor structure. I am for both, with balance and flexibility. The best therapy (my opinion, remember!) gracefully combines the two, more or less of each, depending on what's needed: not empathic to the point of losing objectivity, obsession with feelings, caring too much; not overdoing structure and losing touch with the patient's experience or mine.

Such a demanding craft! It has taken many years to develop an artful, seamless synthesis. I am not alone. Supervisees and patients struggle with this dialectic. When exposed in training and therapy to only one side, they are not aware of what is missing. Overempathizers fumble with structure and underempathizers focus little on the inner world. I underscore these two dimensions because they are among the most common stumbling blocks. Thesis–antithesis–synthesis applies to the wisdom of the "middle way." Not too much, not too little. I think of it as the "Goldilocks way."

Reflections

- Put yourself on an "empathy scale" from 1 (underempathic) to 10 (overempathic) for each current patient. Has your position changed? How is each patient doing? Do you want things to change?
- Think about your last mistake or break in empathy. How did you discover it? What did you do? How were people affected? What interface issues were at work in them? In you? How did it affect therapy—interfere with it, strengthen it, or both? What did you learn?
- Do you have overempathic moments? If so, how do you handle them? (If you never have them, perhaps you don't care enough!)
- Do you have underempathic moments? If so, how do you handle them? (If you never have them, perhaps you care too much!)
- Next time you have a severe acter outer, try the "Kramer three-step."

10

The Therapist's Own Therapy

Therapists satisfied with their own therapy favor that modality. Yet when asked, they usually disavow it. This bias is too subtle to figure planfully into most choices. Being invisible, the bias has great power to influence clinical decisions. Therapists are reluctant to speak of their therapy in conferences, group supervision, or with consultants. Training programs in structural, strategic, and problem-centered methods discourage, some forbid, such revelations as inappropriate at best, or unethical and intrusive at worst. Dynamically oriented programs make it clear that discussing one's own therapy is verboten. Thus an unknown factor skews decisions.

The Down Side of Individualism

Therapists want "the best" for themselves, regardless of the therapy they were taught. In many places, this still means analysis or analytically oriented therapy. Even therapists who disparage analysis are hardly aware of the psychoanalytic bias that permeates their work and choices.

Since 1968, over 1,000 students have entered the two-year training program at the Family Institute. They complete a lengthy form that includes questions about the therapy they have been in. I am amazed at the answers Nearly all have been in individual treatment. Less than half have had couple therapy. An even smaller number have had family therapy with their children (some don't have children) and fewer yet with their family of origin (they all have one). Still others have been in some form of group therapy, 12-step program, or experiential workshop. It is rare for a student never to have been in some type of therapy.

This situation says a lot about students' lack of trust in the very modality, family therapy, they are setting out to learn and practice. I am convinced that a therapist who practices a therapeutic modality not personally experienced cannot be authentic. And without authenticity, therapy is a charade—meaningful change is elusive and bound to be incomplete.

The individual is assumed to be the building block of American society. Our mental health world shares this limiting view. Colleges and graduate schools in psychology and related disciplines typically begin with individuals. Only after a "foundation" in understanding the individual are family, group, and community brought in, often as an afterthought. Some never get to family and group; mine didn't. Every school of psychology, social work, counseling, nursing, divinity, psychiatry, and psychoanalysis I am personally familiar with teaches working with individuals before working with families and groups.

I have heard of a few exceptional programs that teach individual and family therapy at the same time—my preference. Academics, trusting in logical orderliness and with no actual teaching or practice experience in family therapy, tell me this would be much too confusing for students. But therapists who have been through such programs disagree. Simultaneously learning individual and family therapy may be a bit difficult at first, but integration of the two comes readily. These therapists are at home with one person or many. Only rarely do students begin by working with families, groups, and organizations before zeroing in on individuals. They learn family therapy fast and well, but may be uncomfortable with individuals at first, I haven't heard of training set up in this way.

Given this widely favored slant, most students become comfortable and confident with one person at a time. Here is their deep loyalty, their sense of what is right, their sure-footedness when the going gets tough. When they begin family therapy, their background subtly nudges them to focus on individuals, often to the detriment of seeing the system as a whole. Therapy going reasonably well gives a false impression that the therapist is solidly family oriented. But under stress, when things go badly, resolve crumbles and the therapist regresses to the modality first learned.

> *Therapy with a family or couple is rocky, yet moves erratically ahead. Sooner or later, for any number of reasons, treatment bogs down. Threats of suicide or harming another may suggest involuntary hospitalization. Or scapegoating is impervious to intervention. Or family members disrupt sessions, fail to cooperate. Or destructive, dysfunctional relationships escalate. Desperation over a deteriorating situation calls for decisive action, but what?*
>
> *The therapist, never confident about this case, is at her wit's end. Nothing works. Feelings of responsibility, anxiety, and guilt mount. Under such a burden, the therapist falls back on the therapy she has confidence in, namely, individual. There is a powerful pull toward splitting the family into one or more individual therapies by referral to other therapists or an institution. Typically, this move is vigorously rationalized: He needs help "in his own right"; the more disturbed one is more to blame for the family troubles and, therefore, needs "more help"; mentally fragile patients need "deeper" therapy; family therapy is no longer indicated, and so on.*

Splitting therapy is devastating. It replicates and aggravates splitting in the family and accelerates family dissolution, a recipe for more pathology. This denouement is explained away by the severity of the family's mental illness. Psychiatrists and managed care readily endorse individual psychotherapy over family therapy, and the distraught therapist is off the hook. The danger of splitting therapy is ignored. This failed strategy has been undertaken because of personal bias, not clinical experience. That bias is the sum of cultural and mental health allegiances to individualism, the introduction to therapy of one person, and the therapist's own individual treatment.

There are many ways to resolve this impasse.* What is chosen should be based on experience and calm consideration of possibilities, not bias. This situation requires more, not fewer, people. We can bring in the family of origin, children, consultants, cotherapists, clergy,

---

*My preference for an attempted solution is integrated individual and family therapy as described by Larry Feldman[31]; also see Wachtel and Wachtel.[32]

probation officers, respected teachers—any family stakeholder. Couple and family groups are often more effective than seeing the family alone. We may arrange for sessions viewed by students and teachers, or with videotaped feedback. Therapist creativity can solve the impasse when conventional methods cannot. Above all, the same therapist should continue with the family, unless deterioration is beyond repair.

Therapists who began with an individual orientation and personal therapy make an unacknowledged assumption that "what worked for me should work for them." In the 1950s and 1960s the paucity of family therapists was a legitimate reason to enter individual treatment. And although there were many places to learn individual therapy, family training was seldom available. But in the 1990s there are thousands of systems-oriented therapists and many training programs. Ironically and unfortunately, the analytically oriented therapists most sought after are the least trained and least skillful in family and systems work, a fact they seldom admit.

Psychiatry and Psychotherapy

A quarter century of teaching family systems to psychiatry residents, relatively unsuccessfully, illustrates this problem. Medical school is structured around dissecting one cadaver, listening to one heart, writing one prescription. Physicians pride themselves as progressive when they talk about the "whole person." Dealing with the whole family is beyond most of them.

Psychiatric residency is also heavily oriented toward individuals, whether psychodynamic as in the past, or medical-biological today. Learning about families and systems is decidedly secondary. Many think, correctly, that most couple and family therapy does not require an M.D. and so can be delegated (relegated!) to social workers, nurses, members of the clergy—the "softer," less medically prestigious disciplines. Or systems therapy is so simple and superficial that highly educated M.D.'s can do it without special training. Just read a book, go to a lecture, or talk in the hall to a family therapist not yet disillusioned about educating doctors.

Now that family training is required for certification by the American Board of Psychiatry, many programs offer lip-service classes that haven't a chance of succeeding, especially if taught by non-M.D.'s. Family therapy is not respected. A psychiatry resident needing therapy is influenced by the proclivities of the faculty. Since residents choose programs and programs choose residents in the hope of mutual compatibility, the faculty typically suggests (too mild a verb, in some instances) the therapy perceived as "best." I have taught in all six Chicago psychiatry training programs. Residents get either medication or individual psychodynamic therapy, or both. Do they go into what is often needed, couple or family therapy? Or integrated individual and family therapy? Almost never. Even the married ones.

Once they have attained benefit from therapy—and most do despite their reluctance to be in *any* therapy—many residents approach patients with a pallid imitation of what they have chosen for themselves. If medication helped, that is what the patients get. If individual therapy worked, *that* is what they get. Residents are referred to the "best" therapists, who are psychoanalysts, but the residents are not. Thus, the way they do therapy is based on how they perceive their therapist, rather than on study or training. Typically, they are silent, inactive, occasionally interpretive, periodically repeating what the patient just said with the goal of intellectual understanding. They avoid action, interaction, self-disclosure, and family members. In a perceptive chief resident's annual report, this was described as "watered-down Carl Rogers technique."

This passive style not only is inappropriate, but may be counterproductive for many of the resident's hospital patients. Schizophrenics, manic depressives, and borderlines can hardly tolerate a silent therapist who does not actively engage them. And when a crisis involves family violence, child abuse, acting out, or suicide, an inactive style just feeds the turmoil.

Being in individual therapy reinforces the resident's dislike for families and systems. Besides, without adequate training, they have no confidence. Only after a few years of postresidency practice does the young psychiatrist realize the importance of understanding systems, but by then, training and supervision are unlikely. As a result, many psychiatrists practice halfhearted, unskillful couple and family therapy. Of the 141 members of the Illinois Council of Child and Adolescent Psychiatry, 92 (65%) say they do family therapy. That usually means seeing the family as an adjunct to child therapy, not as a primary modality. Many of these are recent graduates who have had a smattering of training. This percentage has been steadily increasing over the last 25 years, for which I should be grateful, having given the first talk on family therapy to the Council in 1968. However, only 17 have had what I consider adequate training and supervision. Having taught most of these, I am comfortable with their competence. But the horror stories I hear from patients, colleagues, and supervisees about some of the others are disheartening. Not surprisingly, their lack of effectiveness is seen as confirmation that family therapy is an inferior approach.

Only after their marriages are in disarray, their children in trouble, and individual therapy for everyone has had little effect, do these psychiatrists finally seek a senior family therapist. I have had 41 psychiatrists and their families in treatment. The array of presenting problems is no different than for any other profession. They usually do well. They know how to use insight and are motivated to improve. Symptoms and relationship difficulties subside fairly rapidly. Since this is what they came for, and since they have all had previous individual therapy or analysis, they see little need to continue once things have calmed down—which is okay with me. Six of these psychiatrists have moved beyond 15 sessions into work over several years that is as successful as with other patients.

In Therapy, Doing Therapy

The relationship between the kind of therapy we do and the kind of therapy we are in is illustrated by my professional evolution.

In *general medicine and surgery*, I didn't give any thought to therapy for myself or anyone else. I listened, gave Ann Landers–type advice, tried to be supportive, and never went beyond skimming the surface. Making two or three house calls a day, I was acquainted with some family members and dealt with them the same way. A few times I invited a wife to join her husband, for example, when a change in diet was indicated. I'm glad now I didn't exceed my limitations. But I wish I had known then what I know now about systems.

When I didn't know what to do with a problem patient, I referred the patient to colleague Alan Lieberman for diagnosis and recommendations. Examples: Huntington's chorea and acute psychosis for hospitalization; a man who refused what the surgeon said would be life-saving surgery; puzzling neurological conditions; severe melancholia for electric shock. None of these wanted, needed, or received psychotherapy. I made more psychiatric referrals than did most physicians.

Between 1969 and 1980 I consulted regularly with four family practice training programs consisting of about 60 physicians. I also have had a dozen family physicians in therapy and have gone to three myself. So I know family doctors well. When it comes to psychological and psychiatric issues, they practice much as I did in the 1940s. In addition, today they do refer patients to therapists, most commonly because of marital conflict or trouble with adolescents. If you find a psychologically minded physician for yourself or for referral, hang on to the rare bird.

When first practicing *adult and child psychiatry*, I was more knowledgeable about what I was doing, but still awkward and only modestly useful. Like most beginning psychiatrists, I saw a collection of individuals with little motivation for therapy or for paying their bills: alcoholics, drug addicts, dischargees from state hospitals, delinquents, petty criminals. Most had been sent under threat by schools, courts, hospitals, spouses, or bosses. The ones who got my name from the yellow pages were the worst. Only the dependent ones came for enough sessions to call it therapy.

I must say, though, that I received a tremendous education from social workers. Between 1955 and 1980 I consulted with a dozen social service agencies for over 1,000 hours. I learned about family breakup, child placement, adoption, foster care, juvenile justice, immigrants, ethnic groups, a wide range of family dynamics, various treatment groups for various purposes—and social workers.

These influences expanded my horizon and helped me become not only more knowledgeable, but also more savvy about life and more compassionate. I saw how complex—and important—life is for many people. I gradually perceived the beneficial effects of direct intervention into a family or group. And my private practice became more manageable and gratifying.

Once Jan and I entered analysis and I was accepted at the analytic institute, I began practicing *individual dynamic therapy and analysis.* What I did was much like therapy that residents do: passive listening and reflecting, trying to fit the patient's needs into what I could offer, rather than vice versa. Typical beginner. The occasional patient who did not need a lot from me and who could afford the fee did rather well, but slowly. I was oblivious to the effect patient changes had on family members: "That's *their* problem." They were referred to friends on an analytic track if they could pay, to the analytic institute clinic if they couldn't. My teaching, supervising, and consulting were very analytical.

I was a strong proponent of people going into dynamic individual therapy. If they refused, or did poorly, I shrugged my shoulders: "Not *my* problem." Whatever happened to them was not my concern. Sounds callous, and it was. But at the time I thought I was upholding the unyielding analytic standard I observed in senior analysts. I was purer than the pure and narrower than the narrow. Now it is obvious that I advocated analysis out of personal bias, not out of objective evaluation. But when you only have a hammer, everything looks like a nail.

When doing *family therapy* was more or less forced on me while I was doing child therapy, my outlook changed again. I was able to grasp a wider view of clinical situations and to offer more possibilities. The therapy I did and taught and advised became systems oriented. I recommended family therapy for everyone, whether they wanted it or not. It was still hard to sit through movies with a psychological twist. Where before they should all be in analysis, now they should all be in family therapy!

I was in analysis, studying analysis, doing analysis, being supervised by analysts, and at the same time teaching myself family therapy. It took a while to integrate the two. Going from a family to an analysand, or vice versa, required a rapid shift in consciousness. The longer I did it, the easier it got. Eventually, I made that shift smoothly, and cases were seen in a combination of individual, couple, family, couples group, and other formats, and it was these people who benefited the most from working with me.

We regularly refer prospective patients, including colleagues, to specific therapists practicing specific modalities. Whom we choose is influenced by a bewildering array of factors: friendship, buddies in training, instructors, fame, geographic convenience, fees, the wish to please the one referred to, hope of reciprocal referrals, and more. The literature ignores the influence of the therapist's own therapy. Yet it is a major factor in choosing a particular therapist and modality.

In recent years, my practice has become more *holistic, humanistic, experiential.* Again, the practice, teaching, and referrals reflect personal bias. I am immersed in reading, workshops, conferences, and personal experience; in studying creativity, meditation, Eastern philosophy, mind–body medicine, and spiritual practices. Referrals reveal this experience.

- Usual medical and psychological specialties
- Testing for Myer-Briggs Typology Inventory
- Biofeedback for headaches and hypertension
- Message therapy for relaxation of muscle tension

- Tai chi for balance and serenity
- Homeopathy for stubborn allergies
- Body work or chiropractic for postural misalignment
- EMDR to access early traumatic fixations difficult to reach otherwise
- The Mayo Clinic for comprehensive physical evaluation
- Clergy and meditation masters for spiritual discipline
- Self-help and support groups for nearly everything

Thinking over this chapter, I wonder why I am belaboring the obvious. *Of course*, our personal life affects our professional life. How could it be otherwise? Yet I am reminded how few see it this way. Colleagues imbued with a need to appear "scientific" make a determined, if unsuccessful, effort to maintain a wall between personal and professional—two different domains. They are slow to give up separateness and to embrace connectedness. You will develop your own unique combination.

Reflections

- Check out the last few referrals you made to other professionals. Were the referrals first class? How did they work out? How much were the referrals influenced by your personal experience in therapy?
- How is your evolution as a therapist similar to mine? Different from mine?
- In what ways has your practice been influenced by your own therapy, and vice versa?
- Reflect on your last serious crisis in therapy. What was the outcome? You may want to check with the people you consulted. Was handling the situation in any way influenced by your personal experience in therapy?
- From time to time, step back and evaluate how your personal and professional worlds are interrelated.

11

Exploring Psychospirituality

Living is an art. We thirst after clinical facts, statistics, mental health tricks. We learn many theories and even more techniques, all "scientific." We gain experience and confidence. But putting a life together and living it to the fullest is an art. Psychotherapy is a slice of life, a special art. Making it happen calls for the full expression of our artfulness. And we learn about the various arts, including therapy. But at bottom, art is a spiritual experience, whether we are creating it or appreciating it, whether realized or not. Neglect of the spiritual dimension in patient care leaves a vacuum in our practice. I, too, have been remiss.

> *The two-hour emergency meeting with Rachel is painful and difficult. She struggles with an agonizing dilemma. Her husband, Sam, is brain-dead after cardiac arrest. The physicians are recommending, "Pull the plug." She is leaning in that direction, but is torn about what is right. Her daughter has an appointment with their rabbi. The whole family is in turmoil. Rachel frets over what she, Jan and I, or the physicians should have done differently. I feel as helpless as Rachel. I point out how much has been done to get Sam to turn his life around, with little result. I offer sympathy and availability. She leaves feeling better. I'm feeling worse.*

While writing my notes, I feel disappointed in myself. This crisis comes as I am exploring spirituality and philosophy, but have not yet mustered the courage to use them in therapy. Rachel and her family not only are in a clinical crisis but, more important, a spiritual, moral crisis. I wish I had started a dialogue. What are her beliefs, and how do they relate to Judaism? How does she feel about death? Does she think about the afterlife? For Sam? For herself? What about God? How prepared is she for all this? How could exploring answers ease despair about past "failures," present agony, and future uncertainty? Would things be different if we could have been joined by the family or the rabbi?

It would be logical for her to talk to me about these things, if only I were capable. The family has much trust in me and Jan. Rachel, Sam, and four teenagers were referred in 1974 by Julia Heald after a daughter's hospitalization at 61 pounds for anorexia nervosa. In her referral letter, Dr. Heald said, "This is probably the most manipulative family I have ever encountered . . . If I have ever seen a case in which illness of one member is only the visible part of the underlying pathology, it is this family . . . hope you break through the fog of contradictory, constantly changing attitudes and information." Quite a statement from a physician renowned for treatment of anorexia.

We had worked together in various combinations for a dozen years. Things quieted down after months of stormy family sessions, and the daughter regained weight and health. Rachel and Sam were in many months of couple therapy and a year in a couples group with us. Rachel and her daughter each saw Jan for months, and the daughter was in a group with us for a year. Periodically, we saw family members together. All made progress, even Sam. But his motivation for better physical health hardly changed. Working with Sam convinced me to take care of myself, to learn how spirituality makes for better therapy, and how it can be taught.

Comparing Psychology and Spirituality

I thought a great deal about "spirituality." The word has a multitude of meanings, many off-putting to colleagues—the audience I most want to get through to. I reflected on how this word has come to hold a natural place in my vocabulary. I usually speak of the spiritual, rather than the religious.

"Religion" is the mainstream answer we put on a form: Catholic,

Methodist, Jewish, and so on. The word conjures up thousands of organized communities, each with a different theology, worship practices, and turf sensitivity. Some too readily defend the faith by bloody combat. Western religions, in contrast to Eastern faiths, are exclusive, with boundaries dividing those who are in from those who are out. They have "the truth." They don't accept that their truth is at odds with the truth of other religions. There is little effort to sort out superstition from reality. Mental health people turn away from religion, dismissing it as irrelevant. Or leave it to the chaplain.

"Spirituality" is what religions have in common. Most were founded by mystics who had profound out-of-the-ordinary experiences: Moses receiving the Ten Commandments from Yaweh, Buddha's enlightenment under the Bodhi tree, Jesus' experiences in the desert, Mohammed's messages from Allah, the visions of Joseph Smith and Mary Baker Eddy that led to Mormonism and Christian Science respectively. These mystical experiences were similar in many ways, but given contrasting interpretations and eventuated in separate traditions. A religious group would coalesce around the original figure. As this organization burgeoned and splintered, it would sharpen its differences from others, and the mystical core would become veiled, diminished, almost unessential. This transcendence, its mystery, and its many permutations, I call spiritual.

Just as the fine line between the physical and the psychological is blurred, so are distinctions between the psychological and the spiritual. Qualities expressed by spiritual leaders of every persuasion—compassion, love, serenity—are old friends I call empathy, cathexis, and mature adaptation. Religious concepts, such as hope, confession, repentance, atonement, forgiveness, reconciliation—seldom heard in psychiatry—are important in therapy. At first I translated: What spirituality refers to is really psychological, what psychology refers to is really spiritual. Today the two domains are inextricably intertwined and translation is no longer necessary. So psychospiritual comes closest to my meaning.

I have changed my belief about God. Until medical school, God was an old man with a long white beard who sat on a throne. Heaven and hell were realities, not metaphors. In medicine, those ideas seemed superstitious. Until about 1980, like most of my colleagues. I was an agnostic secular humanist (only 5% of psychologists believe in God). When I thought of God at all, I vaguely imagined a supernatural thing somewhere out there. I was skeptical that an anthropomorphic being existed. Science demanded *objective* evidence, not dependent on self-deceiving subjectivity. But miracles are hard to come by. However, in philosophy and Eastern religions, God has many meanings for different people.

Separation and loss are the bread and butter of therapy. Behind separation, usually hidden, is the ultimate loss—death. It behooves us to know death in all of its sometimes gruesome manifestations. Such knowledge engenders wisdom that cannot be acquired any other way. The certainty of death raises spiritual questions. Awareness of death is woven into the fabric of our existence, and so also is spirituality. When a chronic, life-threatening illness similar to Sam's stared me in the face, I no longer could disavow the spiritual dimensions of life and of therapy.

As I explore spiritual practices, I am steadily transformed. Patients say I am more serene and at peace. Things don't upset me so much; we open up intensely private realms. Most are eager to discuss their philosophy of life, their puzzlement over life's mysteries, their beliefs, their religious tradition, and how these played a part in their coming to me. A few are not ready and may never be. I am content to wait and see.

This kind of sharing has been so gratifying that I encourage students and colleagues to explore their spiritual views and background. When they are comfortable, they too find that patients open up. Therapy is enriched and people discover that many of their difficulties have roots in a belief system of which they are only dimly aware, and yet has a powerful influence on their lives. My son, Dan, family philosopher and a fine therapist, came up with this.

- The therapist would do well to examine and develop his or her *personal philosophy or belief system*. All our actions come from our philosophy, whether we examine it or not. Some ideas:
- What is suffering? Healing? Is suffering punitive? Does it have a purpose? Is it fair? Is there order or chaos?
- Are health/illness corollaries? Is sanity or health intrinsic?
- Good/bad. Can bad things have value?
- Relationships. Are persons intrinsically separate? Or is there an underlying connection, a universal oneness?
- A good practice, which would fit with journaling, is to trace back a particular therapist/client conflict (or any other conflict) to discover what basic beliefs are operating. There is usually a platitude that is taken for

granted, such as: Life is unfair. Suffering is bad. Everyone is ultimately alone.

- Organized beliefs are not simply intellectualizations. They are what we act on, a combination of mind and heart and gut. And beliefs don't have to be justified. I share my beliefs with clients to keep hope alive. It's a philosophy that works for me. It's so rewarding to have beliefs you can pour your heart into. This means that my rational mind has to be satisfied.

Truth and Authority: A Personal Evolution

Reflecting on my spirituality elicited a life review. The moral truths I live by have gone through a rich evolution. My beliefs are maturing, less black and white, more complex. I was hardly aware of these patterns as I was living them, but I can see them in retrospect. Moving from stage to stage followed a natural sequence. I evolved through five stages. Each began with reliance on external authority. Dependence lessened as questioning and internal authority flourished. By a stage's end, deepening insight into my beliefs, at odds with external authority, stimulated me to move on. Again I looked to authority for guidance until I mastered the new view. Then personal conviction came again as past influences faded, but never disappeared.

Conventional Presbyterian Morality

My early moral influences were parents, Presbyterianism, and Boy Scouts—unquestioned authorities. What was taught was believed: Bible stories, lectures about right and wrong, sermonettes delivered in sepulchral tones from the robed minister above my head, and ethical precepts of the Scouts. Sixty years later, these are still among my values.

Mom was a soloist in the adult choir, so singing in the junior choir was natural. Music was vital in our family. Only recently have I realized what a shared *spiritual* experience music is. Hearing melodies my mother and I sang brings bursts of emotion, a sense of uplift, of mystery, of something bigger than myself, beyond feelings and memories. Hard to put into words. Spiritual.

Acceptance was automatic, but by adolescence I found church boring—no mystery or thrill in Presbyterianism—and skipped when

I could. Skepticism and questioning troubled me. There was no way to argue logically with predestination. When I explained how something might happen, Mom's sanctimonious, "But it wouldn't have happened if it wasn't always meant to be," ended the dialog. I could not prove she was wrong; she could not prove she was right. I later learned that is true for all beliefs. And I disagreed that we are sinful at birth. Babies looked innocent to me. Fairness was important; this was *unfair*. People gave convoluted, implausible justifications for contradictions in the supposedly infallible Bible. War, rape, destruction, greed, the wrath of God did not fit with the sunny, *good* image of God I learned about at Sunday school. The fatal blow to weakening Christianity was Van Loon's *Tolerance*,[33] a fascinating history of *in*-tolerance. I was shocked that Presbyterianism founder John Calvin had burned Servetus to death for questioning the Trinity. Not understanding it myself, my heart went out to *Doctor* Michael Servetus. I reached the end of rigid adherence to the letter of the law and attachment to the forms of religion, Scott Peck's Stage Two, and was entering Stage Three, principled behavior characterized by religious skepticism and disinterest, but curiosity about other areas of life.[34]

Transition to a Liberal World View

Once I decided at the age of 13 to become a physician, *science* was my religion, my philosophical guide to life. I loved chemistry, physics, and physical geography. I could get my mind around these tangible *facts*. Nothing irrational like the Immaculate Conception.

Weather was an eye-opener. Nature's patterns were clear on weather maps. We made predictions for two days that were 75 to 85% accurate. Turns out that percentage holds for a lot of predictions in life!

I was also learning to sail, a risky chance to study weather first-hand. I can't safely ignore the relentless force of wind, waves, and storms, nor can I passively give in. Nature's power can't be attacked or changed; it has its impersonal way. I need to align the boat, the sails, the rudder, and myself so that wind and sea are beneficial, not destructive. These lessons are a metaphoric foundation for my life and my therapy. Alan Watts[35] says, "The art of life is more like navigation than warfare, for what is important is to understand the winds, the tides, the currents, the seasons, and the principles of growth and decay, so that one's actions may use them and not fight them."

Two other influences liberalized me. On the track team, for the first time, I met with blacks my age. Success was measured by who won, nothing else.

I also wanted a close group, and found it in jazz. From the age of 15 until the end of my internship, I played piano and bass in dance bands. Musicians of all ages and personalities, different instruments, all ethnic groups. The only thing that mattered was how well we played—*together*. A jazz group is great for learning how to get along. Within the limits of melody and chords, we would take turns improvising. Democratic coordination of harmony and rhythm, innovation, belonging, commitment make for great music. Winton Marsalis[36] says, "Playing jazz means learning to respect individuality. It teaches you how to have a dialog, with integrity." Well-moving process and therapy groups remind me of well-moving jazz groups—each participant is allowed to express himself or herself freely within limits, and often creatively going beyond those limits. Jazz is another metaphor guiding my life and therapy. Its soul is deeply spiritual.

Morality Based on Physical Health of the Individual

I divided life into two unrelated domains, science and religion. I loved science and thought the other irrelevant. I was yet to learn the truth of Einstein's, "Science without religion is lame, religion without science is blind." Religion seemed useless. I went with Jan and her parents to church, but my heart wasn't in it. I went to win them over.

I loved medical school. It was real, no dubious religious notions. I grasped the unspoken morality of my instructors: *being physically healthy is good, unhealthy is bad*. Members of the clergy might say sinful or evil, but we avoided such terms. Medical research and clinical practice were my authorities for the true and the good, at first perceived, then internalized.

A physician has a moral obligation to provide whatever is likely to result in a healthier patient, and is free to use any resources to make that happen. Materialistic and patriarchal. The Golden Rule prevails without being mentioned: Do unto others as you would have them do unto you. And the patients we do unto should be compliant and grateful.

> *To illustrate, let us follow a hypothetical two-year-old child with leukemia. I would be eager to find a judge to order transfusions, against the wishes of the parents, who are Jehovah's Witnesses. This would result in hostile polarization: self-righteous upset par-*

ents, and self-righteous angry staff. Whether the child would be better off after a transfusion is uncertain. Both sides are frustrated, yet feel morally right.

In general practice, Presbyterianism never disappeared, but just became a background to the medical morality foreground, implicit. No church attendance or interest. I did not see a contradiction: I was medically materialistic, yet relied for healing on the mysterious intelligence of the body. I ignored the saying to the effect that the physician treats and God heals. Not for nothing do M.D.'s have a reputation for playing God.

But materialistic practice was monotonous. I discovered the importance of emotions, psychology, family, lifestyle—the things I knew least about. Allegiance to science began to wear thin as I kept coming up against clinical situations that could not be understood or treated materialistically. I moved toward more comprehensive life diagnoses and psychosomatic medicine. I looked into psychiatry with curiosity and apprehension. I attended staff meetings at Elgin State Hospital, psychiatry consultations for rheumatic children, and psychiatric conventions, and I read books on the psychology of illness. At the age of 29, I was propelled into a professional world with a new set of moral standards.

Morality Based on Mental Health of the Individual

When I entered the Air Force, I seized the opportunity to get into psychiatry and have never regretted it. What I feared would be two wasted years turned out to be two of the best. I joined those who believe that *mentally healthy is good, and mentally unhealthy is bad.* The doctor is free to use all legitimate means to attain that goal. The implicit Golden Rule is, "Do unto the patient whatever you decide is mentally healthy."

For example, a closeted gay serviceman is miserable and wants out. He can't handle the overstimulation of living with naked men. I agree to diagnose him as "homosexual" so that he can be discharged as "undesirable." I believe that leaving the service is mentally healthy for him. The psychology and morality of homosexuality do not enter into the issue. Later I found I was also projecting my *own* wish to get out of the service. This is how the Golden Rule works.

Duty over, I began a long, fascinating journey through inpatient and outpatient adult psychiatry, child psychiatry, adult and child analysis. Each discipline was firmly based on the morality of the patient's mental heath. Individualism was the unvarying theme. The authority for mental health and illness—all behavior—was Freud. As with my Presbyterian and medical phases, authority began with teachers and was internalized during 12 years of analysis. The success I had attained failed to acknowledge the innate healing power of the mind and relationships.

> *I would have sessions with the mother of the leukemic child, doing all the good things that therapists do. I would try to get her to see that it would be mentally healthier for both her and the child if she could soften her beliefs, let the transfusion proceed, and find a way to still love her "changed" child. I doubt that this could have been done, although the atmosphere might have been less hostile. Probably we would each feel self-righteously correct, but not so hurt and angry as with the old-fashioned authority model.*

My professional world was mainly psychological, and physical when necessary, but distinctions between the two were blurry. Unfortunately, I carried psychologizing over into my personal life. Presbyterian and medical morality hovered in the background, subtly influencing the new morality. As before, I began to feel my approach—radical individualism—was not the best answer to human problems, and commitment weakened. My views were changing yet again. The next transition was less abrupt, extending over several years beginning at around age 35 in the late 1950s.

Truth and Morality Within Systems

In child therapy, I do as taught: Focus on the child and limit parents to giving the child's history, bringing the child to sessions, and paying the bills; perhaps send the mother to a therapist. Soon, unexpected complications. A few kids improve, only to relapse. Others improve, but then I'm asked to see a sibling who has developed emotional problems. Most alarming, nine children get well and stay well, but their parents divorce "out of the blue." Clearly, the unrecognized forces in many families are more powerful than therapy. Of course, certain divorces are healthier for everyone. Yet I wonder whether, in some families, the child's symptoms might be the glue that holds the parents together? Is it ethical to help the child and dissolve the family?

I began seeing parents together, and then whole families, and helped pioneer the family therapy movement.

Nontherapists comment with scorn, "*Of course*, you can't treat children without their parents. How stupid can you be?" They are right. I plead unwitting innocence in a psychiatry committed to the blinders of individualism, embedded in a society entranced by the lonely cowboy, the rebellious hippie, and Freudianism that understands one person at a time—a sick one. To say nothing of my authoritarian indoctrination.

I give up preoccupation with what is right for one. With two parents and three teenagers, five truths are convincingly defended, five conflicting values. And the moment I am partial to one, I am in trouble with the rest. A one-person search for truth does not work. What works is honest negotiation, mutual empathy, finding a fit that more or less satisfies all, respecting differences. Compromise may be required. But solutions can be found that account for everyone's needs. Few solutions for many problems. Takes more time and patience, but good results last longer.

A good resolution calls for clarity about what everyone wants, exploring options, weighing each against what is right and wrong for each person, and coming to mutually agreeable conclusions. Often hurtful anger bursts out and tears flow. Our formidable job is to protect the self-worth and dignity of each participant. These encounters leave us exhausted, yet exhilarated. A successful outcome is typical, but not inevitable.

Intriguing things happen. The number of divorces falls dramatically. The few couples who separate do so with less animosity and distress for the children. The number of children removed from the family— rescinded adoption, placement in residential treatment, hospitalization, incarceration—plummets almost to zero. I am impressed by the power and healing intelligence of family relationships. I am onto something that facilitates lasting benefits for people in all areas of their lives. So, in 1968, I founded the Family Institute of Chicago to study, teach, and conduct family and systems therapy—the third such group in the world.

It is hard to describe the mysterious power of biological relationships without sounding sentimental. In consulting with child welfare agencies for 25 years, I have learned a lot about adoption. The search for a child is intense, persistence is amazing, success is overwhelming—and preoccupation continues after adoption. I became fond of these families, and considered the adoptive bond as strong as the biological. No doubt it can be. But statistics make me wonder. Twenty-five percent of children in residential treatment are adopted, ten times the percentage in the population. In juvenile court, far more adopted children are removed from the home than are biological children. The adoptive bond is strong in some families, but weak in others. I have treated several families in which, after years of trouble, both parents and child give up on each other. "Blood is thicker than water." The inheritability of behavior is a sticky and controversial subject. A biological tie is powerful.

> *Twin girls, born 12 weeks early, are put in separate incubators. The larger sister gains weight, breathes well, her strong heart circulates red blood, she moves and sleeps normally. But the smaller baby is in trouble: her pulse soars, her breathing is labored, her skin is blue, she cries weakly and moves feebly. Despite devoted care, vital signs worsen; she isn't expected to live. Desperate, a nurse places the dying infant next to her sister.* Within minutes *her heart rate, breathing, and skin color become normal and stabilize. The larger twin reaches an arm around her, pulls her close and holds her.*[37]

Successful treatment of the family may be attained, but only treating them may not be enough. A family sent by the court for counseling might agree among themselves that Joe's brush with the law is no big deal, but the court disagrees. Or parents' siding with the child against a teacher makes more trouble. The family's morality clashes with the community's. We must add grandparents, aunts and uncles, teachers, principals, school psychologists, social workers, clergy, probation officers—whoever has a stake.

I find that family systems methods work even better in a large group. Everyone feels heard, more usable ideas come up, more enduring solutions are found. Family techniques apply to any group that spends time together: in businesses, hospitals, social agencies, institutes, and nursing homes. A compatible group arrives at better solutions than one person can, no matter how knowledgeable. It feels like a miracle when self-organizing moves us toward workable conclusions. Not everyone is always happy; most outcomes are not perfect. So *workable* is the criterion.

Family and group processes make it clear that the Golden Rule, so universally revered as a guide to human relations, is counterproductive for therapy and negotiation. What works for therapists and others who offer service is the Mutuality Rule: Do unto others *as they would have you do*—provided they know what they need (they often don't); provided what they need is congruent with your standards; provided there is mutual understanding of possible, even unintended, consequences (be careful what you wish for, you might get it); and provided you have their fully informed consent. Mutuality means less doing *to and for* and more doing *with*.

Including a large system does not mean abandoning earlier views. My new perspective takes the foreground, informed by Presbyterian, physical health, and mental health moralities. Although I read voraciously about family systems and attended workshops religiously(!), my strongest influence was working with families and in the nursing home. The self-corrective vitality of a cohesive group is awesome.

> *The child with leukemia (discussed earlier) is better served by expanding the field, including the father and siblings and other family members with the mother. Meetings of medical staff, lawyers, and clergy is advisable, though hard to accomplish. After preparation, a joint conference of professionals and family could be called, an encounter requiring skilled leadership that might not lead to agreeable conclusions. Still, unanticipated beneficial outcomes are possible in such groups. With unskilled leaders or recalcitrant participants, there is only disaster!*

Universal Morality

The psychiatric and nursing home practices are successful and never boring. But again something is missing. Only after I am well into a spiritual quest do I realize a need for spirituality in my work.

In the late 1970s the near-death experience burst on the scene. Ken Ring's[38] books fascinate me and I share ideas with him. I tell the family, "Near-death experiences open up neurological, psychological, philosophical, paranormal, and afterlife questions. I'm not a spiritual person, but these reports have me reconsidering what I believe." My son Greg, long-time meditator and student of philosophy, disagrees, "You are a very spiritual person, but you don't think of yourself that way. I think you are very Buddha-like."

Not asking if this is a compliment (Buddha the sage) or a criticism (a motionless fat statue), I begin a continuing search for religious and spiritual answers. I am inquisitive about matters of the spirit—beyond psychology and toward the *mystery* of life—aspects neither the physical nor the psychological deals with, for example: long-distance prayer has demonstrable benefits. Character *Chris* comes back, and I am in Scott Peck's spiritual Stage Four—mystical, communal, a state of spirit of the law, as opposed to Stage Two, the letter of the law

I believe that therapy in general—and family therapy in particular—is a spiritual process, though seldom so defined. Therapists who do not consider themselves to be spiritual or religious are engaged, nevertheless, in an enterprise with many hallmarks of a transcendent experience. For therapy of two or more to be successful, each surrenders a bit of self-interest to the group, and benefits from the family's greater good. The whole unit becomes more—different, greater, better—than the simple sum of its parts. The family possesses qualities not derivable from its constituents. Therapy is a sacred quest.

When therapy flows well, members pay empathic attention to what is happening, become exquisitely attuned to each other. They share joy in living together harmoniously. Therapists who are fully present model listening without a hidden agenda. Our offices are sanctuaries where the spirit of the therapeutic process originates, where safety, intimacy, and deep emotion change lives. The space and time wherein people are exclusively and seriously devoted to the work feel holy.

Reflections

- Define your idea of spirituality and how it applies to your therapy.
- Describe a recent clinical crisis where moral and spiritual issues were paramount. How satisfied are you with your understanding and how you handled the crisis?
- Trace the evolution of truth and morality over your lifetime, identifying the authority for your beliefs.
- Can you see the direction of your continuing evolution? How would you like it to go? What are the obstacles and how might they be surmounted?

Developing Creatively

I have no special gift—
I am only passionately curious.

—Albert Einstein[8]

When you become creative in any field, your creativity is released
in all other fields.

—Paul Tillich[39]

12

Enhancing Our Selves

Increasing Creativity

Until a few years ago, the prevailing belief was that some of us are creative, others not, and we are stuck with the genetic makeup Nature has handed us. We could only pick students we judge creative and hope for the best. Many educators were more interested in conventional achievements, and still are. The "inborn" theory, so comforting in its certainty and so relieving of responsibility, has been dispelled by research.[40,41] Investigators, taking creativity seriously, believe that *everyone* has an inborn capacity for inventiveness. To our great loss, creativity is often derailed by families, schools, religions, government, and therapy training. We can correct this derailment by using new methods to enhance creativity, despite how "uncreative" we might appear, and regardless of the endeavor.

Trying to force creativity is counterproductive. But we can generate circumstances and states of mind that greatly increase the probability of intuitive innovation. This calls for three basic, complementary strategies.

1. Encouraging creativity already available in us.
2. Diminishing blocks to creative impulses.

3. Bolstering creativity that emerges when blocks are removed.

Symptom-oriented therapy relies on the first strategy, which may be all that is needed, but is limited to the logical use of creativity already present. So too with most psychotherapy training. What is known is what is taught. Conforming to standards brings approval, credentials, and reimbursement. Coaching students to explore their unexplored limits takes much longer.

Strategies 2 and 3 carry us to deeper intuitive levels. All three go on together, do not depend on each other. Weakening blocks frees creative impulses, which makes removing blocks easier. And enhancing the creativity we already possess not only improves it directly, but reveals blocks needing attention—circular and mutually reinforcing. There are examples of creative development throughout this book. Here, I emphasize several that are useful for strategies 2 and 3.

Meditation

My best advice to aspiring therapists: *Practice meditation.* Techniques of meditation and of therapy are different, but the goals are similar. Meditation complements and strengthens psychotherapy, and vice versa. Both calm the mind, deepen self-awareness and understanding, relieve inner conflicts, and inspire simplicity and equanimity. Each leads to creative transformation. Together, they are potent.

> *As one state of mind arises,*
> *Another state of mind ceases;*
> *Uninterrupted the process*
> *Unfolds like the flow of a stream.*
>
> —*Sumangalavilasini, 1.193*

Therapists beginning to meditate are amazed at the never-ending bustle of unstoppable thoughts—things done and not done, lists, plans, memories, anything. We think instead of relax, evaluate instead of accept. If you learned free association, the reflex is to follow these wild animals. In meditation, the goal is to let them come and go without following them by focusing on an object, phrase, breath, or nothing. Persistence pays off as we gradually tame our monkey mind.

Mindfulness for just 10 to 15 minutes suffuses the day, fostering serenity in all we do. The secret is simple: We become our meditation. Repetition fixes the experience deep in the psyche, making it integral to our person. It finds expression in how we act, how we speak, how we think, how we feel, everything. The better we are at meditating, the quicker we calm ourself when tensions arise—which is all the time in therapy. I center and calm myself in a few seconds between appointments—clear clutter from previous appointments and empty the mind for the next. And a few deep meditative breaths are quieting when chaos threatens to spin an interview out of control.

Meditation is training for heightened awareness of the present moment, so crucial to psychotherapy. Beginners can't believe that disciplined, focused awareness is self-corrective, until they do it. When we do therapy with a calm mind and an open heart, the people with whom we work calm down and open their hearts. A student writes: "In a family session when the young children were restless and distracting, I introduced meditation with remarkable results. It was the first time I had done this. I learned it in class."

Try a few of the meditations in "Suggested Readings," or make up your own. How you meditate is not as important as doing it and making it part of your life. Meditating with ones you love is even more powerful.

Right Brain/Left Brain

Neurological research has made great progress.[42] When the right cerebral hemisphere is anesthetized, left-brain functions take over, making the person rigid, narrow, compulsive. Anesthetizing the left produces right-brain dominance: unmanageable, profuse, scattered thoughts and feelings that are difficult to integrate. Harmonious balance between the two synthesizes these characteristics. When upsurges of intuitive thoughts and feelings combine with logical evaluation, optimal creativity results. Although the right-brain, left-brain concept originated in neurology, it has become a metaphor for functions not necessarily proved to belong to one hemisphere or the other.

Schooling heavily favors left-brain skills: rote memory of facts, linear problem solving, making logical distinctions, having correct answers, taking multiple-choice tests, conforming. We need these skills. Unfortunately this education minimizes right-brain functions: feelings, intuition, ambiguity, spontaneity, connection.

Many therapists bring this emphasis to their work, making it chiefly an intellectual exercise. Emotions, presumably the core of our interest, are dealt with cognitively. Those therapists with strong right-brain abilities mainly express them outside of therapy. Many are fine musicians, painters, writers, yet their therapy is cerebral, awkwardly logical, and lacks creative liveliness. If one sign at a fork in the road said, "The way to Heaven" and another said, "The way to a lecture on Heaven," they would go to the lecture.

Most of us need to enhance right-brain proficiency and integrate it with the left brain for greater therapeutic creativity. We need regular, mindful devotion to right-brain activities: music, poetry, art, communing with nature, spontaneous play, humor, fruitful solitude. It matters less *what* we do, but only that we do.

There is neurobiological evidence the brain/mind can be trained as we age, disproving Freud's dictum: "Near or above the age of 50, the elasticity of the mental processes on which treatment depends is, as a rule, lacking. Old people are no longer educable."[43] The key is novelty. When we undertake a task not typical of our work, we break old patterns, open doors, become more creative. The richer the intellectual and artistic life, the richer is the brain's neuronal network. Retirees who continue a pattern of using their minds in new ways conserve, even augment, brain metabolism. Like aerobic exercise, "brain aerobics" require discipline. Don't take your mind for granted.

Optimal Physical Health

Several therapists and I meditate. Later, one reports that she fell asleep. We explore this, getting nowhere. I ask about her typical day. She races about morning until night, never feels finished, sleeps as little as possible in the vain hope of getting it all done tomorrow. She knows her therapy is not as creative as it could be—starts to fall asleep. No one demeans her by giving advice— she knows what to do.

Three years later she reports, "That meeting was a turning point. I really looked at how my hectic life affects the way I do therapy. Now I make sure I take plenty of time for myself: hobbies, music. I'm not placing my patients' time before mine. Now when I am tired in a session, I use it as a diagnostic tool. I shortened sessions to 50 minutes to give myself a break. Even my husband has been meditating and finds that he is more at ease and less tired."

We are more sleep deprived than we realize, making us less efficient, more irritable, with lapses of attention, reduced short-term memory, and impaired judgment—all interfering with creativity. Sleep deprivation accumulates a sleep debt that we can't prevent by storing up sleep. Grandmother was right when she said that we need at least eight hours!

Maintaining a healthy body hardly seems worth mentioning. Yet we push ourselves to exhaustion. Everything suffers—health, work, personal relations, spiritual growth, sex. Those who don't break down have family members who do: "I don't get ulcers, I give them." Many who come to us are devastated, weak, shaky. A therapist showing similar distress is not what they need: "How can an exhausted person help me with exhaustion?" Patients are sensitive to their therapist's health. Two nurses observed my gray skin and shallow breathing before I learned that heart surgery was urgent.

Hope is rekindled with a therapist in radiant good health, especially one who has dealt with exhaustion and found antidotes. Good health makes good therapy. And there is sound scientific evidence that satisfaction with our life's work is the single best predictor of longevity. Of course, severely depressed patients see a healthy therapist as one more "proof" they do not deserve the good things others have. Grist for the therapeutic mill.

Listen to your body. Most women do it better. Men have been trained to use their bodies in sports: strength, coordination, achievement, competition—and boys *still* are, despite a few gender-role reversals. We try not to fuss over pain or malfunction; just patch it and get back into the game. We are impatient with infirmity and inactivity, want to get moving. Ignoring body messages has been ingrained since we were primitive hunters.

Family and social pressures reinforce innate aggressiveness. Newborn boys are more active, fussier, and harder to satisfy. But only on average. Baby girls can be restless and wiry. With sports more available to girls, young women also defy injuries. At 15, my granddaughter, colicky as an infant, reminded me of myself and her dad as she threw herself headlong into a soccer game—and performed well on the *boys'* team.

But macho socialization does not take girls over completely. Female physiology is hard to ignore. Jan says I suffer from not being a woman! She started caring for her body with menstruation. Conceiving, carrying, delivering, nursing, and raising six children taught elemental lessons about patience, body intimacy, and caring for self and others. Only recently have I begun to do as well for myself.

I must be clobbered repeatedly before I get the drift. In the late 1940s, I practiced medicine all day every day and many nights. After a bad hay fever season, I developed a sinus infection. Nearly blinded by headache and fever, I finally collapsed in bed—this happened three years running before I saw the pattern. Infections stopped when I rested more in August and September. Today we know the immune system builds up during sleep. When sleep is lost, killer cells that fight invaders decrease, making us more vulnerable to a host of diseases, from infections to diabetes to cancer.

Twenty-five years later, not having learned my lesson, exhaustion and illness recurred with stress and sleep loss. This time, having abused my body for decades (poor eating habits, little exercise, overweight, few vacations), the messages were more serious: hypertension, diabetes, gout, headaches, arteriosclerosis. All improved with reducing stress; eating a low-fat, low-sugar diet; jogging; losing 45 pounds; working shorter hours and taking more time off. Only half kidding, an analyst said, "Young analysts go back for more analysis. Old ones take longer vacations."

Good health lasted ten years before another period of feeling trapped, angry, and powerless brought back stress diseases. Except that this time the diabetes is persistent, blood pressure is higher, arteriosclerosis is more advanced. More lifestyle changes and four major surgeries were necessary before achieving ten years of sound health. We can get away with misusing our body in the short run, disdainful of complications, recovering without disability. But when we get older, we are fragile, have less stamina. Don't let the quick-fix ethos interfere with your care of your body.

Physicians play a part. They are seldom examples of optimal health. Moreover, they are trained to treat "real disease." Preventive medicine is least popular although patients consider it the *most important*. Orthopedists know more about back carpentry than back exercise. Pediatricians are better at treating pneumonia than colds. Cardiologists offer angioplasty rather than coaching preventive changes in lifestyle.

Surgeons cut rather than talk, even though talking might be healthier. This is understandable, but not excusable. Physicians believe their hard-won skills should be devoted to grave problems. The less serious, meaning not fatal for years, are relegated to assistants, nurses, or health educators. They may be right, as long as the relegatees are capable. But, ultimately, we must take our health into our own hands. We cannot depend on others, no matter how caring, to be as concerned about us as we ourselves should be.

New Tools for Creative Growth

Today there are many healing arts for enhancing wellness that were little known a few years ago: new ways to treat and prevent chronic illness and disability, to actively recover from disease, to heal and transform ourselves. We now have many avenues to optimal physical, mental, and spiritual wholeness. Use them.

> *Organized training for enhancing creativity.* Options for courses, workshops, and study are listed in "Suggested Readings." *Integration of spirituality and religion into psychotherapy.* Some resources also can be found in "Suggested Readings."
>
> *Fitness programs.* Judicious exercise combined with rest, healthful nutrition, and stress reduction. People benefit from unaccustomed strenuous activities, properly supervised. They are faced with situations that challenge them to draw on underused resources. They learn the value of risk taking, so necessary for creativity. They move beyond competition to cooperation.
>
> A therapist recalls an Outward Bound week. The task is to climb a steep hill. Conflict over how to do so erupts. One faction wants to charge straight to the top. The other wants to meander back and forth, finding the easiest path. Each heatedly accuses the other of going about the task all wrong—and being wrong. Finally, someone points out the polarization—most men are in the first group, most women in the second. Cooler heads prevail, they agree that either method would get them to the top. They work together, meandering in steep places, going straight up where less steep. Lots of lessons learned, in-

cluding new perspectives on the practice of psychotherapy.

Treatment of diseases that previously responded poorly. I would not be alive to write this book without bypass surgery, not available in my father's day, plus the application of research less than ten years old on the importance of regular aerobic and strength exercise, nutritional improvement, and stress reduction.

Other tools include:

- *Alternative treatments* coming into the mainstream: homeopathy, acupuncture, energy healing, massage and body work.
- *Psychodynamic advances,* such as self-psychology, object relations, and briefer, more effective individual therapy
- *Methods growing out of the family therapy field.*
- *Self-help and 12-step programs,* effective alone or as adjuncts.
- *Mind–body research*: spiritopsychoneuroimmunology
- *Eastern methods*: meditation, martial arts, spiritual practices, herbal supplements, integration with Western medicine
- *Paranormal and altered states of consciousness,* reported by researchers with mainstream credentials.
- *Focus on the healer,* his or her significance in the therapy–patient interface

Reflections

- Describe a creative moment in therapy. How can you have more?
- Develop a simple meditation practice and stay with it. If you can't, find a teacher.
- Take up an art in which you have some skill. Find a new (to you) style to express it: painting, playing an instrument, writing poetry. Or learn to draw or do other artwork with your nondominant hand. Or try a brand-new

art form. The tougher it is to find time, the more you need it.

- Assess your health. Get advice on exercise, diet and supplements, stress management, and so on. Stay healthy!
- Identify obstacles to being more creative in your life. What have you done about them? How has that worked? What else can you do?
- What beneficial changes have you made in your life? How did you make them? Have they lasted? What's next?

13

Learning from Practicing

I have learned much from therapists, supervisors, colleagues, reading, conferences, writing. Yet patient dilemmas stimulate creativity the most. Clinical learning is empirical, pragmatic, trial and error. We try something, note how it works, correct our course, try again with new data, and check to see how people turn out. We unendingly practice our practice, evaluate our creativity. We need all our perceptions, outer and inner, to give the best we can. Our presence is healing, even in the face of dying and death. There is no substitute for becoming more creative than by doing a lot of therapy. It's irresistible.

Clinical Notes

Keeping notes on our work is basic to amplifying creative impulses. We traverse several note-taking phases. As new students, extensive records are required for learning, anxiety reduction, memory, legal protection, supervision, accreditation. Erroneously called "process notes," they are an undigested hash of too much content, too little process. The writer is hardly discernible behind the verbiage. Very uncreative.

With experience, notes become more useful, closer to reality, more to the point, more reflective of *us*. Rather than mimicking a method, we should evolve a personal style that meets these purposes. With training over, many give up note taking. I asked a friend how it felt to be in private practice. "It's wonderful. Freedom from notes and supervision!" I could hardly wait. Once graduated from the analytic institute, where I wrote more garbage than I could possibly use, I kept few notes—relief from what I saw as an unneeded, time-consuming chore. I was on a fast, high-output track, also not very creative.

Jan joined me as cotherapist in 1970. At Plum Grove she did a wealth of interviewing, but this was new. Writing notes after every contact was essential for learning, and a key to our working together. She puts down the gist of what happened, themes and feelings that strike her, and a summary of what she said and did. She encloses in a box afterthoughts to be discussed with me or patients. I add thoughts, usually complementary. Should agencies or lawyers object, you can keep personal comments separate from official records. I am delighted with this arrangement. To equalize labor and forestall guilt, I handle intake, DSM diagnoses, appointments, fees, billing, insurance, and correspondence. She is relieved of these left-brain drudgeries; I am relieved of taking notes.

Occasionally, Jan misses a session, so I write notes to discuss later. Surprised to find that I enjoy this and that the review is so helpful, I now make notes for solo practice. They are different from those of my student days—understandable, interesting, self-revealing, practical, alive, short. They suit my current mode—few patients, worked with more thoughtfully; every case a jewel creatively polished.

A thought for readers who plan to grow older: Notes are invaluable as we struggle to recall names, dates, and content. But I am pleased to report from the high side of 70 that feelings and processes are more accessible than ever. Remembering specifics of patients' lives is not nearly as important as I thought. Besides, they never forget! I agree with Jan's claim that being unburdened of so much remembering makes it easier to be fully present and open to creative ideas.

Records create dilemmas, as illustrated in "To Share or Not to Share? Notes on Myself" by Marcia Davis.[44]

A man keeps asking to see his therapist's notes. The therapist keeps refusing while trying to use the request therapeutically, even though she believes patients should see their files. Interpretations have no effect. She has several concerns: the personal nature of her notes; fear it would undermine therapy; fear the patient might use them against her. She agonizes for weeks, discusses it with her husband, brings the issue to classes she teaches. Some colleagues think she should say no; others would have dismissed him long ago. She confronts many new issues about ethics and attitudes. She finally decides that therapy will not move until he sees the notes. She is tempted to edit them, but doesn't. He studies the notes and is depressed over what he sees about himself. He is angry at her for not always being the perfect therapist. But reading them helps him move on to difficult sexual issues he was avoiding. He feels safer and more trusting. They eventually reach a successful ending.

This honest and caring therapist puts it well when she says, "One of the excitements of therapy is that it continually stretches me, continually makes me think about my values, my contradictions, my behavior, my views, and the messages I am giving to others."

Notes are a potential clinical and legal issue, so develop a clear policy before trouble arises. Attitudes toward notes reflect the personality and theoretical orientation of the therapist. Since I am inclined to share myself, I feel the same about notes. I tell patients I write notes to make therapy more efficient, and they are welcome to see them. They seldom ask; permission dissolves distrust. When we can't recall something, reading portions of the notes aloud or asking patients to read them clears up uncertainty and cements collaboration. Patients are not as fragile as we imagine, and letting them in on what we think and feel is not as harmful as we might anticipate. I also tell them that notes are for our eyes only. I emphasize, especially with conflictual couples, that they will not be shown to anyone else for any reason.

Terminating after months of tumultuous therapy, a couple decides to divorce. The husband's attorney phones and wants my records. I tell him they are confidential and would not be given to anyone. Angrily, he threatens me with a subpoena. I say, "I saw them together. He is as much at fault as she. If I go to court, you will have a hostile witness on your hands." Never heard from him again.

This works with relatives who refuse to come in, authorities deciding on annulment, courts ruling on custody, insanity, and so forth. I only give out information (insurance, schools, courts) after the patient and I agree it is in the patient's best interest, and he or she has edited the material.

Our position on the confidentiality of patient records has been confirmed by the highest court in the land. A former student of ours refused to testify or produce her records in response to a subpoena. That confidentiality privilege was recognized by the United States Supreme Court on June 13, 1996, in *Carrie Jaffee v. Mary Lou Redmond*, No. 95-255.

A good working relationship that evolves over a long time makes a solid foundation for trust and flexibility.

> *A family returns several years after therapy for a few once-a-month sessions. To make the most of the time, we suggest that the parents and four young adults each jot down a few reactions to each session and send them to us. We will use them for planning. They say it's a great idea, if we do the same! They do, we do, and the sessions are lively and productive. A creative technique worth trying.*

Journaling

Recording sets off associations to patients, personal and family reactions, reading and training recollections. These are worth putting down after a session or at the day's end. Too tired? Fatigue weakens defenses and useful, less conscious material comes up. Even a few words are valuable. Worried about remembering? Freud listened all day, wrote all evening.

Journaling is excellent for creative growth: bolsters memory and deepens insight, augments understanding and accepting life, benefits health by supporting the immune system. A periodic review offers special perspectives that can lead to significant life changes. Amplification is at work. Reflecting on and writing down whatever strikes us—within or outside of sessions—we become more aware and attuned. We discover, for example, that dreams become more numerous and revealing when we record them. This is also true of intuitions and the other experiences discussed below. Research shows that writing about personal traumas aids not only mental health, but physical health as well.[45,46]

Many ways work. Devise an easy one, not too ambitious. M. H.

141

Vorse [47] advises, "The art of writing is the art of applying the seat of the pants to the seat of the chair." Address emotional issues, especially negative ones. Writing for your eyes only, you feel freer to put down anything. Write without pausing—stream of consciousness. You'll be surprised at the creative ideas you come up with. Here's what students who did this have written.

1. *How I became a better, more creative therapist today.* We have moments when we feel on target, say or do something that is just right. Capturing them fixes them in our minds; in similar situations we will be reminded of what worked before and might work again.

    — Journaling has become a valuable technique for patients, now that I'm doing it.
    — Having patients write their long-term goals on a big flip chart as we do in class has focused and accelerated my therapy.
    — I laughed more today. As I have loosened up, so have several of my more rigid patients.
    — Allowing them more responsibility lifts some of my exhaustion.
    — Instead of giving assignments to a family that brought in a problem, I engaged them in creative problem solving.
    — Brief centering before each patient enters my office works well for me. I'm less likely to be worrying, "What should I do next?" Meditation has increased awareness of myself in the here and now. And patients look forward to readings on meditation I suggest.

2. *What I wish I had done differently.* We wonder if what we did or did not do was the best. We fine-tune and grow by reflecting, not obsessing. Mistakes can be so impressive that we remember and learn from them all our lives. Good judgment comes from experience, and experience comes from bad judgment.

    I missed a good opportunity to keep my mouth shut.
    I think I hurt her feelings. I must ask her first thing next time. If I did, apologize, we can figure out what happened, repair the damage, and make it a springboard to understanding for both of us.
    I'm surprised and relieved that I enjoy making a "creative mistake."

I aligned with the mother against the daughter and the teenager refused to come back. I phoned her directly and owned up to my
mistake. I asked her to call me on it if she sees me doing this
again. She's back in therapy and acting more free.

Questions to ask: How can I spot a tendency to repeat this, so
I don't do it again? What self-inquiry is necessary to understand
myself better? Is this an isolated mistake, or part of a pattern? Can
I handle this, or should I talk to someone? If so, to whom?

3. *Night dreams.* Freud said that dreams are the royal road to the
unconscious, as true today as it was a century ago. Dreams are
priceless gifts, honest critics, guides. They reveal our deepest self,
holding out direction for the future, confirmation of the present,
and meaning for the past. They are wiser than our ordinary mind.
A dream faces two ways—toward the world of relationships and
outer events, and toward the world of thoughts, feelings, and inner events. We gain insight into both worlds, clarifying our part
in the outer and illuminating the inner. Being a personal production, every detail represents some part of our psyche, accurately
portraying unconscious processes so salient for a therapist.

Having a detailed account of a dream makes analysis more revealing. Records of successive dreams show trends not apparent
from one dream. When dreams reveal our reaction to a patient,
we have a sensitive indicator of what is happening beneath the
surface.

> I'm jarred awake, heart pounding, mouth dry, dreaming a
> big black monster is after me. Breathing deeply, I calm down
> as I wonder what this means. Earlier today I saw a black
> man in session who was half a foot taller and a hundred
> pounds heavier than I. In the session I felt comfortable, in
> good rapport, even when he told of slugging a man with
> whom he disagreed. But the dream reveals a contrary re-
> action. Next session we share early impressions of each
> other. With trepidation, I tell the dream. He chuckles, "You
> don't have to worry about me. You're just a li'l ole honky."
> Honky and monster become staples of our lexicon during a
> successful individual and family therapy of several years.

Share dreams with someone you trust: spouse, therapist, good
friend, dream group. When partners share dreams, both are en-

riched. Honesty is an aphrodisiac. A puzzling dream may be clear to someone who cares about us. Mutual sharing is exquisitely intimate, hard for couples to do before they have a strong and candid relationship. Sharing dreams contributes to further strength and candidness, a virtuous cycle. Dream sharing among family members is even more beneficial.

Once we learn how to work with our dreams, we are ready to help patients with theirs. Working with dreams is a neglected, yet rich technique with couples and families. Take workshops, use "Suggested Readings," get consultation on how to use your dreams for creative growth.

4. *Daydreams*. Daydreaming has a bad press. Daydreamers are considered a problem. Jan and I talked to our son Greg's fourth-grade teacher:

> "I don't know what to do with him. He spends most of his time gazing out the window, daydreaming."
> "Well then, why don't you just flunk him?"
> "I can't do that—he passes all the tests!"

Greg quit college after two years. He liked his classes and teachers, but still had no spark for schoolwork: "Being taught cheats me out of the fun of finding out by myself." Daydreaming evinces a healthy, creative mind, readily distinguishable from preoccupation that impairs functioning. Greg's success as a person 35 years later makes it clear his daydreaming was more creative than not. He is the most creative of our six.

In daydreams we experiment safely with ideas, explore life directions, try actions. Visions of the future are crucial to reaching that future. Vivid daydreams show us the bliss we should follow. Objectifying fantasies in a journal shapes a sense of the life we want to lead, the person we want to be. Daydreaming, we align conscious goals with deeper trends in our psyche. From his many years of scientific creativity, Einstein tells us, "Imagination is more important than knowledge."

5. *Intuitions*.[48,49] Therapists have hunches. At first I was cautious about voicing them aloud. Growing more daring, I decided that when an idea or feeling comes back three times, it's okay to voice it. As I learned to trust hunches, I put them into words after they came up once or twice. Now I often think out loud. When it adds to what is happening, great. When it doesn't, people tell me. Until

intuitions are confirmed, I'm tentative, recognizing that we will each be tentative in our own way: I have a hunch that . . . Since I saw you last, I thought several times about what you said (quoting) and I wonder if . . . Correct me if I am wrong, but it seems to me that . . .

Intuitions, like dreams, are eruptions from the unconscious. Like dreams, they guide us to deeper understanding of both therapist and patient. Checking them out clarifies whether they belong to us alone or are truly a product of our interaction.

6. *Synchronicity.*[50] Synchronistic events are meaningful coincidences closely related to intuition, a path to wisdom. Like intuitions, the more we are interested in them, attuned to them, and write about them, the more they occur. They help us see covert connections. They widen our horizon, hint at the mystery of life. Acknowledging these events in our own lives, it is natural to help patients do the same. Jung tells of his frustration with an overly intellectualizing patient who recounted a dream in which she was given a piece of jewelry, a golden scarab. He heard something tapping at the window, opened it, and a gold-green scarabaeid beetle flew in. He handed it to her saying, "Here is your beetle." It broke the ice of her intellectual resistance, allowing healing to proceed. Honing such awareness can be crucial in discovering meaning, magic, and purpose in life.

7. *Observations on your evolution.* Put into your journal anything you are doing to enhance your life, in and out of therapy: comments on meditation, right-brain work, health, and so on. Check how well what you observe fits with your vision for your future. Are you taking committed action that will get you to your vision? Look for isomorphisms—similar, parallel patterns that show up in the therapy you are in, therapy you are doing, intimate relationships, dreams and daydreams, and threads that connect. Reviewing your journal provides larger perspectives. Note items to discuss with a trusted other. Look for discrepancies between thoughts, feelings, and behavior. Colleagues report that the journaling workshops of Ira Progoff[51] are useful.

Experiment with Greater Self-Disclosure

How much personal information we should reveal to patients is highly controversial. Some therapists believe that the less, the better. Others disclose as much as possible, even sexual details. The style of most therapists falls between these extremes. This is an issue for every therapist, and so important for creative development that Part IV is devoted to it.

Transformational Experiences

Nearly all of my new patients have been in therapy. We learn what was helpful, what was not, and why. Too commonly, nothing much happened. Oh, they had a few insights and made a few changes, but there was little impact. Pivotal questions were left untouched. Trivial gut involvement. No aliveness. Therapy was not consequential in altering life.

Impact, transformation, aliveness, confrontation with meaning and purpose in life—these are both goals and means in our therapy. Getting to the core is a formidable task. Analysis on the couch for 12 years didn't do it. Requisites for deep change are seldom present in one-hour-at-a-time talk therapy. We just get rolling when it is time to stop. By the next session, defensive patterns of internal characters have regrouped, sealed over, the "Monday crust." Openness to the deeper psyche has to be initiated again and again. And the anchoring of psychological conflicts within the body is untouched.

For many, talk therapy is enough. Pushing to go deeper not only is forbidding, but could be hazardous to a fragile psyche. But many of us want more. Not satisfied with merely shuffling interior furniture, we want radical change. We refuse to go on as we have. Most therapists rightly belong in the second group, especially those who thirst for life transformation for themselves and selected patients. We have the necessary psychic sturdiness, perseverance, and capacity to tolerate temporary turmoil. We can postpone gratification when convinced it is in our best long-term interest. We have been doing it all along.

In experiential encounters, I dealt with many potent issues untouched by analysis. Among the ingredients that make deep change possible are an isolated indoor–outdoor retreat atmosphere; 24-hour immersion for five to 14 days, or even longer; heightened openness to unconscious processes; becoming swept up in the collective energy of a safe group similarly engaged; and bringing forth hitherto untapped inner resources for survival.

All of these encounters have been guided by leaders who have spent years opening their hearts and minds, and helping others to do so. In retreats with Brugh Joy, Richard Moss, Thich Nhat Hanh, Bob Goulding, Bob Drye, and others, Jan and I took part in powerful experiential exercises: gestalt empty-chair work, high-intensity music, whirling, rock climbing, fasting, sweat lodge, holotropic breathing, "sing until the song sings you," body scanning for altering energy patterns, group meditation, the rising and setting sun, walking meditation, dharma talks, dream work. Surviving the exercises altered us in ways that were impossible to predict, and yet beneficial. We made decisions about careers, family, ideals, life goals. We became more compassionate therapists, able to work flexibly and creatively with anything at all.

Having experienced transformational encounters, we coach patients to do something similar. They prepare for what might come up, and what comes up feeds back into therapy. Negative reactions to a workshop—they do happen when change is the goal—are handled in sessions. Even physical and mental casualties can contribute to learning and growth.

Reflections

- Trace your history of note taking. Does what you do now meet your creative needs? Are there changes to make?
- Was Marcia Davis, who showed notes to a patient, being pushed around or was she demonstrating flexibility? What would you do? How genuine are we if our notes tell a different story from the person we are in sessions? Would we be wary of what we write if we knew that the patient might see it? Is sharing notes a valid technique? Whose notes are they? Who is the best person to judge if a patient should see notes? How does your attitude toward notes reflect your attitude toward therapy?
- How would you handle a patient's request to see your notes? Under what circumstances would you agree? Refuse? Give your reasons. Do patients have a right to see your notes? Why or why not? If you agree, would you edit out comments about yourself?
- How did you become a better, more creative therapist today?
- What do you wish you had done differently? How can you fix it?

- Describe a creative mistake. Be easier on yourself and more creative next time you make an error.
- Pay attention to your daydreams and night dreams. What do they tell you about your characters, ideals, regrets, conflicts, therapy, the future?
- Describe a correct hunch in therapy. What did you do with it? How did it affect progress? Have you had an inaccurate hunch? What did it tell you about yourself?
- Have you had a creative, life-changing experience?

CHAPTER

14

Evolving Every Day

In *The Psychopathology of Everyday Life*,[43] Freud throws light on common miseries, such as forgetting, slips of the tongue, bungled actions, superstitions, errors. With this insight, we can get beyond irritation over "loss of control," and use everyday life for creative development.

Pay Attention to What Upsets You

A man explains what brings him to therapy. "My ten-year-old son gave me this look that I hate and made a sarcastic crack, just like people say I do. I'm usually pleased when anyone says he looks and acts like me, but now I realize how annoying I am and shudder to think of him—and me—going through life like that."

The gift of discomposure is hard to appreciate. Annoyances fill our day. Patients frustrate us; so do partners and children, news, movies, TV, neighbors, colleagues. We may criticize, or stew, or ignore, or take action to change what is bothering us. But left at only that, we miss an opportunity. The upset is *our* upset, no one else's. Others might have similar, different, opposite, or no reactions. The incident

149

triggers something in us that is supersensitive, unfinished, in need of attention and change *within* us. There is great wisdom in the commandment to love our enemies. They reveal our selves to us. Life's Rorschach.

We attribute to the outer world unacknowledged aspects of our psyche, a subtle, powerful projection. When I point a finger at someone, there are three fingers pointing back at me! Abraham Lincoln said, "I don't like that man, I have to get to know him better." Prejudicial self-deception blocks self-awareness and restricts inner freedom, yet can be a path to greater self-awareness and freedom.

Social schemes fail when they are designed logically and do not take projection into account. Linear thinking blames a single cause "out there" for behavior deemed undesirable, ignoring underlying roots and unintended consequences. Politicians are nonplussed when a "desirable" law strengthens the behavior it is supposed to suppress, like the "war on drugs." The failure of punishment, so obvious nationally, may be harder to see in everyday exchanges. But we ignore it at our peril.

Brugh Joy[52] tells of catching himself to prevent disaster. In charge of training, he listens to an emergency room intern describe a woman with rectal bleeding. The cause is obscure because, according to the intern, examination reveals nothing abnormal. But Brugh does a rectal exam and feels a bleeding mass. He tells the intern to meet him in 45 minutes. Back in his office, Brugh is enraged. Pacing angrily, he silently berates the negligent physician. Inexcusable not to examine her! He will put such a scorching letter in this liar's file that getting a decent job will be impossible. Calming down, Brugh wonders why he is so upset. He recalls the horrendous night he was deluged by 12 rapidly admitted emergencies. Struggling to do his best for each, he cut corners by making up much of what he put in the charts. Brugh is calm and clear when the intern arrives. Instead of blasting him, Brugh tells his own story of deception under pressure. It is a moving moment. Brugh learns a lesson, as does the intern, who goes on to become a trustworthy physician.

There is wisdom in the Sufi prayer, "May your troubles increase." When we accept what is desirable and suppress the undesirable, the latter do not vanish; they become unconscious and press for expression. We see it outside ourself, and then attack it with vengeance. Pogo said, "We have found the enemy, and it is us."

Pay Attention to What Turns You On

A similar projection process is at work if we accept our negative qualities and suppress the positive. We deny our idealistic urges, attribute them to others, then admire those others: hero worship. We keep ourselves from becoming the best we can be. Worship of inimitable heroes has stunted many a student of therapy. We have a fear of becoming godlike, as Maslow[19] suggests.

We don't give enough credence to inspirations that energize us, things we plan to do some day when we have enough time. "Not enough time" is our favorite, weakest, most transparent copout. We hope to avoid offending, soften a turndown, sound innocent. We con ourselves. Used habitually, it invalidates legitimate use. It solidifies a tangled mass of self-deceptions that become what we live by, hiding from ourselves what we really want. Humans are the only animals who make excuses, or need to. We must give up self-deception, let our complete self unfold.

The simple fact is that we can make time for what really matters. If we give ourself to something that does not matter in the long run, we waste what is most precious—our life. Pious precepts of duty, hard work, responsibility, and doing what is expected override acting upon whatever the deeper psyche is trying to tell us about our direction and purpose.

The Unity of Opposites

What turns us off and what turns us on are inseparable aspects of an organic whole. For every quality we harbor its opposite: tenderness and harshness, joy and sorrow, generosity and selfishness, love and indifference. We cannot have one without the other. They are opposite ends of one stick—when we cut off one end, we still have two ends.

This aversion–attraction law of the mind is the universal principle of yin-yang. We describe the world in adjectives: hot and cold, long and short, near and far, happy and unhappy. We go through a long evolution in understanding, from seeing things from one narrow view to a broader philosophy. We eventually see that "opposites" are contrasting views of the same thing. I wish I had read sooner Lao-tzu's wise words[17]:

We join spokes together in a wheel,
but it is the center hole
that makes the wagon move.

We shape clay into a pot,
but it is the emptiness inside
that holds whatever we want.

We hammer wood for a house,
but it is the inner space
that makes it livable.

We work with being,
but non-being is what we use.

And musicians know that the spaces between notes are as essential as the notes themselves.

As infants we define boundaries by moving toward and accepting what feels pleasurable—warm milk, cuddling, lullabies—and pulling away from and rejecting what is painful—cold, falling, pin pricks, loud noises. This necessary sensing of what is me and what is not me remains basic to our existence and identity. Then as we mature, we discover that discomfort cannot be avoided entirely. Moreover, some things we want require putting up with a certain amount of discomfort. When we make a painful mistake at a more immature stage of development, we react by getting upset, looking back, blaming, vowing to do more of the same, only better. We try to maximize the things we want and minimize the discomfort necessary to get them. Only slowly do we learn that discomfort need not be an enemy. Properly understood, pain is an ally. When more advanced we react without much upset and use discomfort to tell us what is needed to forge a path toward our ideal. We welcome mistakes as error-correcting information from the universe, mistakes that guide us toward what we ultimately want to do and be.

Congenital dysautonomia is a condition in which babies are born unable to detect pain. They have no warning of appendicitis, fractures, etc. They die young of catastrophes that would have been prevented were they able to feel pain. Our mental pain serves a similar protective function and must be respected.

Just Pay Attention

Once we are familiar with how easily we project onto the world, we see that this goes on subtly all the time. We do not have to be upset or inspired. Full attention makes us aware of hidden sides of our selves.

> A gestalt workshop opens with a deceptively simple exercise: "Describe any object in the room." An attractive woman describes what looks to me like a nondescript vase. "It's very lovely. But it's fragile. I would like to hold it in my hand, but I'm afraid it might break." The leader asks, "Does that say anything about you?" Suddenly sobbing, she stammers, "That's the story of my life. Everyone tells me how beautiful I am. But inside I feel weak and fragile and in danger of breaking apart at any moment."

Every day gives opportunities to sharpen your attention. Here are some I find useful.

> Waiting to warm up the car or at traffic lights, relax, breathe slowly and deeply, focus attention. Listen to your body instead of the radio. Release tension. Drive smoothly and reasonably, instead of rushing through yellow lights. (A famous golfer prepares for a tournament by driving side roads to the course at 15 miles per hour!)

> Do everything slower, with mindful attention. Smile and center yourself and let the phone ring three times before answering; notice the lilt in your voice and positive response. Stretch out on the floor for two minutes between appointments. Live slower, live longer.

> Meditate for 30 seconds before entering the office. Walk more slowly, listen, look, feel muscles move. Take more time for transitions—between home and family, work and lunch, work and vacation.

Treat yourself to less stress. Relaxed attentiveness will serve you well in every interview for the rest of your life.

Work with Your Own Families

Nothing is more mundane than our families. Familiar to us year after year, we take them for granted. They may upset us, annoy us, depress us—yet we put up with them. After ill-conceived efforts to show them the light, our resigned attitude is, "They will never change."

Changing family relationships has been extensively documented. Read Murray Bowen and his followers. Their theoretical ideas are valuable; but use your own techniques. *Family Interfaces*[53] recounts Jan's adaptation to humanistic therapy and to her family. Here I underscore a few ideas salient for psychotherapists.

Genograms and family-of-origin work are useful for patient families. But often we neglect *our* family work.

> *A "comprehensive and integrative" training program requires family-of-origin work. Early on, a supervisor has students do their genograms at home and then show them to the group. Once that onerous task is over, families and genograms of the supervisees are never mentioned. Not surprisingly, the supervisor's family and its genogram is neither referred to nor presented.*

This hierarchical teaching—directives from administration to supervisor to supervisee—promotes hierarchical therapy: third parties act unilaterally on therapists to unilaterally change patients. Students are cheated out of learning the nuts and bolts of a complicated technique, and the genogram's value for beneficial change is not taught. Patients of supervisees are cheated also. The intricacies of how the construction of a family tree reveals diagnostic and treatment information are ignored. A dynamic, evocative process is degraded to a static, pointless diagram, put together out of sight of the group. More important, the family roots of the student's assets and liabilities, so central to creative supervision, go unexamined. Substantial evolution is sacrificed to insubstantial expediency. Such is the impotence of mandated requirements.

Furthermore, the prevailing culture of training in which therapists are taught strongly determines how therapists learn and do. I discovered this on a site visit to a graduate program that prides itself on teaching brief, solution-centered therapy.

I watch a therapist with a bickering couple. The student unimaginatively goes back and forth, clarifying communication, negotiating a compromise. Tension mounts with no progress. When time is up, all look exhausted. Ready to leave, the wife mentions her parents are coming to campus tomorrow. The student says something banal and ushers them out. No connection is made between the parental visit and the bickering, no exploration of family dynamics, no coaching about how they will handle the weekend, no invitation to a session with the older generation. Nothing that might move them beyond the impasse that now includes the student, who has dutifully done what was required. Student and couple alike have been short-changed. So have her parents.

Family-of-origin work is best done in surges over a lifetime. Stretches when nothing special seems to be going on alternate with events that bring the family members together from great distances. Each phase is different, yet promising. Lack of turmoil is deceptive. Unfinished business percolates internally, silently. Therapists, who should know better, but do not, are lulled into hoping all problems will be solved and equanimity will reign. Family contacts, if any, become perfunctory. But these are times when meaningful staying in touch, however briefly and casually, could bring disproportionate positives. Strike while the iron is cold. Sincere tokens of affection pay off handsomely. Our responses to children's and grandchildren's cards, phone calls, photos, and valentines keep love flourishing.

Eventually, fallow calm is disrupted by milestones: weddings, births, bar mitzvahs, anniversaries, medical crises, funerals. These are natural occasions, undervalued by individual-oriented therapists, for reconnecting with family members. Our families are not exempt from the laws of systems. Their reactions to stress are entrenched, unhealthy. New ways of relating stir up pressure to go back to the old. If anyone has the necessary insight and stick-to-itiveness to make changes that pay off and last, it is the therapist in his or her own family.

Relating in a new way is difficult. We find a million reasons not to. Respected teachers, but committed only to treating one person at a time, brainwash us and validate excuses. The likelihood of family healing is rationalized away. They have a limited supply of ideas about dealing with the family, ineffective at best, destructive at worst.

1. "Stay away from your toxic family" is their theme song.
2. Go through the motions, keep up your front, get out quick.
3. Rev up your gumption. You don't have to take it any longer. Tell them off good and proper. They need confrontation.
4. You understand psychology. Interpret their motives. Show them how wrong they are and how psychologically minded you are.
5. Stick with individual therapy and there will be no need to change family relationships.

The pseudosophisticated therapist who offers these misguided tactics rarely prescribes them forthrightly. Rather, encouragement is by insinuation, well-timed silence, adroit questions, or approving tones. Failure confirms the need for more individual therapy. Such failures are predictable by systems therapists.

The error is in the goal of changing the family. It may or may not change, no matter what we do. What can change is how we relate to the family and the internal world derived from the family. When unhappy about our family—as all of us are at times—the most certain locus of change is within us. We can always change ourselves and how we respond. And when we can handle ourselves with family, we can handle ourselves with anyone.

The false assumption is that working through family-originated issues with the therapist is all that is necessary. Colleagues of various persuasions—Freudian, Jungian, Transactional Analysis, Gestalt, Neurolinguistic Programming, client-centered, Eastern spiritual practices—all get stuck on this point. Their position: When I resolve my relationship with my mother in therapy, this accomplishes whatever could be done in person with her. These therapists have either used bound-to-fail tactics, or have never worked with their family under systems-informed guidance. Their disparagement of family work is theoretical. They are against something they have never succeeded at. Their objections are abstract, not experiential.

After talking about my mother for 12 years on the couch, I'm sure I've resolved all issues with her. Visiting in San Jose, I invite her to drive with us along Highway 1. She objects, "It's so dangerous on those cliffs above the ocean. Let's go somewhere else." My heart starts pounding just as it did as a teenager when she foisted her

*fears onto me about driving, football, swimming, almost any-
thing. I retreat to the bathroom to calm down, telling myself, "Relax, you aren't a teenager any more." Composed, I tell her we
have decided to leave for Highway 1 at one o'clock and she
doesn't have to come if she doesn't want to. At one she is in the
car waiting! None of us say a word as we enjoy the view along
the cliffs. From then on, my relationships with all women undergo
subtle improvement.*

Another fallacy to dispel is that family change only comes about
through group encounters. That happens. But the more dysfunctional
and the larger the family is, the more likely it is that chaos will result.
Bowen[54] found in the 1960s that working *systemically* one-on-one
with psychiatric residents is more manageable and more effective with
disturbed families. Being a person with a person, one human with
another, is as rare as it is transformative. The best way to understand
a relationship is to try to change it. The best way to change it is to
change your part in it. When change endures, amid some turmoil,
good things follow.

Another neglected point. Hundreds of my family-oriented patients
and students have settled matters with parents, yet often do not improve their relationships with brothers and sisters. Present-day sibling
connections are distant, shallow, inconsequential. Remarkable, when
we consider that sibs are the people whom we have known the long-
est and with whom we share a common childhood and heritage. And
getting together at funerals and weddings, for instance, can hardly be
avoided. How we relate to sibs is a fundamental template that prefig-
ures how we get along with peers, and especially with spouses. Robert
Bly[55] labels our emotionally distant, superficial buddy–buddy culture
a "sibling society." Becoming true peers in marriage, with balanced
respectful give-and-take, is rare. Many marital problems orbit around
inadequate peership, originating in unfinished business with sibs. The
proof is in the easing of couples' problems when fixated sib conflicts
are resolved.

Also, the literature tends to neglect the family of procreation. True,
resolutions in the original family can pay off handsomely in the current
one. Still, we should not overlook the power of our present family.
What happens professionally affects our partners, and what happens
with them affects us. Early in teaching I was surprised by a development I didn't expect. Students learning to treat families found their
immediate families reverberating, both positively and negatively.

Since most had not been in family therapy, we offered optional work-shops and supervision for student couples, which were well received.

Therapists who do not include both original and current families in their therapy leave huge areas of life untouched, potentials for trouble. Jan writes about her groups for therapists and their families in *Family Interfaces*. Safe exchanges with colleagues are a powerful impetus to family and personal growth. Her group is still spirited in its tenth year. Supportive peer groups, with or without a leader, can be stress re-ducers as well as vehicles for learning and healing. Therapists who steadfastly work with their families over many years harvest great ben-efits. Furthermore, firsthand knowledge makes for more effective coaching of patients and students. Every facet of life is enriched.

Grow Through Life's Transitions

Periodically, we become caught up in a crisis that summons neglected inner resources.

> *When I awaken from coronary bypass surgery after being uncon-scious for 36 hours, I am high. I made it! Two days later I collapse. I glimpse my skeletal, haggard face and speak to the image, "I don't know if you are worth saving." Staggering to bed, I mutter unfamiliar words, "I'm not fighting any more. I can't handle it. I did my best for this surgery and survived. Now I just have to surrender to whatever." I fall on the bed exhausted. I wonder, "Is this the 'giving up to a Higher Power' I have heard about?" Too tired to think, I slip into welcome sleep. From this moment on, I steadily recover. The surgeon attributes it to depletion of hormonal reserves. I attribute it to sadness as children and grandchildren go home and Jan stays away because of purulent sinusitis. Prob-ably we are both right!*

Useful for both professionals and patients has been *Transitions* by William Bridges.[56] He defines: 1. Old phase. 2. Neutral zone. 3. New phase. These stages unfold whether we are coping with a "negative" crisis, such as illness, or with a "positive," such as a job promotion. The neutral zone is a necessary interim, and should be accepted rather than fought. Confusion is unavoidable but temporary, as we consol-idate and resolve leftovers and prepare for whatever comes next. When in haste to leave the past behind and uncomfortable with a pause, we exaggerate its negatives. Makes it easier to leave. But this is a shortsighted gain. Plunging into the future, we drag along unfinished business that contaminates our new life. According to Bridges, transitions present several tasks.

- Realize that you are, in fact, in a critical life transition.
- Patiently monitor the process as it resonates interiorly.
- Explore internal characters who can help with problems.
- Finish unfinished business from the earlicr stage.
- Say a wistful goodbye to the old consciousness.
- Cherish just being in the disorienting neutral zone, in not doing.
- Welcome the unfamiliar new phase as it comes into view.
- Relax into ambiguity and uncertainty.
- Find your right functioning in the new life.

Gain wisdom from the lessons learned. Hang out with people who have struggled through similar transitions, a basic 12-step dynamic. Enjoy the enrichment that a new perspective in life brings.

Relationships with Nontherapists

The people with whom I spend the most and best time are psychologically minded students, colleagues, patients, and family—five of eight are therapists! It's only natural to seek out like-minded souls, so long as other ways of living are not excluded. But that is what happens in a busy life, especially to an intuitive introvert who prefers a few deep relationships. My less favored extraversive side needs cultivation.

Dean Ornish's *Love and Survival*[1] summarizes extensive research showing that a profound sense of loneliness, isolation, and alienation is a major cause of serious physical and mental disease, and that intimacy plays a powerful role in prevention. For example, patients about to undergo open-heart surgery were asked two simple questions: 1. Do you participate regularly in organized social groups (clubs, church, etc.)? 2. Do you draw strength and comfort from your religious or spiritual faith? Those who did not participate socially had a fourfold risk of dying, and those without religious support had a threefold risk of dying.

I find bowling refreshing: no psychologizing over motivations, no intrusive "analysis." We just roll the ball, cheer strikes and spares, commiserate over bad breaks, and act like adolescents. There is little talk of age, illness, family, what we do for a living. Bowling brings out parts neglected for decades. I am enriched every time I go bowling. So make friends with people who have nothing to do with therapy. They can teach you a lot.

Reflections

- What does the most recent upsetting event teach you about yourself?
- Think about the people you most admire. Identify admirable traits you want to emulate. Are you developing them?
- Find three small situations where you can sharpen attention.
- Try a little experiment. Next time you are alone with a family member, notice how the conversation turns to a third person, to outside events, to trivia. Say something personal and meaningful about the two of you. See what happens. Notice how hard it is to stay with that theme.
- Here is a simple, yet profound, measure of how far your family's mental health has come. How able are you to say *anything at all* to your mother? Your father? Your sibs? And how able are you to hear anything at all?
- Using a recent life transition, apply William Bridges' model and see how it fits. Add anything you need for full understanding.
- Inventory your life. Are you seeing enough nontherapists to keep you sane?

15

Doing, Undoing, and Not Doing

Much of life goes like this. We make decision based on what we want right now. Since *all* decisions have down sides, we get boomeranged. So another decision tries to counter the effects of the first. But it is also impulsive, there are new down sides . . . Some bounce from one ill-considered choice to another, like the divorce epidemic from which therapists themselves are not immune; and the rate is even higher for second marriages than first.

Therapists get into a hectic doing mode that brings so many of life's goodies that getting off the merry-go-round seems impossible. But we get stale, tired of doing, flirt with burnout. When we do finally get off, we suffer withdrawal symptoms and jump back on. Doing and undoing become knee-jerk reflexes, not mindful actions.

Therapy is stressful under the best conditions, impossible under the worst. For many therapists today's scene verges on the worst. We are besieged by requests from third parties, well-meaning groups trying to make psychotherapy more businesslike by rewarding speed, efficiency, and conformity. Be brief, follow the DSM, get rid of presenting problems and quit, document everything for everyone. Therapists spend their days trying to do it all.

Many managers are clinicians who do the best they can under a dysfunctional system. But it is difficult to "first, do no harm," having no direct contact with patients. A focus on the cheapest way cannot be supported for long in this system. (Imagine how my already fragile security would have been undermined had open-heart surgery been assigned to the lowest bidder!) Most people can be helped by non-physicians, yet psychiatrists are reimbursed more than nonnpsychiatrists. My experience tells me that good outcomes are more dependent on the quality of the therapist than on his or her discipline.

The threat to our livelihood is coercive. Management technology appears so logical, so reasonably devoted to the common good, that fighting against it seems irrational. And refusal to go along looks irresponsible. Plus, new practitioners coming off graduate-school production lines are eager to conform. Most important, "scientific" management blocks creative alternatives. Change will come about when all therapists, represented by their national professional societies, are able to creatively modify the reimbursement system.

Obsessive doing-at-the-behest-of-others is destructive to our spirit, creativity, and mental and physical health. I wish I had known sooner what I know now. Here are some things that have permanently stopped my doing–undoing busyness. I finally am in charge of my orderly tendencies; they are not in charge of me.

Practice Not Doing

Drivenness precludes mulling over a life, playing creatively. Fr. Anthony de Mello[58] advises, "To become creative, learn the art of wasting time." But wasting time sounds insane. It's not reimbursable! And it's certainly not something that needs *practice*. Yet busyness is precisely what makes it essential that we planfully waste time. Until we get over guilt and restlessness, and make it a regular habit, it's just another good idea that is rarely carried out. Lao-tzu[17] cautions:

> *Fill your bowl to the brim*
> *and it will spill*

> *Keep sharpening your knife*
> *and it will blunt.*

> *Chase after money and security*
> *and your heart will never unclench.*

*Care about people's approval
and you will be their prisoner.*

*Do your work, then step back.
The only path to serenity.*

Recognize when you are going flat, then do something about it. Son Chip (now a busy therapist) once challenged, "Dad, let's you and me go sailing Saturday and not talk about our relationship." Being together and "wasting" a day cruising aimlessly was wonderful, and a turning point for him and me and the family. It's not easy not to be doing something useful or efficient or with a goal. I wish my father had. Advised by his physician that golf would help hypertension, he clutched the club, clenched his jaw, smashed the ball, cursed under his breath as the slice disappeared into the rough. Clearly, golf was not relaxing for him.

Lest the reader be disheartened that workaholism is hereditary, be advised that I am not as work-addicted as my dad, and Chip is far more happy-go-lucky than I am. When Chip was told he could get into medical school by taking chemistry in summer school to change a C to B, he declined. Too many plans for wasting time with sailboats, guitars, singing, girls, ballroom dancing. Two months into social work school, he phoned exuberantly, "This is what I've been looking for. I can help people without going to med school!" Sometimes families really do learn something from generation to generation. Incidentally, the preference of medical schools for chemistry over a healthy lifestyle still persists.

My creative impulses come unbidden while wasting time. Tinkling the piano, lounging in bed, strolling through the woods—moments of peace that allow upsurges from the unconscious. Biographies of inventive people speak of flow from activity to rest and back, even from frenzy to collapse and back. Your reactions to vacations measure how addicted to work you are. The more energy you have been pouring into work, when finally taking a vacation, the more you will:

—be haunted by an undercurrent of anxiety;
—bicker with your partner while packing or traveling;
—sleep the first few days;
—be impatient with trivia, frivolity, celebration;
—think, talk, dream about patients;
—be restless and itch to get back to work.

And if you take work along or call the office, you have advanced, possibly incurable, workaholism!

Doing and undoing are codependent, symbiotic. They depend on each other for their existence. We undo after too much doing, do again after too much undoing, endlessly going nowhere. But when we do not do in the first place, there is no need for a cycle of redoing. The dilemma vanishes. Buddhists say that grasping is the cause of suffering. Letting go of grasping is not doing, giving up the old grasping way, seeing things in a new and different light—enlightenment.

Meditation is not-doing training in serenity. We reach the heart of tranquility when nothing is happening. Healing is allowed. The beauty and nurturance of not doing sustain us, no matter what the world's turmoil. Convalescing from life-threatening crises, coupled with growing older, has curtailed my need for doing. Now it is easy to say no, to plan inviolable times for respite and recuperation from everyday miseries.

In the 1940s I assisted a fine, Mayo-trained surgeon with a huge practice. He announced that he would be on vacation for all of August. I was stunned. So much time off. I had trouble taking two weeks! He explained, "I can do a year's work in 11 months, but not in 12."

What does all this mean to you, the reader with a lot to do? It means that the pressures I tortured myself with are like yours. They are not as momentous as you think. Much doing is meaningless. You will look back and realize that some problems are never resolved, just outgrown. Don't wait until you are old and decrepit. You can waste your time, forestall burnout, and save your life right now.

Lao-tzu again:

> *In the pursuit of knowledge*
> *every day something is added.*

> *In the practice of the Tao*
> *every day something is dropped.*

> *Less and less do you need to force things,*
> *until finally you arrive at non-action.*

> *When nothing is done,*
> *nothing is left undone.*

True mastery can be gained
by letting things go their way.
It can't be gained by interfering.

Accept and Appreciate Mystery

My busyness was fueled by a kinetic need to learn more about health and illness. Moving from one modality to another, I gained much knowledge buttressed by a multitude of facts and experiences. I am overeducated. It's shocking to read in Paul Pearsall's[59] *The Heart's Code* that research shows that one's number of years of education is a more important risk factor for heart disease than are all other risk factors combined! The more we know, the more we don't know. The horizon retreats as we move toward it. Scientific fields—medicine, psychoanalysis, family systems—promote demystification. I am all for learning. But time-wasting daydreaming reveals that the fantasy of knowing everything, of once and for all getting in control, is just that—fantasy. It's an illusion of safety that invites obsession.

Outer-space discoveries expand the known and open to the unknown. So too with inner space. Each new theory, new technique, new finding poses more problems than it settles. We are reluctant to acknowledge the mysteries never to be encompassed. Frantic searching makes no difference. But be not disheartened. Relax into acceptance of what is. Stop stewing about what might have been, what might be, what should be. Albert Einstein tells us, "The most beautiful experience we can have is the mysterious. It is the fundamental emotion which stands at the cradle of true art and true science. Whoever does not know it and can no longer wonder, no longer marvel, is as good as dead."

Clamoring after knowledge—epistophilia when balanced, epistomania when compulsive—has family roots. Children love learning, thirst for mastery of life, pester parents with questions to confirm observation. Why is the sky blue? Where do babies come from? Why are boys and girls different? Who made us that way? Who is God? What is death? These "childish" questions are profound. Experts engage in social, political, and scientific struggles over the same issues. They seem unaware they are trying to answer childhood queries, reluctant to step back from doing to look at the larger mystery.

I am not against learning. I am against the obsessive need to learn.

I am against an obsessive need for anything, no matter how noble. Obsessions become destructive: houses of worship that are home to a different faith are attacked in the name of religion; the war on drugs increases drug use; humanitarian efforts intensify the problem, instead of solving it. In psychotherapy, we see the same needs, disguised as professionalism. Therapists cling to a method they know despite evidence that it is ineffective. They subtly push political agendas onto patients entitled to unbiased support. Distorted sexual desires, unrestrained by morals, are acted out with patients.

Obsessions, compulsions, addictions—these are today's slaveries. They take us down a road that starts with satisfaction and ends with disaster. The need to help, to do good, to see patients prosper backfires unpredictably and tragically. The need to have all the answers and to rack up all the achievements almost killed me. Accepting life's mystery saved me—along with surgery!

The more medicine I learned, the more it seemed I understood the body. When I prescribed antibiotics and once-fatal infections vanished, I thought I was in command of life and death. When a psychoanalytic interpretation struck home, my sense of power inflated. Small wonder that physicians act is though they are God. I was conditioned to judge the immediate by what happened next. Nothing wrong with that. But I was consumed by cycles of stimulus–response, I was lulled into thinking that that is all there is to healing. I lost the feel for mystery I had glimpsed when I played the piano while Mom sang, "Ah, Sweet Mystery of Life!"

Materialistic medicine has no place for mysterious happenings. We know how wounds heal, and how the inverted image in the brain looks right side up. But we do not understand the basic forces—why things work the way they do instead of some other way. To say that God does it just gives a name to the mystery, a name with many meanings for many people and causes as much disquiet as succor. Sometimes I envy those who are certain about uncertainties. But when I am at my best, I simply appreciate the sweet mysteries of life.

Master the Fear of Disability, Dying, and Death[60]

Death is the biggest mystery, and fear of that unknown is the universal fear—of painfully dying alone, of death itself, of whatever happens afterward. Defenses against this deep anxiety are so ubiquitous that it is easy to pooh-pooh this claim. But there is much evidence. To the best of current knowledge, signs of anxiety—*terror*—begin when we pass through the birth canal. (Cesarian is no exception.) We must feel overwhelmed by crushing, inescapable uterine contractions. Annihilation threatens after we have been floating effortlessly in warm amniotic fluid for nine months. The very young fetus is more reactive than we thought. Reflex alarms are deeply ingrained in our physiology. Throughout life, these danger signals lie in wait, ready to potentiate the most trivial fears.

Thus, anxiety runs like a red thread through our lives, now hidden, now obvious. It brings people to therapy. Anticipation of every loss resonates with death, the ultimate loss. This primal fear is dealt with incompletely in most therapy. In 12 years on the couch, we barely scratched the surface. Fortunately, in the postanalytic years, when I engaged in the various self-helps for helpers described here, I became conscious of deep pervasive anxieties. And coming face-to-face with the imminent possibility of dying forced me to make peace with the prospect of my demise.

"Making peace" means going toward unambivalent acceptance. I have sat with dozens of dying people. For days before death, many are restless, full of forebodings, fussy. Yet shortly before death, still conscious, all are calm, even blissful. (I have heard of, but never witnessed, terror at the time of death.) Rarely can we fully divest ourselves of dread in advance. But even a fragment of peace is worthwhile. It helps to know that death can be peaceful. Mine will be. Those convinced they are passing into a better life, to be with loved ones, seem more willing to go. Who can tell a deep-seated illusion from a deep-seated truth? Another mystery.

Knowing cognitively that everyone dies is vastly different from experiencing in my guts that, in fact, it will happen to me, and that it could catch me unaware at any time. Here are some of the ways in which I have deepened my awareness of death and moved closer to acceptance:

- Making sure that grief and mourning are dealt with well in therapy, like coaching a family to invent goodbye rituals 20 years after an unacknowledged suicide.
- Grieving at funerals, wakes, and memorials for family, friends, colleagues, and patients (the last are avoided by therapists).
- Looking at losses and endings with death as a prototype.
- Reading first-person stories about dying and grief.

- Caring for dying patients (and their families) in the office, at home, in hospitals, in nursing homes—wherever they are dying.
- Visiting dying friends; they have a lot to teach.
- Learning from nurses about deaths I could not attend.
- Doing a workshop with Elisabeth Kubler-Ross; we integrated my views on families and hers on death and dying.
- Using guided fantasies of dying; wishing to be with my family; talking now to lessen their regrets later about what we should have said.
- Learning from psychiatrist Stan Grof's Holotropic Breathwork, ventilating death anxiety that originated with birth anxiety. It brought out my most powerful emotions and reduced day-to-day anxiety.
- Utilizing Buddhist meditations on impermanence and death.
- Speculating with Jan about possibilities and inevitabilities.
- Planning directives for health care, wills, trusts, bequests, inheritances, cemetery plots and markers, funerals, memorials.
- Dedicating a family burial place; visiting relatives' graves and including children and grandchildren; talking with them about life and death.
- Studying religious and spiritual views of death and beyond.
- Learning about near-death experiences and reincarnation.
- Writing down my beliefs about dying and death.
- Doing audio- and videotapes, photo albums, and writing my life story for those who come after me.
- Living mindfully each day, as it could be my last.

Each of these has brought me a step closer to mastering fear, and made me a more effective and creative therapist. If this sounds like full-time busyness, remember, I have dealt with dying and death since we bought the nursing home in 1953. Death is inherent in life; there is no life without death. This wisdom is integral to everything we do. Starting therapy means ending therapy. The birth of a child means the child eventually will die. Relationships end. Transitions demand the figurative death of the old and the birth of the new. Life is a parade of starts and stops and yet we live as though only the starts matter.

The therapist who has worked through fears, attitudes, and beliefs about death as fully as possible reaches equanimity that serves well in all of life, and especially in therapy. Once you have truly accepted the inevitability of your death, you can fully accept your life. And vice versa.

In comparing individual and family therapy, it has struck me that family work involves us more intensely and poignantly. When seeing one person, the human drama is played out at a distance. We don't deal directly with illness, accident, surgery, disability, hospitalization, dying, death. Most analysands are young and rarely die while in analysis. None of mine did. We only hear about what happens to their important others. But the therapy Jan and I do is different. We treat families in homes, hospitals, nursing homes, emergency rooms. We sit with dying patients. We go to wakes and funerals, grieving together with families. Attend weddings, graduations, confirmations. When we take our work as family healers seriously, we are impelled to do and be whatever is needed. Life doesn't wait for controlled elegance. It grabs us—ready or not.

I want to say at the end of every course of therapy, as at the end of life, "I have fought the good fight. I have finished the race. I have kept the faith."[61]

Reflections

- Assess your busyness. Imagine the end of life approaching. How much of your current doing-undoing will mean little at that time? Does this suggest changes to make right now? Make them.
- What is your favorite way to loaf creatively? Are you doing enough loafing? Too much? Recall a creative insight that came at such a time. Arrange to loaf more.
- List aspects of life that are mysterious. Do the same for therapy.
- How do you cope with disability, however temporary? How do you handle not being able to do some things as well now as you did in the past?
- Recall your thoughts and feelings the first time you saw

a dead person. Trace the history of your experience with dying and death.

- Write out your thoughts about dying, death, the hereafter. With your primary partner, discuss power of attorney for health care, wills and inheritances, trusts, funeral arrangements, and other end-of-life matters.
- Explore these issues with your patients and follow up their responses.

Revealing Our Selves

All models are wrong, but some are useful.

—W. Edwards Deming

If you knew what I do about the power of giving, you wouldn't let a single meal go by without taking the opportunity to give.

—Buddha

16

Modeling and Self-Disclosure

Finding acceptable solutions for the thorny issue of self-revelation is central for therapists. In any meaningful encounter, it is impossible *not* to reveal a great deal. How we dress, the questions we ask, the information we are or are not interested in, reveal our attitudes, philosophy, and lifestyle. Significant events are hard to disguise: marriage, divorce, pregnancy, parenthood, illness, death. And when we try to be a blank screen, we reveal that we are concealing something, a message of deception. Furthermore, therapists and patients share a small world. They are likely to hear about us from others, to see us at meetings or around town. The longer we practice, the more other therapists come to us, which blows a contrived cover.

Once we accept that we cannot *not* reveal ourselves, the questions are : What is revealed? To whom? How much? In what way? For what purpose? With what timing? In what relation to the dynamics and stage of therapy? With what result? Nothing simple here. Answers to these complex questions hinge on our personalities and styles. We engage in unique interactions with people who have unique personalities and problems. We evolve a practice that suits our style.

A crucial point is the intensity of transference, which arises in every sustained relationship. Transference and self-revelation are reciprocal. The less self-disclosure there is, the greater is the patient transference.

More self-disclosure, less transference. Control of intensity is the therapist's responsibility, and is guided by self-disclosure.

In four-times-a-week, on-the-couch analysis, the analyst builds transference by minimizing personal information. The patient fills in gaps with fantasy, a transference neurosis that partially replicates the childhood neurosis. Analysis then may produce a resolution. This technique has been fine-tuned and standardized over many decades.

But in once- or twice-a-week sitting-up therapy, a regressive, dependent transference is not desirable. Should an intense transference be created by the therapist's silence, it results in a jam that cannot be resolved by the same therapist. Judicious revelation of personal material minimizes this denouement.

In the beginning, I believed that perfect therapy proceeds using standard techniques and theories without interference from my personal life. I soon found that not only is this impossible, but that the closer I approximate a blank screen, the more sterile the therapy.

A numbers lover once counted 250 varieties of psychotherapy. Categories are bewildering. One valuable way of thinking about therapists and the therapy they do is from the perspective of modeling and self-disclosure. What sort of a person should the therapist *be* with patients?

Therapists range from those who try to reveal as little as possible to those who reveal as much as possible. To be at either extreme is to take an irresponsible position and one based on ideology, not on what is right for this patient with this therapist at this time. The following principles for disclosure take into account many variables in both individual and family therapy.

Modeling

I use *modeling* as follows: We cannot help but be a model. Whatever we are, we are. Those who spend time with us will make what they will of what they see and hear. Simply by being in the same space, we present a style of being that may or may not be emulated. We may set a good example, be a warning, or both. Posttherapy research confirms that the kind of people we are is the most important factor in a positive outcome.

In this example of modeling taken from couples group therapy, husband and wife argue bitterly while Jan and I try unsuccess-

fully to help. At the next session, the other three couples report how much they learned from watching, fruitful conversations, new insights. The first partners propose: "Someone else fight today so we can learn. We fought all week and still haven't settled anything."

The fighting couple and our lack of success provided models from which to learn. It wasn't helpful for the couple. It didn't demonstrate how to do it right. The couple's pain and discouragement actually were heightened. (We should have cut it short. This happened early in our first group, where we learned as much as the participants.) Yet it was a lively example of their problems. The observers resonated, and were stimulated to explore related issues. The couple was consumed with attacking and defending. There is a seminal difference between being a participant and being an observer. The participant is upset and defensive. Energy is spent dealing with assault. In therapy with two or more people, there are many opportunities to observe, and observing may be more helpful than participating. When we reveal ourselves, patients are the lucky observers.

What I do *not* mean by modeling: Presenting an ideal image, perfection, a "model person" to be imitated. Beginners mistakenly believe they must appear as paragons of mental health. Self-disclosures must show maturity and positive adjustment. Since we don't *feel* mature when we embark, it's not surprising that we are afraid to open up.

I also do not mean an act put on just for the occasion. Patients see through pretense. Analysts object to Alexander's[62] "corrective emotional experience," considering it artificial. "Acting is for actors," one purist snorted. No one would disagree. But when the relationship is what it should be, there is no acting. Patients' experiences are both different from and corrective of their lives as children. They are corrective because they are compassionate and unambivalent—different from their experiences in their families. We are not contriving, we don't need to be. Internalization of the new modulates the old, becoming a fixture of the inner world, correcting longstanding dysfunctional patterns.

The paradox is that when we make no attempt to be perfect or to tell patients how to be, by the end of therapy, they have taken in much of our thinking, feeling, and behaving—whether we like it or not. They pick up both our faults and our assets. This is why we have an obligation, to our patients and to ourselves, to keep growing.

Self-Disclosure

This chapter emphasizes the importance of self-disclosure, not because it is a large part of my technique, but because it is *central* to it. The best therapists are authentic, fully present, and open to speaking about themselves, without sacrificing power or expertise. I may make only one or two brief personal comments. I am convinced from experience—mine, patients', and students'—that these are heard and molded by each person's interpretation. At the same time, it is essential not to distract from patient concerns or be self-centered. I am careful to make sure that my comments are in the patients' best interests, not mine. Their best interests serve mine, but mine rarely serves theirs.

For 40 years, I conducted my practice in my home. Patients knew our taste in decorating a house—and when it needed painting. They glimpsed my wife, my kids, many details about my life outside the office. And when Jan joined me in cotherapy, our relationship was evident. So I have had plenty of practice handling "distractions."

> *A couple, experienced therapists, arrive for their first appointment with Jan and me. In the office, the husband is flabbergasted. "In the 10 or 15 feet between the waiting room and the office, I was nearly overwhelmed by a feeling of being back in my parents' home again. Only this time it feels safe." Instant positive transference.*

People in distress are searching for inspiration, guidance. They want to be sure they can trust enough to offer their most precious possession: their story. Small personal facts show that you know about life, and will help them reveal themselves safely. Self-disclosure, like cooking spices, makes the difference. Like spices, the pinch must be just right—too little is flat; too much spoils the dish.

I stress disclosure because the topic is seldom addressed in publications or by teachers! Instructors ignore it, supervisors don't demonstrate or discuss it, and many students are content not to be troubled about it. Years later, no longer safe within the protective embrace of a training program, they struggle to understand why they cannot keep patients long enough to be effective. It is never too late to look at ourselves with an eye to effecting real change.

Why Self-Disclosure?

When we share our life experience, we connect with our patients and they connect with us, and all of us connect with life. We present a personal handle. Therapy is more effective when we are seen as persons, not as scientists, robotherapists, walking textbooks, acolytes espousing someone's method. Vivid images from everyday life, expressed without pretense, convey powerful messages. The therapist who is not frightened away from any subject, including the self, inspires confidence. We like being with, and more easily trust, someone who is relaxed and having a good time, especially when we are in trouble.

I want patients to know, too, I have wrestled with therapy and with life and will share my journey. I want them to relate to it, to know their journey is also personal. I want them to know my way has been a saga of stress, frustration, humiliation, anger—mellowed by hope, success, joy, romance. And without burdening them. It's a difficult task, but doable and worth doing.

> *I ask patients about disclosure in previous therapy, and often hear this story. "I always complained about others—bosses, lovers, friends. I lost them all before I realized that I must be doing something to bring this on. I went into therapy to find out. I asked my therapist how I came across, what his reactions to me were. He always said, 'What do you think?' When I guessed at his experience of me, he bounced it back. He wormed out of saying anything about what he thought or felt about anything. I felt rejected again, and I wasn't learning what I do to people. I tried to provoke him. Just the usual focus on me as though I were the only one in the room. After a year I was more confused than ever, so I quit. He said I was once again acting out an old pattern, and that his reactions were irrelevant."*

This story, not as rare as some might think, sets the stage to propose a collaboration, again paraphrased.

> *"If we decide on therapy, I'll let you know how you come across, and you do the same. I may not realize how you take what happens. I may say things you don't want to hear. You may get annoyed and be tempted to quit. That will be the time not to quit,*

but to keep our appointments, maybe have an extra session, and work on it."

I watch for nonverbal signs of acceptance, puzzlement, rejection. Nearly always the response is positive; this is what they want. Later, however, they may not be so sure. Ambivalence shows when they ask for examples of the kind of feedback I might give. Typically, I comment on something that has already transpired.

"You seem overwhelmed by what you are going through, and I am reminded of times when I felt overwhelmed." (No details.)

"I know how sad you are because I feel sad just listening to what's happened between you and your mother."

(Said after evidence of some rapport on both sides.) "Several times I asked John a question and he looked frustrated when Mary answered. That must be an important pattern."

"The death of your father might be a big turning point in your life. It was for me." (Again, no details.)

These comments, and others like them, are brief and without elaboration. I do not want to detract from the flow. I do not go on about myself. Yet I want to put out an opening statement that if the time is right, I am open to further discussion of my experience.

I comment on something that we all could have observed, without making an interpretation. I pick whatever is moderately significant, neither trivial nor a blockbuster. Trivia have no power for change, unless artfully embedded in a speech. Blockbusters are for one-shot consultations or after much preparation.

I want patients to know they will be getting something useful from me, not only relief at pouring out their story. I want them to realize that this is a mutual relationship with a human with feelings, opinions, life experiences—and who is not reluctant to talk about them when the time is ripe. Revealing glimpses of my world teaches about life, sometimes using apparently positive examples, sometimes negative. I say "apparently" because events have both positive and negative aspects. What at first looks positive will ultimately reveal a negative. And vice versa. As Lao-tzu[17] puts it:

Success is as dangerous as failure.
Hope is as hollow as fear.

What does it mean that success is as dangerous as failure?
Whether you go up the ladder or down it,
your position is shaky.
When you stand with your two feet on the ground,
you will always keep your balance.

What does it mean that hope is as hollow as fear?
Hope and fear are both phantoms
that arise from thinking of the self.
When we don't see the self as self, what do we have to fear?

See the world as your self.
Have faith in the way things are.
Love the world as your self;
then you can care for all things.

The principles invoked in teaching patients about life are much like those involved in teaching students. The teacher's presence is a sustaining model, stronger than words and theories.

A Jewish tale tells of a man who came back from visiting a famous
rabbi. His friend quizzes him as to what great knowledge he ac-
quired from the learned man. The answer, "I didn't go to the rabbi
to learn his theories. I went to watch him tie his shoelaces."

Patients are keenly interested in watching us "tie our shoelaces." Should I tell a story, secretly hoping that others will do as I did? Will I be disappointed if they don't follow my "advice"? And they may rightly feel that they are being told to do it my way. I felt frustrated after early attempts to tell about my life. But I learned that patients seldom do things just the way I do—and things turn out okay. Listeners, whether students or patients, hear according to their needs at that moment, and in the light of a lifetime. We often agree on the facts. But what the facts mean, and how those facts apply in one's life are different and individual matters.

Guidelines and Suggestions

The big self-disclosure questions are: Will I enhance therapy or interfere, not just in the near future, but over the whole course of therapy and after? Is there a better way? What risks are associated with disclosing—and with withholding—and how do they balance out? How much is for their' benefit, how much mine? What are patients' reactions likely to be? How can what is disclosed be integrated into therapy and keep it flowing? This is a lot of imponderables for the beginning discloser. But the more extensive our clinical experience, the easier the answers. After years of practice, I still fine-tune.

1. Jan and I plan for possible disturbances, often sharing these with patients. Every therapist should have a plan for illness, interruptions, family crises, any distraction. We don't know *what* will happen, but we can be prepared for almost anything. If something is likely to interrupt a session, I say so. (There is no telephone in my office. I hated it when a therapist used my time to talk on the phone.)

2. Start with small, relatively safe disclosures. If these do no harm, and perhaps even enrich the process, be a little bolder, experiment with greater freedom. It feels appropriate to patients for me to begin with comments about how I experience them—what I see happening, how I feel and think about it, what being with them is like for me, and so on. My manner is nonconfrontational, neutral, curious, inquiring, not blaming. With more than one in the room, I address all in the early sessions.

3. I usually start the second session by asking each person to tell his or her reactions to the first, adding that I will do the same. I elicit how they felt and what they thought during the session that they didn't say. What were their afterthoughts, afterfeelings? Their reflections since then? Conversations about how it went? Did anyone have any dreams? We work for a little while on whatever is brought up. A subject not directly related to presenting issues is discussed briefly and tagged to return to later.

   I probe for negatives. When eager for therapy, getting started is such a relief that they do not think of negatives. Wanting to please, they limit comments to the positives they imagine I want to hear. Why jeopardize a good start? If they don't mention negatives, I offer a few: getting the family together, traffic, insurance, budget, painful subjects. I propose a ground rule: negative thoughts and feelings about therapy—theirs or mine—must be brought out in sessions. When they are not, I say, they accumulate and interfere. People agree, but later need reminding when I suspect them of having unexpressed negatives.

After exploring their reactions, I tell mine: thoughts and feelings not mentioned, ponderings since, and mild to moderate interpretations. I want to estimate their readiness for change. I say both positive and negative things, on the principle that my negatives will influence therapy unfavorably when not expressed and resolved.

With psychologically minded people, this exploration often starts near the end of the first meeting. But if ongoing sessions seem likely, I prefer to wait until the second session so we can reflect on the first. First impressions may change, so I usually set up two get-acquainted appointments. I explain that our goal is to see whether we have the right "chemistry." I also get clues to the prognosis and some of the difficulties to be expected—a minitrial. The longer I practice, the sooner I know whether we can work together.

4. With more practice in revealing myself, I began to make small personal comments even in the first interview. These are brief, not elaborated, and only made if relevant to what is happening.

> *I interview a family while the adolescent-inpatient staff members watch. With gusto, the father rattles off his son's misbehaviors. After listening respectfully, when he pauses for breath, I say, "Yeah, my six kids about drove me nuts when they were teenagers." He smiles, relaxes, sits back, and we hear from the rest of the family. The son angrily recites all that is wrong with his father, sounding just like him. When it feels right, I say, "Yeah, I remember when I was a teenager. My parents nearly drove me nuts." He looks understood and relaxes. That consultation succeeded because of my self-disclosures.*

Triggering both comments were flashes of specific incidents. To go into these in detail would burden a one-shot consultation. In the beginning, my responses to the session are more important than going into personal matters. But with a family in treatment, I later might bring up an incident from the past. Emboldened by my openness, someone may say, "You mentioned that you and your kids had problems. Were they anything like what we've got? How did you handle them?" I usually oblige.

5. How to decide whether to express a memory, feeling, or hunch? What will be useful, what will not? I had a rule-of-thumb: When something came to mind during a session, I silently evaluated how useful saying it might be. Being an intuitive introvert who prefers thinking over feeling, this took a few moments, interaction moved on, and the idea vanished. If it came back, I took it more seriously and thought about what to do. Again we moved on. If it came back a third time, I was convinced of its relevance, if not its guaranteed utility. Unless it was clearly out of line, I tentatively put into words what was on my mind. I go through a similar rehearsal when patients come to mind between sessions.

The rule evolved further. Now I speak with less hesitation. Sometimes I say, "I don't know whether it's useful, but I keep having this thought (feeling, image, fantasy, memory) and I wonder if it has any value for you." If it *is* relevant, we take it from there. If not, I say, "I could be wrong. Maybe it's my own thing. I'll look into it. You might do the same."

More often these days, I am on target for something hidden from their easy awareness. Or perhaps one family member sees a connection that others do not and is reluctant to say so. An analytic dictum has served well: We are able to gain insight into a feeling, thought, or memory, when it is *preconscious*, that is, made conscious by focusing attention on it. An interpretation that goes deep into the unconscious will be rejected as untrue, even if correct. If we do this too often, credibility is lost. Furthermore, a too-deep interpretation increases resistance.

By trial and error, I have learned to trust intuition and usually do not wait until the second or third time. I wait if the timing is wrong, or if I don't want to interfere with a person's discovering it for himself or herself. With a powerful, positive flow, I stay out of the way, especially if I think highly of my brilliant insight. Good therapy is precious and hard to find. We do not want to do anything to harm it. When in doubt about speaking personally, it's better to wait. You are held back by what you do not yet understand.

6. A patient's interest in knowing about our lives should be honored. If you don't know whether patients are interested, ask them early on. Some do not want to know, especially if they heard too much

from another therapist. Jan or I may say, "We had a similar incident, but will tell you only if you want to hear." If they don't want
to hear about it now, maybe they will later. Some never will.

7. For some therapists, self-disclosure is natural and comes easily.
For others, family reticence and the pseudoprofessional blank
screen can be unlearned. Jan claims that when we first knew each
other, I was spontaneously self-disclosing. Only after years of indoctrination in "judicious silence" did I become a strong silent
type. This worked well for me as a general practitioner dealing
with life-or-death medical crises, but set a harmful hard-to-change
pattern.

8. The more disturbed a patient is, the greater is the need for openness. Schizophrenics, borderlines, the psychologically primitive,
and the severely abused are exquisitely sensitive to nuances, eva-
sions, and the unconscious of others. They need to test and confirm reality, especially that of the therapist and therapy. Trying to
put anything over on them, despite good intentions, will backfire
and destroy the trust they badly need.

9. Hostile, seductive, or competitive feelings that have not been resolved need disclosure, lest therapy collapse. Strong negative reactions are most difficult to disclose and, paradoxically, most
important. We must work on ourselves before sharing with the
patient. This may mean a consultation with our therapist or a
trusted colleague. Disclosure is less likely to be disruptive if done
calmly with a sincere interest in teaching patients about themselves and shoring up the foundation of treatment.

Patients, too, must be prepared. Shock is tempered by recalling
previous helpful disclosures and by advance warning. "Some of
the things I have pointed out about you have not been easy to
take. But you have used them well. (Mention one or two.) There
is something else I want you to know, but I worry that you will
take it badly. I've thought about this a lot and decided that our
relationship is strong enough for strong feelings. Ready?"

10. Over the course of therapy, I am increasingly self-revealing. Natural, effortless progression toward greater self-disclosure is a sign
of deepening intimacy. I check to see how personal comments
are coming across, identifying which are useful and which are not.
Impactful stories have parallels in their lives. Areas are opened up
to explore that might never have been touched, had I not first told
my story. By the end of a long therapy, patients know a lot about
me and my characters, my wife and marriage, my children and

their families, and how we have handled—or mishandled—various crises. People tell me that this knowledge has been valuable.

11. Timing is the essence. Early on, when patients are in pain, they are not in the mood to hear about our lives. "We came here for help with *our* problems, not to help you with *yours*." I hold my tongue while we struggle with the crisis, focusing on what they can do to help themselves. The most I might say about myself is to identify my experience with theirs in brief, perhaps nonverbal, ways. When a family is grieving, I might nod and say, "I know how you feel." Or, "Yes, I've been through that." Or Jan and I may look knowingly at each other without words and someone takes note. We do not go into details. It is enough that the message was received.

12. When therapy becomes growth oriented, the task is: Do not stagnate. Effective leadership is essential. Of the many ways to keep therapy moving, none are certain. We need a range of things to say or do or recommend. Most useful is simply commenting, "I have been thinking we are in the doldrums," and recall when we were stuck before. Or I may recount a similar stuck time in my life. This stimulates talk about solutions for stalemates. Sometimes what are needed are simply patience and observant waiting to see what comes next. A few key pages from William Bridges' *Transitions*[56] are useful. Commonly, the block is caused by unspoken positive or negative feelings toward me or Jan or the whole treatment. Nearly always, we have corresponding feelings as well. These need to be talked through and understood. Corrective action may be necessary.

13. Self-disclosures are related to what I hope my patients will disclose and work on. However, keep an open mind about this. Sometimes the mere fact that I disclose something is more important than the information itself. Patients may be encouraged also to disclose, but the content often is unexpected. My preferred stance—not always achieved—is to be ready for anything at all, and for nothing.

14. Occasionally, a self-disclosure causes the wrong reaction—it is inappropriate, results in hurt feelings, disrupts the flow. This is the time to acknowledge the error, apologize (once is enough), make corrections, and learn a valuable lesson. Some people tell me immediately when a self-revelation is not useful. This puts the process out front so that repairs can be made—the sooner, the better. Others do not own up to being offended or distracted. Watch for

clues that the flow has been interfered with: symptom return, irritability, awkward silence, argumentativeness. Gentle probing usually brings out the break in empathy. Until this is done, therapy flounders. Some people harbor a hurt long after being asked. I make it clear early on that it is essential to let me know if my comments are hurtful. Even then, many test out whether I mean it. Unwillingness to reveal when they are hurt is an opportunity to change a disadvantageous trait.

It's important to recognize subjective signals telling me that I have goofed: a sinking feeling in my stomach, an uneasy suspicion that something is not right, preoccupation with a session long afterward, any of the foregoing patient indicators. When I get internal clues and others seem unaware of them, I describe what I am feeling so that we can look for a break in empathy. Putting sensations into words suggests that it's safe for them to do the same.

"We don't know when we've had enough until we've had too much." We may not know when we disclose optimally until we overdo it. This is the value—and the risk—of gently, firmly pushing until we do. But why take an unnecessary risk? When you have never upset a patient, never had a break in empathy, the therapy has lacked power, was not transformative, was not deep enough. It has been unreal, not true to life. Life is full of mistakes and messes—we bounce from one to another no matter how many years we have been bumbling through. Effective therapy is no exception. The sooner we accept our "imperfections" and use them to enrich our work, the better.

Reflections

- How did your family view your expressing your thoughts, feelings, and behavior? Your response? Has your attitude changed? Trace it.
- Have you ever said anything personal, only to have it backfire? How did you handle it? What did you learn? Did it change your style?
- Have you developed a pattern of self-disclosure? How does it fit your personality and therapy style?
- Experiment with a little more self-disclosure. If it works,

push it farther and see what happens. Try this with a therapy patient in deep trouble. What can you lose?

- If speaking about yourself is new for you, it will take a while to get comfortable in this heretofore forbidden world. So be patient with yourself and be willing to suffer through awkward moments.

17

The Risks and Benefits of Self-Disclosure

Disclosure can go wrong in many ways. Risks decrease and benefits increase when disclosure is done well, and we learn from mistakes. Two errors: (1) saying too much, at the wrong time, in the wrong way—bad disclosure; (2) saying little, putting the onus back on the patients, not knowing how this will affect them—avoiding disclosure.

We are shocked by a bad disclosure. We lose confidence, and realize we must work hard to save the alliance. It seems that revealing personal material is damaging, that our cautious supervisors were right, and the value of the blank screen is confirmed. I learned a lot in an early group supervision in 1973 at the height of the encounter craze.

> There are four students in groups supervision, their spouses, and
> Jan and I. We tell how we got there, what we hope to accomplish.
> I describe being propelled into medicine by my father's illnesses,
> and feeling responsible for them. Out of the blue, I sob hard for
> several minutes. The group is stunned. An ambivalent member is
> absent, but listens to the tape. She is upset, makes feeble excuses
> to miss the sessions, stops listening to tapes (a ground rule). Re-

*actions are worked through and the group is stronger in the long
run. Not long after we end, she and her husband divorce.*

Error 2, guardedness, is insidious and cumulative. Some withhold
for years, not realizing the effect they have. Cautiousness kills liveliness. Patients quit after achieving little, leaving therapists without a
glimpse of why they did so. "Untreatable" is the rationalization. Unfortunately, beginners are taught to say nothing personal, "to establish
boundaries," instead of how to disclose optimally.

Errors of commission are more obvious than are errors of omission.
Yet guardedness is more common, is professionally validated, is more
damaging. Beginners are careful with patients and supervisors. There
is much to learn, silence is safe. The drawback comes when therapy
hits an impasse. The frustrated therapist reverts to what was first
taught. We fall back on what we learned as insecure beginners, regress
to what seemed to work.

What we first teach should be methods that support students in
emergencies. That means training in appropriate self-disclosure. Any
short-term gain from blank screening should not be promoted at the
cost of becoming open, authentic, and giving. Reticence signals that
we are not free with thoughts and feelings, and yet we expect patients
to be free with *theirs*. Being nagged to put everything into words—
the "fundamental rule"—by analysts who did nothing of the kind was
frustrating. No example, no forthright expression of what was going
on behind my head. Professionalized withholding is a deterrent for a
young therapist who aspires to be authentic and responsive.

Whether it's harder to keep your mouth shut or open depends on
your personality. Introverts turn thoughts and feelings inward, and
don't speak until they know what to say. Extroverts turn outward,
aren't sure what they think or feel until they say it. These types have
similar tasks: bringing forth less natural parts of themselves.

When a former therapist has made unhelpful disclosures to patients,
I do not repeat the mistake. I explain, "Usually I tell more about my
life than I do with you. But I don't want to upset you again." I work
with the response and see if the patient can accept being told, "I had
a similar thing in my life. But I don't want to tell you unless you want
to hear it." Eventually, curiosity overcomes apprehension and the patient asks. What the therapist said or did that was off-putting often
was on target, but the patients were not ready to hear it. With plenty
of preparation, patients eventually understand the vulnerability causing their extreme reaction.

Early on, check reactions to disclosures: "How did you feel about my telling you of my experience?" Some negative reactions.

"I had enough on my plate and didn't want to hear about your problems."

"We came to get therapy, not to do therapy."

"At first I wondered how you could help us if you had the same problems, but later realized that having been through it made you more understanding and better able to help."

Self-aggrandizing turns people off. Name dropping, religious and political advocacy, competitiveness, and self-inflation may be hard to identify, given the prima donnas in our field and the payoffs for speed and quantity. The tidal wave of therapists of every description aggravates dog-eat-dogism, inflation is the norm, "marketing" the catchword. The "Yellow Pages," magazines, flyers, professional publications trumpet appearance over substance. Solo practitioners with undecipherable "degrees" present themselves *"and associates,"* practicing in one-room "suites." If you want a good, long practice, improve yourself. Word-of-mouth is the best advertising, effectiveness the best marketing.

With narcissistic and borderline patients, self psychologists withhold to promote idealization. My experience has been that these patients will idealize regardless of withholding, as long as the therapist is gentle, interested, and not confrontative. There is little danger that idealization will *not* occur. It will be less intense and more amenable to resolution if not artificially heightened by silence.

In telling about personal events, beginners may attribute them to others. Freud did. It's easy to get away with this harmless subterfuge, but I do not recommend it. If therapy is to be genuine, it must be based on honesty, however painful. Better to self-reveal in small comfortable doses. The sugarcoated white lies we were raised on need to be seen for what they were and not repeated in therapy. White lies are contagious, spreading until the white liar loses track of them. Sooner or later, a cover will be blown that was not necessary in the first place.

You might well ask: "What's the big deal about self-disclosure? If it can interfere with therapy, why bother? Sounds like stirring up unnecessary trouble. I'm very private, and my personal life is not their business." Well, much research[63,64] shows that when an interviewer makes a self-revealing comment, the interviewee soon does so as well. And the number of revelations by the interviewee is greater than when the interviewer does no revealing. Follow-up of our patients several years after termination shows that no harm was done by these disclosures. On the contrary, stories about ourselves were often mentioned as helpful.

I believe it is most satisfying and mentally healthy to know the self as fully as possible—good, bad, indifferent. Knowledge of the self is blocked by defenses against deeply knowing. Most of us have an unreasonable fear of knowing our deep inner life. The rich self-awareness that helps us most is the very thing we keep ourselves from discovering.

If we accept the value of self knowledge—and some do not—then openness in therapy is an excellent way to learn more. Parts are triggered that might never be touched in other work. We are stirred by events to which we have not personally been exposed: incest, pedophilia, murder, cannibalism, sexual perversions, criminal behavior of every variety. Working with extreme situations, we are challenged to examine our most depraved impulses, impulses that are as strong as the energy it took to repress them. If we are open to the internal, illusions of innocent childhood are hard to maintain.

Benefits from Risking Openness

The most important benefit of self-disclosure is *diminished transference*.

In contrast to psychoanalysis, psychotherapy requires that negative transference be kept from becoming intense. This is done by letting people know the human being we are, thus minimizing the false image they manufacture when they have few facts. It is done by interpreting transference reactions as soon as they appear. It is done by responding rather than evading, talking rather than stonewalling, giving opinions rather than withholding, being open rather than closed, by having two or more people in the room, by audiotape or videotape feedback. Knowing about the therapist undercuts idealization.

Greater openness also teaches us to *take risks and make mistakes*. Taking risks is sine qua non for an authentic therapist. In fact, risks are unavoidable, not only in therapy but in life.

We are developing guidelines to eliminate risks for frail nursing-home patients. It is impossible to prevent all accidents. At first it seems we could eliminate risks by keeping them in bed 24 hours a day. But this risks hypostatic pneumonia, osteoporosis, muscle deterioration, and loss of zest. So we shift to educating patients and families and ourselves. Accepting certain risks is the best we can do, knowing there may be unavoidable complications. Balancing risks and rewards not only builds rapport with the patient and family, but also keeps malpractice suits to a minimum.

It's the same in therapy. When we don't take risks by revealing ourselves, therapy is one-dimensional, self-limiting; "no-risk therapy" causes complications, just as "no-risk bed rest" does. When we do risk self-disclosure, sooner or later we make a mistake that disrupts flow and jeopardizes the relationship. Welcome to our no-risk world!

The irony is that when we gather courage to ever-so-tentatively say or do something pressing for expression, it almost never turns out as bad as we expected. For many of us, it goes like this. We have a strong impulse to say or do something personal, "use of self," not use of theory or of technique. Anxiety arises: The heart pounds, the mouth is dry, there is queasiness, tension—familiar signals. Inhibition takes over and nothing is done. Anxiety subsides, leaving us mildly incomplete. Afterblame or reassurances go on for a while. Then it happens again while we build the nerve to be open.

After hesitant false starts, a risk is taken with little confidence. Waiting for a reaction, anxiety with a flash of dire consequences. The patient notices something different, something interesting and personal, perhaps picking up the anxiety. Both parties feel relief, loosening up, a block unblocked. We have taken a creative leap, an unprecedented risk—and no debacle. Therapy moves forward, enlivened, richer. A cycle has been broken, but not forever; it must be repeated. The vicious circle becomes virtuous: success prompts more attempts, more success, more confidence on both sides. Not all choice points work well. Mistakes reteach us. Nudge self a little farther, check results internally and with the others, be miniexperimental. Results are immediate, rarely with delayed reactions. We train for awareness by gently probing for reactions, suggesting they may appear if delayed, inquiring with neutral interest.

Two things are happening, both necessary for long-term success: (1) patient issues are worked on, and (2) *how* to work is savored.

Learning about ourselves expands throughout therapy, a mutual collaboration. Fears engendered by this "dangerous" exploration are replaced by fascination. Discovering nuances of one's inner life, motives, and defenses becomes practical and fulfilling.

A lifelong benefit of therapy, difficult to acquire in any other way, is an approach that few achieve, the skill to analyze thoughts, feelings, and behavior—*to be therapist to oneself.* The therapist who shares thoughts and feelings offers a rare gift: an insider's view of what goes on in the heart and mind of someone who compassionately cares about us and who may have insights we have yet to grasp. It does not matter if some perspective are off the mark. It is the *process* of thinking and feeling that is absorbed. I would be delighted if patients and students only learned how to take a risk, correct mistakes, take more risks. After I disclose my inner process, they are more able to help themselves, aided by the internalized memory image of me—portable, permanent, always available. Later when occasional pretherapy symptoms do recur—slight headache, mislaying keys, slipping into overwork—they trigger reflection and resolution, not panic.

There are also many benefits for therapists. Working out effective self-disclosure enhances our psyche, thus enhancing our therapy. Especially if we have a background of inhibition.

Babies are free of inhibitions, gradually learning what is permissible and what is not: normal sexual, aggressive, and curiosity instincts are repressed because of parental disapproval, necessary for the survival of society and the child. But repression inhibits spontaneity, artistic expression, and emotion. The baby had freedom without responsibility, and then had restricted freedom and increasing responsibility.

By school age, we have a repertoire of prohibitions. Thus begins a career in benign deception. As Dan says, "A firstborn *has* to be sneaky." The same is true for later-borns. What normal child willingly tells parents about behaviors that will incur unpleasantness? Most children, to protect their privacy, don't fully level with the most receptive parent. A child who tells parents "everything" is a child with problems. Adolescence accentuates this pattern, as does leaving home. By graduate school, self-concealment is well honed. This is not a value judgment, but describes what most of us go through. Kids of all ages lie, cheat on tests, and otherwise protect themselves.

Simultaneously, parents construct walls to keep *their* lives private. Families have a host of topics that are off-limit between generations. Depending on the child's age, some are appropriate to withhold (sexual practices, financial arrangements). But much is withheld for "protection" (an impending divorce, a death in the family). Both generations build walls of silence that grow more problematic with the passing years.

A similar situation exists between spouses. It is routine in marital therapy to find that neither has mentioned a vital subject. Openness between siblings is more common, and yet with many limitations. Protection rackets are *projection* rackets. The fact that it is *true* the other may be hurt or angry disguises projection. Assuming the other is fragile is another projection. And failure to appreciate the hurt when concealment is discovered keeps the destructive pattern going.

In most graduate schools, needless secrecy continues. When personal issues affect learning, individual therapy is advised. We are accused of "doing therapy" when countertransference is pointed out. So training programs turn out incomplete therapists. Still, therapy is so difficult and takes so long, it's probably unfair to complain about grad schools.

It is a misconception that development is completed in adolescence. In child psychiatry training in the 1950s and analytic training in the 1960s, adult personality growth was ignored. Since then, the gap has been partially filled. Still, childhood and adolescence are considered *the* most important periods developmentally. Major changes late in life are dismissed, except by elders, who know better. Young therapists, not far from adolescence, are still caught up in the trials of those years. They have little appreciation of changes yet to come. This is a fact of life, not a criticism. Are we better off not knowing?!

Thus, young adults mistakenly assume that they are emancipated: living away from parents, self-supporting, married, raising children—and being superficial with the family. We do not realize that for each family cut off in the *external* world, there is a comparable *internal* void. Disowned parts unknown to the self and not expressed carry energy, wisdom, and resources. We are impoverished when these are not available. This can go on for so many years and be so ego-syntonic that we don't realize what's missing.

Self-deception is fostered by the individually oriented therapists young people seek, therapists who have little appreciation that early adulthood is a fine time for connecting with parents and sibs. We can be open and self-revealing with each other. When the older generation shares life experiences, the younger finds new options. We can repair narcissistic injuries, right wrongs that can be righted, forgive those that can't be. The typical reaction is, "Why talk about those old hurts? Can't change them now. That's the dead past. Why bring them up and feel bad?" Well, the reason is that unresolved feelings are not over, hurt is *not* dead and *not* past. The unconscious knows no time limit.

> *Middle-aged brothers and sisters disagree on their 85-year-old mother's care. Antagonism makes consensus impossible. The mother reacts with anxiety; her health is deteriorating faster than explained by her ailments. Through a daughter's private aside, the root of the trouble becomes clear. These sibs, now grandparents, are still upset over childhood sex play, with no lessening of shame, mistrust, hurt, and anger. The subject has never been discussed. Thus they cannot agree on plans for their ill mother.*

What does all this have to do with self-disclosure in doing therapy? Openness in the family determines our pattern. When we make changes to produce greater family openness, it transfers into therapy. And as we are more open in therapy, it's easier to be open in our family. That is the experience of those who have done family-of-origin work.

A frequent criticism of therapist self-disclosure has to do with boundaries. To the slippery-slope mentality, if you tell a little, where will it end? Individual treatment, whether purely medical or psycho-therapeutic, supposedly maintains professionalism, assures confidentiality, and averts overinvolvement. This position is difficult to support when 5 to 10% of physicians have ill-advised sex with their patients. I have never heard of sex between a therapist and a patient in conjoint therapy.[65]

Boundaries are established in every therapy, usually without conflict. Try thoughtful experimentation with greater self-disclosure. Borders are not breached by a few honest comments. Trust is built and boundaries established out of mutual experience, instead of arbitrarily imposed by an "authority" presuming to know what is good for everyone.

When you tell people about your life, you offer a bit of yourself for identification. A template—one way, among many, of being in the world. Therapist examples, undistorted by transference, are useful to identify with or reject. They make changes more real, more under conscious control.

Self-disclosure is effective because it demonstrates empathy. People who come to us are deficient in this quality, most noticeably between husband and wife and parent and child. They repeat the same, dysfunctional pattern without knowing or changing how they affect others. Training in empathy is one of the world's greatest needs.

Disclosure works because an authentic encounter is corrective. Middle-class therapists are raised by poor self-disclosers, using deceptions from benign little white lies to malignant big lies. We are poor managers of anger, inept at resolving conflicts when our most influential teachers don't show healthy disagreement and healing resolution. Kids miss out on learning how to handle emotions, believing that niceness is loving and anger is not loving. They don't learn that loving includes being nice at times, and being angry at other times.

Those who come to us are impaired in healthy emotional expression. As parent figures, we are corrective when we do not "protect" patients from the truth about our differences and fumblings. In co-therapy, most helpful are disagreements that Jan and I resolve, often while the family or couple watches. If not resolved, we report later. If they do not ask, they wonder, so we tell them. To be corrective, we don't use white lies. At times, we might say, "It would be better if we didn't go into that at this point." Or, in answer to problematic questions, "We will tell you, but we must understand what you hope to learn. What do you imagine we will say?"

As in raising children and in teaching, information is gradually unfolded, guided by feedback. We offer ideas a little ahead of where the recipient is, when he or she is just ready. Or we go back over something that needs attention. When anyone hears something new, especially if it counters our belief, we must hear several different versions before it sinks in. We judge how ready others are by staying in close touch with patients, students, supervisees. We fine-tune: taking small steps, noting small results, and making small mistakes, correctable with help from allies. Optimal frustration at work. Learning in manageable steps built on previous learning lasts longer, is understood more fully, can be related to other learnings, and is less vulnerable to misuse or forgetting.

Occasionally, a patient plunges into a dangerous situation. We may try to head off an impulsive disaster. Or the patient may need to flounder before waking up. Or our judgment may be wrong; the person does well despite our well-intentioned reservations. Remember, we are mostly inhibited do-gooders who fear the world's dangers. Willingness to be wrong is an important model for those patients and students whose fear of being wrong keeps them from acting or, contrariwise, makes them act counterphobically. I may give my opinion, "I think you are making a mistake, but I respect your autonomy and will be available no matter what happens."

Sometimes we give patients information they are unlikely to get anywhere else: new ways of thinking about and solving problems, new options for decision making, unexpected consequences of an intended action. Or we may tell how other patients or friends deal with crises of everyday living. Many patients live narrow lives, with few close friends, and out off from their families. Their families wrapped a shield around themselves so that all the child knew was a repetition of a familiar dysfunction. "It stays within the family. You can't trust outsiders."

Nothing is more real than telling stories about our clan. Not only do patients have new information about family life, but they see some-one actually breaking through *their* family secrecy, revealing what went on inside—without catastrophe. They may then have courage to expand their horizons. It's an eye-opener to tell isolated parents about kids staying overnight with a friend or at camp where they taste different lifestyles. It disabuses belief that the family's way is the only way. Knowing about differences eases the shock when the children grow up and discover how limited their families, and they, are.

There is a vital difference between telling a story about someone else or describing what is "normal," and telling about yourself. When we say something is normal, understanding is cognitive. But when we share our lives with traces of anxiety, sadness, or catastrophic expec-tations, people resonate emotionally. The result? Authentic validation, acceptance of self, and expanded awareness of life—those good things we hope will come out of successful therapy.

Revealing our lives is what happens in support and self-help groups. People are surprised that they aren't the only ones to lose a parent, to agonize over children, to consider suicide. Normalizing ex-perience is relieving; for example, learning about normal mourning. They frequently worry that depression, preoccupation with the de-ceased, or hearing the beloved's voice is a sign of mental illness. So too with the paranormal, the strange, the uncanny. Most people who have had out-of-body feelings, near-death experiences, distant view-ings, or precognitions are unlikely to share these with anyone who remains aloof and "scientific."

> *After a lecture on near-death experiences, a man stands up and announces, "I am a cardiac surgeon. I have resuscitated many*

patients from clinical death. I've never had one tell me about this kind of stuff. I think it's all poppycock." After a few moments of stunned silence, another man stands up. "Doctor, I was one of those patients you brought back to life, and I'll be forever grateful. But with your attitude, I was afraid to tell you about my near-death experience, and I'm not going to tell you now." Self-disclosure is strongly influenced by the reception we expect.

Reflections

- How open were/are your parents about their personal matters? How did you feel about it at the time—and now? How open were/are you with them? With sibs? With your children, other relatives, friends?
- Describe your risk-taking style. How did you get to where you are today? Are you satisfied? Are you inhibited? Would you push yourself to take a few more risks? Or have you been burned by too many bad risks?
- What were the attitudes toward self-disclosure when you were in training? How did they work for you? Is your view now different from that of your trainers?
- What have you disclosed to patients about your personal life? What effect has it had on them and therapy?
- What are you willing to tell patients about yourself, if doing so might move therapy beyond an impasse? What are you not willing to tell?
- How do you know what disclosure is appropriate?; When timing is right? What the effects are?
- Review a time when self-revelation backfired. What did you learn? Review a self-revelation that worked well. What were the ingredients?
- Perhaps you were a lucky one who came into this field *without* inhibitions about self-disclosure. How has this worked for you? Any advantages? Any drawbacks?

18

Illness and Other Distractions

Therapist illness compels involuntary self-disclosure. Professional and personal lives intersect. Illusions of invulnerability and availability promoted by the reliable, sacred time and space of sessions are destroyed—a dose of reality. Patients know we are coping with life's vicissitudes, are full participants in whatever comes along.

Our Unbalanced Way of Life

Therapists are not immune to the agitated chase, the nervous unrest. Most spend their days and some nights in a flurry of activity. We let ourselves be ensnared by trivial busyness; we are prisoners of schedules. Preoccupied with making a living, we overdevelop parts that are active, instrumental, quantitative, efficient. The parts that offer nurturing calm, esthetic pleasure, spiritual reflection, and healing repose are underdeveloped. So it is not surprising therapists have a high incidence of psychosomatic problems: hypertension, back problems, depression, alcohol and drug abuse, divorce, suicide. Inevitably, these intrude into the therapist–patient arena.

As a young therapist, I uncritically adopted the view of illness of analytic teachers and therapists: "Tell as little as possible. You must protect your patients. Don't burden them with your problems. Your life is your private business. Don't make it into your therapy."

> *I have diarrhea, but say nothing to the patient. Concentration is hard as my stomach churns; I stonewall, struggle for control. Finally, I bolt out of the room, muttering, "I'll be right back." When I return, the borderline young woman is distraught, convinced that she drove me out by what she said, that she is so disgusting that I can't stand to be in the same room with her that I don't really want to treat her, and so on. After I explain and apologize, she looks at her reaction and its roots. I ask what I should have done. She says she would have been less upset, if I had warned her that I might leave. A simple explanation would do, no details.*

Her parents were euphemistic and hypocritical; it is corrective to work with someone who learned (from her) to tell it like it is. Upset by stonewalling, she was calmed by honesty. We overestimate the negative impact of disclosure. Seeing patients as fragile, we discount their adaptive parts. *They always have strong parts. But our preoccupation with problems blinds us to them.* We deny dependency, attribute it to patients (they do have dependent parts they display to us), and set ourselves up to be perpetual "helpers."

Keeping illness to myself stems from identification with my father. He had grand and petit mal epilepsy from the 1930s to the 1950s. For 20 years, he avoided having a convulsion at work; colleagues and superiors never knew. So being secretive about illness came naturally to me. He did the right thing, given the stigma of epilepsy and his private, taciturn personality. What worked for him is not necessarily right for me. But secrecy augmented the tense emotional containment that contributed to his hypertension, arteriosclerosis, and death at the age of 59.

The Value of Illness

Our frenzied lifestyle—E. F. Schumacher's[66] "forward stampede"—takes its toll, knocks us out of the office and into bed. We rage, pout, whine, but are forced to take time out. Illness is the body's inescapable message to *stop!* As kids, we welcomed a sore throat that kept us home on test day. Illness is a "legitimate" call for retirement from the hurly-burly. When we get past fretting and trying to do therapy from bed, the enforced rest can do wonders, a golden opportunity to break unhealthy habit patterns. "We rejoice in our sufferings, knowing that suffering produces endurance" (Rom. 5:3). Philosopher Paul Brunton[67] writes:

> *"When sickness forces us to bed, do nothing, and be still, it may confer a real benefit by allowing reflection and intuition to become more active and useful . . . a chance to see more deeply into the meanings of past and present circumstances no less than future possibilities. Pressures then begin to lose their urgency . . . people find illness a time when relaxation, reflection or prayer beneficially influences the remaining years of their lives!"*

Therapists who implement the suggestions in this book have a head start on illness. Not only can they engage in a life review, but they have tools for recovery. Meditation, relaxation, visualization, affirmations, spiritual practice, mindful attention—all aid healing. I speak optimistically to each pill I take! And anything helpful can be passed along to patients and students. I sent this letter to a class interrupted by my unexpected surgery.

> *My biggest disappointment this spring (next to having surgery!) is being unable to complete what we started. Still, I worked on some valuable lessons: patience, finding the message in pain, learning how to accept sickness, getting better acquainted with my body (more a male problem), and appreciation—of family, of friends, of colleagues, of life itself in its many offerings. I wish you the very best as you move forward in your lives and careers.*

Naps without guilt speed recovery. We work hard all week, consider sleep a waste of time, are sleep deprived and vulnerable to illness, accident, and mental errors. If we sleep longer on weekends, we throw the sleep cycle off. No wonder that Mondays are miserable! Naps are recouping from a bad press and childhood pride in not taking them. Not only do daily naps aid healing, but they prevent the buildup of stress. Most people have an early afternoon letdown. A nap is more effective than caffeine or white knuckling. Pilots who take naps are sharper on the job than are those who don't. The "too-busy-to-take-a-nap" practitioner is the one who needs to stretch out on the couch with the phone unplugged for ten minutes in the middle of the day. A longer nap leaves you groggy, unless you take an hour and a half to two hours to complete a sleep cycle and preserve circadian rhythm.

Professional Attitudes

Illness of the Analyst[68] depicts illnesses handled by psychoanalysts. They conceal as long as possible. Most deny serious illness by working as though nothing is wrong, in spite of ominous symptoms. They delay asking for help, with catastrophic consequences. They proudly proclaim that the welfare of patients comes before the welfare of analysts, a belief I no longer share. This sacrificial attitude demeans patients as resourceless children. It is repetitive, not corrective, and repeats family alarms: Don't tell children bad news. Protect them from unpleasantness, funerals, divorce. It is a destructive model for both patients and therapists.

Viewing patients as in need of "protection" is disempowering. In this view, the patient is too feeble to deal with life, and the strong therapist knows best. It feeds young characters who feel helpless, and ignores others who do not, who have untapped strengths. This stance is based on therapists' avoidance of discomfort with revealing themselves, rationalized as though it were for the patient's benefit. Freud put patients on a couch where they couldn't see him because he couldn't stand being watched all day. Therapists who "blank screen" are not skillful with personal questions and inadvertent disclosures.

Giving and Receiving

Therapy can be seen as an exchange of giving and receiving. The conventional view goes something like this.

Some things *patients* are expected to do (give):

- Show up for appointments.
- Provide an intimate, probably embarrassing history.
- Cooperate with every life detail asked about.
- Look at and change unhealthy aspects of life.
- Take the risk of feeling rejected and misunderstood.
- Pay, or get someone to pay, a fee.

Some things *patients* hope to receive:

- Guaranteed, exclusive time.
- Accurate, compassionate listening.
- High-powered expertise.
- Empathic understanding.
- Healing.
- Relief of symptoms.
- Love and attention missing in life. (Unstated, yet most important.)

Some things *therapists* are expected to *give*:

- Professional time and expertise.
- Attention.
- Thoughtful, ethical clinical responsibility.
- Techniques based on theory.
- Commitment to success.

Some things *therapists* hope to *receive*:

- Expression of altruistic compassion for people in trouble.
- The satisfaction of caring for and helping others.
- Joy in practicing a chosen profession.
- The chance to see years of training bear fruit.
- Making a living.

Patients and therapists get most of what they want. But there are two discrepancies. (1) Patients are expected to reveal their lives, therapists are not—a one-way street. (2) Love, help, *giving* flow only from therapists to patients—another one-way street. It is considered not only unnecessary, but harmful, to give of the therapist's personal world. And it definitely is not proper to expect caring. Therapists don't need love from patients, which should be found elsewhere. Not receiving from patients, we are drained. Receiving is unprofessional. The unvarying theme has been, "Refuse gifts and analyze the patient's motive," assuming pathology. And we are raised to believe that receiving is weakness. "Better to give than to receive." Receiving obligates, leaves us indebted. Better to give and be one up. Little effort is made in conventional therapy to ensure that learning to give is accorded equal time. I made this error for years.

He was a very disturbed chronic paranoid schizophrenic. Electric and insulin shock, tranquilizers, and long hospitalization helped, but he still hallucinated and got into trouble. We recently celebrated 40 years of therapy, and I believe seeing me kept him out of the hospital and working. After he retired, he was bored, hung around taverns, regressed. Then the woman he lived with had a ruptured aneurysm, requiring 24-hour care, which he willingly provided. Later, she told me that he was healthier mentally and easier to get along with than he had been in 20 years. Giving, a necessity I never thought of, brought healthy balance to many years of receiving from me.

We are increasingly aware of the deprivations and violations that patients have suffered—good reason for compassion. The assumption is that these traumas are compensated for in therapy. That is fine, but incomplete. We overplay pathology and underplay health. Both patients and therapists expect therapy to fix the damage, give what the patient didn't get, fill an empty vessel. "Empty" is a favorite word for disturbed people. Therapists don't go beyond defensive emptiness into the fullness, richness, and complexity of the deeper psyche.

Listen to a case conference. You will hear the bad things that have happened and the good things that have not, the psychic damage and deficiencies, and how therapy must repair and compensate. The patient is in great need of receiving. All true. But this half-truth misses the crucial corrective: The patient is in great need of giving. In the yin and yang of life, giving is as vital as receiving.

Elderly subjects enjoy receiving massages, need fewer doctor visits, drink less coffee, and make more social phone calls. But giving massages to toddlers is enjoyed even more.

Healthy physiology requires the balanced intake of nutrients and output of waste. That patients are given to without giving back violates this body/mind principle. To stay healthy, we cannot receive without giving, and vice versa. Therapists are exhausted, giving our all without comparable return. And the patient hooked on receiving is blocked from growth. A negative self concept goes like this.

"I must be given to constantly because I am a pitiful victim with no resources. I cannot provide emotional support for myself; someone else must do it. Victimized in the past, I still live as a victim,

turning all that happens into proof that once again I have been taken advantage of. My craving for dependency, which I get in therapy, is legitimized because innocence justifies entitlement."

Preoccupation with victimization blocks the recovery patients say they want. Much therapy impairs self-responsibility. Underdogs sometimes become vulnerable to feelings of entitlement. Loving underdogs led me to treat the most rejected of the sick, mental patients, in the field most rejected by medicine, psychiatry. But altruism is susceptible to distortion and politicization and a "me-before-the-others" mentality.

I am not against social advocacy. I am against advocacy in therapy, an incendiary topic. My orientation is consulting rooms, not barricades. Conviction comes from treating underdogs. I am eager to serve, but when I lose sight of the power of their self-centered one-way-streetism, we all suffer. Transformative therapy calls for courage by the therapist and patients to confront humiliating underdogism. With careful preparation and support, this can usually be done. Or the danger seems too great and the patient or the therapist flees.

Twelve-step programs incorporate giving back. The 12th step of Alcoholics Anonymous reads, "Having had a spiritual awakening as a result of these steps, we tried to carry this message to alcoholics, and to practice these principles in all our affairs." The fifth tradition of AA: "Each group has but one primary purpose—to carry its message to the alcoholic who still suffers." Recovery is incomplete without the 12th step. And groups do not survive without the fifth tradition. We have a long way to go in accepting that therapy, to be complete, also requires giving back. Giving to others need not wait until the end. Some are never "ready." They can start in small ways. Unwillingness to give is a good topic for exploration. Giving begins and blossoms with a therapist who gives of self and receives from patients.

Neglecting spirituality is a mistake. Serving others is a tenet of all religions, but therapists believe it is unnecessary for patients to give. This distortion of life metabolism is clear with sexual-abuse survivors. They were terribly traumatized, so therapists insist they continue to need all they clamor for: extra time, attention, love—as though still victimized Small wonder that workers burn out quickly. Unilateral advocacy blinds them to the possibility that memories might be inaccurate or that there are other sides of the situation. I discourage survivors from legal action, which complicates matters further: their victimhood is strengthened, family relations polarize, they might lose.

Suing is traumatic. Their potentially mature internal parts—which every survivor has or they wouldn't have survived—are minimized. Some therapists believe these patients don't have such parts, can't develop them, and unending therapy is necessary. If that is really so, then therapy is a waste of time for there would be nothing to be nurtured into strength. If mature parts did not exist, a better solution would be to take the patient home and raise the patient again. There was such a movement, "Reparenting," in the 1960s and 1970s. Its misuse was devastating. Therapy is a long-term benefit when we help people use disowned, neglected parts of themselves. Once discovered—rediscovered—these resources are forever available, portable, usable. And they can be evoked by mutual giving and receiving in an authentic therapeutic encounter.

To return to the prevention of therapist illness! The gains for the therapists are as great as for patients. Mutual give and take are life-affirming, mentally unconstipating. Once we overcome apprehension about false vulnerability and become authentic, we are exhilarated, not guarded; freed, not constricted; open, not closed. And this translates into greater openness in the family, with colleagues, in life. It leads to fulfillment we never dreamed possible. It counters burnout, makes the career worthwhile. Our addictions and psychosomatic illnesses are due in large part to a stultifying ethic of "patients first, therapist later."

Patients seldom mention their shame, always taking, never giving. Therapists do not realize how they feel. This often is a motive behind giving a gift to the therapist. When patients do something for us, one-sided obligation and dependency are assuaged. The relationship feels more equal, more mutual, more fair, more balanced, more collaborative.

> *Fifteen minutes before a session, I learn that a former student and staff member committed suicide. I am shaken. When I step into the office, the couple, both therapists, know there is something terribly wrong. Overfunctioning **President Frank** acts as though nothing happened, babbling a sentence or two. Then I blurt out that I can't go on. I speak of what my colleague meant to me and the pain, shock, and tears I feel. These fine therapists listen, and are helpful, supportive, compassionate. When I calm down—not more than 20 minutes later—we set up another appointment.*

205

In later sessions, we joke that instead of just not charging them, I should pay them. But they received something more valuable than dollars. They explain that it is a wonderful feeling to give back a bit of what I have given them in three years. It puts us into better balance, makes for more mutual, honest give-and-take. It does not keep me from continuing as therapist. In fact, it opens up discussions about giving and receiving in therapy and elsewhere. Caring is not a zero-sum game with winner and loser; love increases when given. In therapy, it is a two-way street, even if not recognized. Better to own up to it. Then therapists can savor what we get that is rejuvenating. Even the most hard-bitten, blank-screen analyst believes he or she is a better analyst now than before. There must have been something of value coming back from all those analysands.

Guidelines and Suggestions

In addition to guidelines for disclosure in Chapter 16, I have a few ground rules about illness and other disruptions.

- When illness or other events might affect patients, I tell them myself. When not possible, if Jan knows them, she tells them. Otherwise, our secretary makes sure they are told. She worked at the nursing home and is good at explaining medical matters.
- I give headlines without details. If asked for more, I provide it, after exploring their need for more. No one has begged. If they did, I would deal with it as with any behavior. Not saying too much is our responsibility. When I decide that is *all* I will say, they get the message. Being clear, calm, and gentle conveys respect, given and received. Full patient disclosure does not require full therapist disclosure. The better the relationship, the easier it goes.
- Honesty is critical. What they are told is the truth, although not necessarily the whole truth. I respond naturally. When I'd rather not give specifics, I tell them, "I prefer not to go into details right now." "I can't tell you more without violating a confidence." "This is as much as I'm comfortable telling you." Be candid about the fact

you are holding back. No deception. Nothing artificial. Patients rely on us to stand for reality.

- If I am likely to be absent for more than a few days, Jan or I keep them informed of important changes, good and bad.

- I dislike euphemisms. They are evasive and deceptive. They repeat parental dishonesty. I refer to euphemisms in therapy, not those in everyday life. There, they make society's wheels turn more easily, I may not want to reveal myself, and others may not be interested. "Fine" is often the best response to the ubiquitous "How are you?" Most greeters are just greeting, not starting a clinical interrogation.

- When I return to work, patients need to know I have recovered and am fully available. I give a brief, matter-of-fact summary. Candid acknowledgment that I am both fallible and resilient expresses more respect than evasion. They are encouraged to comment as appropriate—condolences, congratulations. A normal human exchange reinforces everyone's grip on reality.

Reflections

- How well do your nurturing characters balance your busy ones?
- What are your body signals that tell you it's time for a refreshing break? How sick do you get before taking care of yourself?
- Recall the last time illness required cancellation. How did you inform people? With what results? Any changes to make when you get sick again?
- What are you willing and not willing to tell patients about your illnesses? How do you prefer to handle this?
- How do you feel about giving and receiving? How do you handle the offer of gifts from patients? Does your answer depend on the patient, stage of therapy, value of the gift, or any other factor?
- What are the pros and cons of how I handled my illnesses? Anything there you can use in planning for the next time your personal life disrupts your practice?

The Pull of a Style

Students who study a smorgasbord of therapists through the literature, videotapes, and in person are easily overloaded; diversity is disorienting. Yet, as chaos theory predicts, a disordered mix self-organizes into a new and better order after six months to a year. Knowing different, sometimes conflicting, methods assists students in evolving a style congruent with their personalities. When free to follow what is appealing, they are attracted to teachers and techniques of self-revelation that match their own way of being and doing.

For both teacher and students, of course, a single, party-line method is simpler, quicker, and less demanding. One-dimensional therapies are easy to research, publicize, present in workshops, and write about. The field has witnessed a parade of buzzword techniques that rocket into prominence and fade when their incompleteness becomes apparent. Because leaders care about and proselytize their own philosophies (and this book is no exception), most training goes the univocal way.

But one note doesn't make a concerto. By examining an array of possibilities, we gain insight into our natural proclivities. After practicing a few years, most therapists experiment, while looking to heroes for hints. If trained in a single method, they find that the practicalities of clinical life demand a broader approach. They become more eclectic, more integrative in their own way. Why not help them evolve that way in the beginning?

Pioneers make good subjects for studying style. Each made a point of delimiting exclusive turf by emphasizing uniqueness—Freud's "narcissism of small differences." Today, with the trend toward integration, it is more difficult to see styles in the sharp relief of 30 years ago. The distinctive originals I know best, personally and professionally, are family therapists, so my opinions are subjective and biased. I am fond of them and learned a great deal from all.

These descriptions are based on the amount and type of self-disclosure. They come from personal contact and are designed to provide guidance in understanding the pull you might feel toward certain therapists and certain methods. They are not exhaustive; others could be included. They describe people whose methods are available via writings and videotapes. Each attracts and does best with those students and patients who are drawn to them.

At the no–self-disclosure end of the spectrum are Nat Ackerman, Don Jackson, Jay Haley, Sal Minuchin, Jerry Zuk. The big attractions: withholding personal reactions and stories, and clever, concrete thinking. Some, like Haley, claim it is unethical to ask students to be self-disclosing. (A ground rule of my groups is optional self-revealing. The timing and amount are in the hands of the student, with only an occasional nudge from me. A mutually agreed upon contract is in no way unethical.)

Haley's stance in teaching is consistent. He scorns asking about the past. At a meeting with students, I ask him to tell us about early experiences that led him into this field. He answers in his pixie way, "I never thought about it." And he does not choose to think aloud about it now. I believe him. He was the only visiting pioneer among dozens, who did not launch into a description of the personal and family events that led them into family therapy. His strategic approach appeals to those who like one-up, hands-off, adroit paradoxes. He was much influenced by master strategists Gregory Bateson and Milton Erickson.

Murray Bowen represents the middle of the spectrum and attracts intuitive people who prefer thinking over feeling. He took a determinedly unique position, selectively self-disclosing in a specific way. He was the first to describe work with his own family in an anonymous 1967 article that knowledgeable people knew was his. He did this to describe the method and theory he was developing. He wanted his ideas to reach and influence a large audience. He succeeded.

Bowen and his followers have a peculiarly objective way of describing their subjective experiences. They downplay emotions, emphasize cognition and behavior, claiming they are *only* guided by Bowen's theory, not by others, and certainly not by feelings. They preach differentiation to students and patients, and try valiantly to differentiate themselves from all others. They succeed, but at a price. I chuckle when a Bowenite rhapsodizes over theory. Bowen had a stubborn streak a mile wide. In the 1960s he said, with determination, "The longer these kids' hair gets, the shorter mine gets!"

Words such as love, compassion, or empathy seldom appeared in his speeches or writings. Bowen never spoke of his feelings. He scorned anyone who did as "part of the encounter crowd." I don't think he ever forgave me for introducing him by telling an audience that I loved him! When asked about his reactions to some event in a session or to what he heard about patients' lives outside therapy, he responded with a minilecture on his theory, or doing what he called a reversal—paradoxically encouraging problematic behavior to ridiculous extremes. He told stories that conveyed a powerful, indirect message, letting it be received however the hearer chose. Stories about himself and his family were devoid of emotion, objective, like moves on a chess board.

Bowen often said that his students should go their own way, not be like him—which worked as a reversal. You recognize his followers who use his pat phrases and party-line concepts. Mike Kerr, his protege and successor, stood at the blackboard, drew diagrams, told stories, and flipped his chalk exactly like Bowen! About half of the students with two years of training with Mike tried his approach, using the theory but different techniques. The rest were too turned off to become more involved.

At the other end of the spectrum are therapists like Carl Whitaker, Virginia Satir, and Norman Paul,[69] who attract those who react with feeling before thinking. Whitaker is famous for his outrageous, spectacular performances. He tells entertaining stories about himself, his wife, kids, and grandkids; many no doubt are true. I have learned a lot from Whitaker and he has done fine work with difficult families.

Virginia Satir uses herself in a personal way that brings out strong feelings and leaves a lasting, positive impression. She has a host of admiring colleagues who have intense relationships with her. She is more likely to *imply* her familiarity with life's traumas than to describe them.

Norman Paul was a creative pioneer in the use of video. He not only played back audio- and videotapes of their sessions to his patients, but used the tapes with others who had similar problems. These cross-family techniques often made therapeutic breakthroughs that more conservative methods hadn't. In the book that he and Betty, his wife and cotherapist, wrote, how they conduct therapy is revealed for all the world to see. It is a fine, yet underappreciated, contribution to the field.

My Evolution in Self-Disclosure

In arriving where I am today, I have evolved through several phases, oscillating between openness and concealing. I examine these in the hope that you, the reader, are stimulated to do the same. As a patient once said, ruefully reviewing the permutations in his life, "I don't mind if the pendulum swings back and forth, just so the clock moves on."

Medical Practice

Medical-student clerkships heightened my excitement and anxiety. Excitement because at last I was a real doctor taking care of real patients; anxiety because I didn't have the foggiest idea of how to be a real doctor. So I acted as though I knew what I was doing, and adopted what I imagined to be a professional, scientific manner. I presented an awkward caricature of probity I did not feel and maturity I did not have, all business, non–self-revelatory. I dealt with people at arm's length—with forceps, not fingers. This was a change, a strain; I was accustomed to being free and silly. I still shudder when I think about my asking a sick old man rote questions from a blue card, "Any diarrhea? Borborygmi?"

Graduates were given Sir William Osler's[70] *Equanimitas*. Theme: no matter how critical the patient, no matter how hard your heart pounds, as the physician, maintain an appearance of confidence. Later, as a teacher and therapist of medical students, I saw this as temporarily necessary for survival when first dealing with disease. The compounding tragedy is that many physicians never grow beyond being guarded and stilted.

Internship reinforced patient-on-the-end-of-forceps mentality. My abrupt initiation was to arrive on Ward 64 and be told by the senior resident, "These 89 patients are yours. Let me know if you need help. Good luck." And she was gone, leaving me terrified. I had never been solely responsible for even one patient. So I plunged in, counter-phobically, and did my best with people facing life-threatening diseases—I had little time for their personal lives, and none at all for mine.

Then for five years I practiced in a Chicago suburb. News, accurate and inaccurate, traveled at lightning speed. Despite no announcement, the day I arrived, a dozen people were in the waiting room. Making house calls, the phone often rang—a neighbor had seen the blue Plymouth and wanted me to come over. If anyone needed me in a hurry, the telephone operator knew where I was. My professional and private lives were open to scrutiny. I was surprised that I was the target of such intense curiosity.

I compartmentalized my mind as much as possible, something I could do even before medical school. When I so chose I could focus on one thing, filter out everything else, typical of thinking introverts. (This valuable "skill" was a liability in the family, to my regret.) The final test of objectivity came when Jan and I walked into a party of 12 young, attractive couples. After saying hello to everyone, I realized I had done a complete physical, including pelvic, on every woman there. Quite an exercise in compartmentalization, and savoir-faire! I became comfortable with juggling hats. Patients told me that when I was not obviously self-conscious they could relax and be whatever was appropriate. This small-town practice laid the groundwork for my being at ease in wearing many hats, in my family, with students, with patients—and especially with Jan.

Psychiatry and Psychoanalysis

Once I entered psychiatry, the situation changed again. Both in the Air Force and in residency, I was a hospital physician, expected to conform to clear, unbreachable boundaries between staff and patient: doctor in charge, patient expected to be compliant, personal exchanges frowned upon, questions the province of doctor, not patient. There was plenty of gossip, but it was easy to be above it with my family living on the grounds. Life shifted neatly into work and personal boxes. The older children remember these three and a half years as the best. Dad was home a lot and emotionally more available than in general practice, or would be later in psychiatric practice.

The Chicago Institute for Psychoanalysis again was different. Between the time I was accepted (1953) and started classes (1960), Franz Alexander had resigned and moved to California. Some of his innovations were disapproved of by many faculty member, so there was a rebound of orthodoxy. Patients were to be treated on the couch four or five times a week, expected to vacation only when the analyst did, and "corrective emotional experience" became dirty words. In the seven years before graduating in 1967, only the work of Freud and of his direct followers was taught. I never heard the names Jung, Adler, Rank, Fromm, Horney, or Frankl unless used disparagingly. Quotes from Freud[71] were frequent and reverent.

> *"The doctor should be opaque to his patients and, like a mirror, show them nothing but what is shown to him. He should not bring his own feelings into play."*

This was interpreted to mean that you must never tell the patient anything about your feelings or your life.

> *"The psychoanalyst should deny the patient, who is craving for love, the satisfaction she demands. Treatment must be carried out in abstinence. Ethical motives unite with technical ones to restrain him from giving the patient his love."*

This meant not only that sexual involvement was prohibited—and I agree—but also that the student was not even to hint at liking the analysand. If rookies foolishly admitted having let an patient know we cared, we were chastised for our countertransference.

> *"Activity on the part of the physician must take energetic opposition to premature substitute satisfactions . . . deny the patient precisely those satisfactions he desires most intensely . . . If everything is made pleasant . . . he is not given the necessary strength for life."*

While there is clinical half-truth in these statements, they were interpreted in a most extreme and arbitrary way: Never tell the patient anything about your life or your opinions. Talmud-like, answer a question with a question. Put the most negative and pathological twist on all that happens, especially questions, because even the most innocuous-sounding question covers an unconscious, and therefore unhealthy, motive.

But the fact is, I was learning psychoanalysis, not psychotherapy. A firm distinction was made between the two. We were striving for analysis: an all-encompassing transference neurosis that could be analyzed. Transference interpretations were to be used nearly exclusively. "Interpret the negative transference; the positive will take care of itself." The most chilling criticism was, "You are doing therapy, not analysis." Therapy was considered supportive and educational, and as producing structural (read: lasting) changes, and was done by social workers, psychologists, and clergy who hadn't gone to medical school, and were unscientific and not qualified to be psychoanalysts.

There have been many changes in over 30 years. A few psychologists and social workers have been trained in analysis. Self psychology makes analysts more humane. But in 1991 in Chicago, the birthplace of self psychology, only 9% of the Psychoanalytic Society identified themselves as self psychologists; the other 91% called themselves Freudians. The psychoanalytic influence has been pervasive, and since World War II, has been the dominant psychological paradigm. Its subtle influence shows up in details of practice, even of therapists claiming to be antagonistic to it.

The other major Chicago influence is Carl Rogers' client-centered therapy, which is interpreted to mean nonrevelatory responses from therapists who feed back the last thing the client said. This is a distortion of what its founder did and was, but that doesn't keep therapists from caricaturing the technique when they don't know what to do. A confused version of analytic and client-centered techniques is practiced by many therapists who adopt such trappings as working only with individuals, valuing frequent sessions for many years, and maintaining anonymity. They have usually been in dynamically oriented therapy and have analysts as supervisors and teachers. Analysis is considered the best, most prestigious, form of therapy. When a psychiatry resident is having marital difficulties, a persuasive referral for analysis is made because, "We want the best for our residents." This, despite the poor research record of individual therapy for marital problems as compared with conjoint marital therapy.

It is easy to see why psychoanalysis was so attractive to me, an introverted, intuitive, thinking, organized personality. Sitting out of sight, speaking infrequently after careful thought, being "scientific" seeming to be in control at all times, having a rationale for not disclosing thoughts, feelings, or personal life—these were appealing and fit my taciturn father's dictum: "If you don't know what to say, don't say anything. People will think you know and are choosing not to say. Open your mouth when you don't know and everyone will know you don't know." So becoming a psychoanalyst was natural.

Child Psychiatry and Family Therapy

I began to experiment by seeing the whole family when faced with a "problem" child. Gradually, I treated couples, families, and groups of couples and families in various combinations. I started out sticking as close to the psychoanalytic model as possible: seldom speaking, keeping opinions to myself, focusing on the transference, dealing with resistance by interpretation. I even went through a brief phase when I sat behind the couple, at right angles to them, and pretended I was dealing with two persons freely associating as one, a pitiful effort to apply what I knew best.

The more couples and families I saw, the more I was impelled to be active and interactive. With lively conflictual families, if I waited to intervene until I thought I understood, I was inundated with more data than I could deal with. Much against my training, I was drawn in very early, being responsive, and taking active leadership, especially with disorganized families with no effective leader.

Because I grew as a therapist, when video became more available, I had many opportunities to see and hear myself in action, a learning shock to which all therapists should expose themselves until it is no longer a shock, merely a dose of reality. For example, seeing over and over a profile of my pot belly convinced me to lose 40 pounds—and to keep off. Videotapes showed I was more self-revealing than I thought. Besides, it didn't seem to do the harm I had been led to expect. In fact, after I told a story about myself, someone often would make a personal comment. When I held my body in a certain posture, others followed. When I stood up or moved around, they livened up. Knowing what to look for, it became clear we were in a well-orchestrated, unconscious dance. Families watching videotapes of themselves gave us a chance to comment on what was before our eyes. I could no longer limit my remarks to objective analysis. They soon commented about me, and not always favorably. Similarly, when interviewing families before an audience, whether present in the room, watching through a mirror, or on closed-circuit video, colleagues would make penetrating comments. This all contributed to my steadily becoming more open—with patients, with colleagues, with students. And with my family and myself. We even videotaped ourselves.

In 1970, when Jan joined me as cotherapist, we saw couples, families, and groups, and did cosupervision, coconsultation, and coteaching. Again, my cover of anonymity was blown. Cotherapy by unrelated people reveals much about their personalities—and all the more so when the cotherapists are married to each other. Patients and students not only discovered my partner of many years, but could see and hear a great deal about our personal lives, both overt and implicit.

We took our six children (ages 14 to 24) to a weeklong family communication workshop in the summer of 1970. We agonized over the instruction, "Tell your family something important you have never told them before." Powerful. And effective in removing more barriers to openness, especially after I told them with anguish about a brief affair I had had 15 years earlier. We learned more about them—and they about us—in one week than we had ever learned before, or since. And that openness continues to this day.

Another influence was the workshops Jan and I attended in 1972 and 1973. The blend of transactional analysis and gestalt made for direct encounters with leaders and with each other. Participants paired up, taking turns as therapist and patient, dealing with personal issues. Bob and Mary Goulding, Bob Drye, Ruth McClendon, and Les Kadis encouraged us to do more nontraumatic and growthful self-exposure. This learning translated into therapy, teaching, workshops, and marathons—settings where we revealed more of ourselves than in conventional therapy.

In addition, the fact that our practices are conducted in our home makes anonymity less feasible. Anyone can see what we spend our money on, how often the house gets painted, our taste in decorating, and other details of family life.

As beginners, we feel more secure learning a single, internally consistent method. Nothing wrong, as long as we don't get stuck in it, a handicap to exploring other possibilities. You will do your best work when your method is consonant with your personality. Experiment and find ways that resonate positively. Invent a fit that feels right, at home, natural. You will save yourself from burnout and enjoy a long, productive career.

Reflections

- Where do you place yourself on a least-to-most spectrum of self-disclosure? Are you the same with each patient?

In each stage of therapy with the same patient? If not, account for the differences.

- Trace your journey on the path of self-disclosure in therapy. Are you satisfied where you are now? If not, what will you do about it?
- Who are the therapists and what are the methods that attract you? Compare and contrast them with those that feel alien. Describe the fit or misfit between your person and these techniques.
- If you were trained in a particular method, how have you adapted it to your practice? Have you been able to use the essence, while finding other ways to compensate for any deficiencies? Are there other limitations to the method that need solving? Is your therapy evolving? (I hope so!)

PART

V

Leadership Beyond Problem Solving

If you want to be a great leader,
you must learn to follow the Tao.
Stop trying to control.
Let go of fixed plans and concepts,
and the world will govern itself.

The more prohibitions you have,
the less virtuous people will be.
The more weapons you have,
the less secure people will be.
The more subsidies you have,
the less self-reliant people will be.

—Tao Te Ching[17]

20

Leadership

This book is for naught, if you fail to lead your therapy. Much as therapists resist thinking of themselves as leaders, effective leadership is crucial. The following styles, all effective in specific situations, may help you find a way that is right for you.

Therapists seek consultation for a host of reasons. The most important reason, usually unstated, is that the therapist is not in command of the therapy, is not the leader of the therapy. The therapist may have been in charge for a while and then let leadership slip. Or it may never have been there in the first place. Without an effective leader, treatment flounders—a ship without a rudder, going in circles. There may have been some progress. But the perception of nonprogress troubles both therapist and patients.

Patients usually grow dissatisfied before, sometimes long before, the therapist does. But it is not expressed because the patient is too shy, polite, dependent, intimidated, or willing to blame himself or herself. Authority problem. Ineffective leadership is hard to put a finger on. Most patients are ambivalent toward authority figures. So are most therapists! Acknowledging the need for consultation is a first step toward clear leadership and progress.

Patients may tentatively, rarely aggressively, request another opinion about how treatment is going. The therapist's response is telling.

The one who bristles, becomes defensive, or doesn't see the need is uneasy with having authority challenged, fears criticism, resents being exposed. The one who welcomes the request, and manages anxiety, is more likely to accept criticism, and be comfortable with sharing leadership, secure with authority, and open to anything that will get things moving. My kind of therapist!

Once the therapist asserts leadership, therapy moves forward. In a few cases, it is obvious that the therapist will never be the leader, the therapist–patient chemistry is wrong, and treatment mercifully ends. These natural experiments—bogging down and renewal—led me to three related hypotheses:

1. Success is governed by whether the therapist is perceived, by himself or herself and by the patient, as the leader of the therapy. When leadership is weak, therapy falters. When leadership is autocratic, success is limited. When empathic and confident, therapy moves forward.
2. Good leadership is more important in effecting change than is theory or technique. And good leadership depends on an authentic, self-possessed therapist. Johnny Carson puts it, "The only absolute rule; *Never* lose control of the show."
3. The essentials of effective leadership can be taught—the purpose of Part IV. Organizational consultant Peter Drucker[72] says, "Innovative effectiveness is not inborn, not mysterious, not the result of genius. It can be learned."

Once I stumbled on these ideas, I looked with fresh eyes and found confirmation. The hypotheses also explain why family pioneers succeeded, despite contradictory theories and techniques. They were experienced by patients and students as effective leaders who could be followed safely. Something good will happen, no matter how hopeless things looks—the key to any risk taking. And taking risks is necessary for patients to heal and grow; for students to learn and grow.

Awareness of the necessity for good leadership impelled me to study group and organizational dynamics. I introduced leadership principles into clinical work and teaching because leadership in our field is virtually ignored. I do not recall hearing about the concept in training, although no doubt it was implied. Leadership is not obvious when therapy is going smoothly. Exchanges flow seamlessly into each other, session follows session without pause. As with a pair of skilled dancers, the leader can hardly be recognized by observation. *Co*leadership is more accurate. Lao-tze speaks:

> *When the Master governs, the people*
> *are hardly aware that he exists.*
> *Next best is a leader who is loved.*
> *Next, one who is feared.*
> *The worst is one who is despised.*
>
> *If you don't trust the people,*
> *you make them untrustworthy.*
>
> *The Master doesn't talk, he acts.*
> *When his work is done,*
> *the people say, "Amazing:*
> *We did it, all by ourselves!"*

I only add: The Master remains the Master.

Consultation is sought when the consultee feels a loss of leadership, although not explicitly stated. The breakdown exposes underlying dynamics not easily seen before. When leadership is resumed, it is inconspicuous. After the therapist has asserted effective leadership, but not before, it can evolve into co- or multiple leadership. But the therapist must continue to be one of the leaders.

Some therapists say that the need for good leadership is self-evident. It is not. Others claim that they do not lead their clients and recoil at such language as being in command, being in charge. They are wrong.

When I raise this subject, I am often greeted with body language showing distaste and mistrust. Many do not think of themselves as leaders and reject the whole idea. They were raised to be self-effacing and modest. "Don't be pushy" is a common family injunction.

Choosing a profession viewed by some as low in prestige, such as social work or psychiatry, suggests a motive to provide humble service. (Upon giving up a good social work job to enter the ministry, a friend was teased, "Why leave a low-pay, low-prestige career for one with even lower pay and lower prestige?") And toiling on the front line can mistakenly be seen as opposition to leadership, equated with manipulating others. Front-line workers believe power is bad, not recognizing that power lies on both sides of therapy. They don't distinguish between power—which is inherently neither good nor bad—and the misuse of power.

Further, many supervisees and consultees work for agencies where they struggle with oppressive bureaucracy, endless paperwork, and meddling higher-ups—sure to bring out passive aggressiveness concealed by self-effacement. For me to suggest this unprepossessing "nobody" should be a leader goes against the grain. I hear, "I don't lead, I follow." "To me, therapy doesn't require leadership by the therapist." "I go side by side with the client, I don't lead."

These comments show a preference for a particular *style* of leadership: accompanying joining, facilitating, enabling, reflecting, accepting. Nothing wrong with these qualities. They describe my own way. Andy Ferber called me a "counter puncher." In boxing lingo, a counter puncher waits for the opponent to swing first, then counters with a blow that catches the puncher off balance. As in aikido, the *fact* of leadership is not obvious, but still there.

> *John Sonne, psychoanalyst, quiet reflective guy, carries his analytic persona into family work. He is listening attentively to a noisy session when the bright ten-year-old turns to him and demands, "Why are you just sitting there? You're supposed to be the leader!" John calmly replies, "Who says I'm not the leader? I make the atmosphere." The family settles down and the session moves on. As kids do, the boy asks for the whole family, and they respond to the simple, direct answer.*

We are fond of saying that we cannot *not* communicate; it's a question of how. So also with leadership—we cannot *not* lead. It is a question of how, and how well or how badly. When we believe we offer a legitimate service, are available to people in trouble, and are paid for it, we take on the mantle of leadership whether we like it or not. Goes with the territory.

Some believe they must be a certain kind of leader. Physicians, for example, are M.D.s in part because they are drawn to an image of the doctor as leader-healer. If they are the take-charge leaders, they will work on a team reluctantly. They believe they should have the answers. The idea of sharing is repugnant, team members may have better answers. Some specialists, such as surgeons, can get away with it, but not psychotherapists.

Psychiatry residents, when uncertain of their skills, assume a know-it-all facade and fume at the suggestion of consultation. Clinical psychologists also fit this pattern, but not as often, as do social workers and nurses, but less so. People with more education have difficulty asking for help. People with less education have difficulty taking charge.

To those who shy away from leadership, I say: "Set aside problems with authority and be authoritative (not authoritarian) in your own way. You owe it to your patients and yourself." To those reluctant to share leadership, I say: "The one who decides to share leadership is the leader." To those of you who fail to express dissatisfaction with leadership you are getting, I say: "Speak up. We have to help our leaders lead. We have to show them how we want to be led so that what we want and what they can provide combine to bring forth the best in us and in them." Mohandas Gandhi said, "There go my people. I must hurry and catch up with them, because I am their leader."

Two Careers Enrich Each Other

Since graduating from medical school, I have had two careers, separate but interrelated tracks, both calling for many of the same skills. The first, always primary, is clinical practice and all its permutations. The second is organizational leadership. The tracks have steadily become more interconnected. Each contributes guiding principles and methods to the other. There are similarities between practice and organizations, especially regarding leadership.

I have always been ambitious. As a person, this means lifelong self-improvement. As a physician and therapist, it means doggedly searching for quality results. As an organization leader, it means experimenting with more effective group functioning. I have toned down pushy ambition, am more accepting of life as it unfolds. But I will never give up my curiosity, my urge to find something better, even while savoring—rarely regretting—the past, and enjoying the present.

From 1957 through 1968, I learned to do, supervise, and teach family therapy, searching for methods and theories that felt compatible. I watched many pioneers work and knew them personally. All used different techniques, many radically divergent from the others. Each was internally consistent, but the inconsistency among them was hard to miss. Yet they all seemed to powerfully affect families. Moreover, their theoretical explanations were also different from each other, whether given to a large audience, in their writings, or in private conversations.

Two examples. Since the earliest years, a cornerstone of Virginia Satir's approach is that family members communicate as clearly and congruently as possible, and she coaches them to do so. Carl Whitaker proclaims that therapists should be as crazy and ambiguous as possible, and shows them how. Confusing. How could this be?

However, I saw there *was* consistency. Each pioneer believed strongly in his or her system and was willing to practice and defend it. Each believed firmly in *self* and self's way. Their personal presence was the force influencing—that is, *leading*—people. They all had it, yet never spoke of their common denominator. They carved out their special turf and pushed their preferred brand (just as I do). Their signature way of doing therapy was an extension of themselves. The principles undergirding their way of therapy were integral to the kinds of people they were, their way of dealing with the world.

During the period of learning to do therapy (the mid-1950s to mid-1970s), we were also hard at work on the organizational track, searching for better ways to create a therapeutic community in the Plum Grove Nursing Home. Jan and I explored and experimented with whatever techniques and theories showed promise, whether from medicine, nursing, rehabilitation, psychiatry, systems theory, or business administration.

At the Family Institute, I applied this experience. I studied organizational development and leadership, observed successful and not-so-successful examples, and came to a similar conclusion. Successful leaders have different styles, different methods, different theories, and different interpretations of leadership. Yet all have excellent results. Belief in themselves is a potent determinant, and their style of leadership reflects their personalities.

The two streams—therapy and organizational leadership—became intermingled. The conclusion is clear. What makes therapy effective and what makes organizational leadership effective must be similar. That does not mean leading an institution is the same as doing therapy, but the underlying principles are comparable. Both are the result of successful accomplishment. Both have a common denominator in *mastery*. Each enriches the other.

Styles of Leadership

Identifying leadership components helps to reveal its relevance. There are many ways to lead and many categorizations. Each involves a personality-compatible style. Whatever we prefer, when we offer ourselves as therapists, we must lead the therapy we offer. By definition, we cannot *not* lead. Our styles express ourselves as people. What kind of leaders will we be? How good? How bad? We can study the essential ingredients of leadership and shape a style that fits our personhood.

These styles came out of suggestions by Family Institute cofounder Bernie Liebowitz.[73] They are useful in business, in families, and in therapy: *authoritarian. egalitarian. nurturant.* Types do not exist in pure form; every leader is a unique mix of all three. The labels are determined by the predominance of one or two. I separate and *stereo*type them for teaching. The key is the structure of relating and the pattern of decision making.

When the predominant style is *authoritarian*, most, if not all, of the decision-making power resides with the leader. There are authoritarian women and nurturant men. On average, however, male leadership is more likely to be authoritarian, female nurturant. The structure is pyramidal, the leader on top, with decisions passed down through a hierarchy. Superiors give orders for subordinates to carry out. Decisions become rules to control how everyone functions. Unless there is a rule covering a situation, action is problematic. How to get work done (on the job), live a life (in a family), or grow (in therapy) in spite of the rules becomes an intricate game.

Threats, bribes, manipulation, and scapegoating become the means by which people try to get what they want. Pressure from without supersedes intentions from within. Pecking orders evolve with superiors (bosses, parents, therapists) making it clear that subordinates (employees, children, patients) should shape up.

On the other side of the battle line, subordinates look for ways to win points with superiors, while chafing under oppression that inhibits their natural inclinations. Surreptitiously, they try to beat the system. Everyone is sneaky, including the leader.

This style has advantages. Life is structured and predictable, decisions get made, people know their places and many feel secure.

But there are drawbacks. Creativity is stifled, valuable dissenting opinions are not heard, compliance is passive-aggressive, and rebellion inevitable. Relationships polarize around "I am right, you are wrong."

Rule breaking warrants intensified control from above—punishment and stricter rule enforcement—in the vain hope of preventing further deviance. The vicious circle snowballs. Sooner or later, the authoritarian leader is confronted with complications. The system—organization, family, or therapy—becomes more dysfunctional and fails to achieve its potential. People have to get out to fulfill their creativity. We hear about failures of authoritarianism: in the military, in government, in large corporations, in educational institutions, in mental health organizations.

Authoritarianism is what therapists have in mind when claiming they are not leaders. They have experienced oppressive authority and do not want to have or be such leaders. They know autocratic therapists and are unlikely to refer to them, except for a quick fix. As long as therapy does not extend beyond the symptom-reduction stage—strategic, structural, problem–solution oriented, deliberately brief therapy—the authoritarian leader can succeed. Once past presenting problems and into growth, relationship and actualization, he or she faces complications. A leader who is only authoritarian cannot nurture creativity.

But being authoritarian has its place and is effective when someone is not in good control, as in highly conflictual, chaotic families. It is necessary in a crisis. It is needed with lower-functioning patients, some of whom may be brain-damaged, are not reflective enough, are confused by too many choices, or can't remember. Often it is appropriate leadership to start with an authoritarian stance, then gradually hand over more authority to them as they gain better control.

The predominantly *egalitarian* leader avoids what the authoritarian meets head on. This nice guy or gal leans over backward to be fair to everyone and is hard to get angry at, yet generates a surprising amount of anger and frustration. Structure is horizontal with the leader on the same level as the rest. Who is leading whom is unclear. All opinions are heard, no matter how unorthodox. Everyone gets a voice in every decision. Many ideas—good, bad, indifferent—are debated at length.

There is no authority for making decisions; many just happen by default, some are never made. Independence and innovation are so idealized that it is laborious to merge individual opinions into concerted group action. This type is strong on new ideas and plans, weak on followthrough. People who are spinning their wheels get angry and competitive. Everyone is disorganized, including the leader.

This system (in business, or family, or therapy) is great for spawning ideas, an exciting place to be. It attracts creative people eager to do something unique. Many small groups with shared goals and common interests work together successfully. The larger the group (more than, say, 10 or 12), the more dysfunctional, without some form of hierarchy.

Egalitarian groups have trouble getting the job done. They are vulnerable to manipulative people who seize on disorganization by playing one against another. Unreasonable demands clash with the wish to be fair to all at all costs. The system risks grinding to a halt due to an excess of ideas and a lack of planful implementation.

So also the therapist who is purely egalitarian. Important issues remain unsettled. Direction and goal attainment are problematic, conflicts are unresolved. No group survives. Even leaderless peer groups either implicitly select a leader, or work out multiple leadership.

This style is effective with high-functioning people who are more self-regulating. The occasional psychologically minded person or family may just need a place in which to explore and the freedom to do so. I get a reading on this when, in the second interview, I ask for reactions to the first and share mine.

The primarily *nurturant* leader wants everyone to be happy and to get personal satisfaction from what they do. He or she warmly encourages the follow-up of ideas, and expects loyalty and friendship in return. Disloyalty and unfriendliness are unwelcome. Structure is an inverted pyramid, with the leader at the bottom, connected to and supporting the others. This leader overcommits and overextends self, cares *too* much about work, or family, or therapy. Members try to match the leader's intensity of involvement, but feel they fall short. Jealousy and feeling cheated emerge as people vie for the leader's attention and love. Although people are productive, they often feel depressed, uneasy, and burned out. Everyone is dependent, including the leader.

The benefit of this style is a strong sense of belonging to a close group, including a group of two, and everything that entails. We all want to be nurtured and cared for. We all need a safe, secure feeling of place with people. A nurturant atmosphere is necessary for job satisfaction and for family well-being. It is imperative for healing and growing in therapy.

But when nurturing prevails, the cost is high. Problems stay hidden. People don't believe what is accomplished is the result of individual effort. Anyone who fails to acknowledge attachment to those who have helped is seen as ungrateful. Anyone not intensely committed to the nurturant style hazards criticism, even ostracism.

Our field attracts many with huge nurturant parts, especially social workers and nurses. When these parts are analyzed, however, the direction of nurturance is almost entirely toward others, not toward self. No wonder we take care of everyone but ourselves! Inhibited, frightened, deprived families need lots of nurturance. But excessively nurturant therapists have difficulty encouraging independence, resolving conflicts, probing into less obvious pathology, standing back to let patients work out things for themselves, and allowing people to leave when the time is ripe.

To show their ultimate dysfunction, I have caricatured each style. Each has strengths and drawbacks. The *effective* leader is not locked into one style, but flexibly and appropriately uses the strengths of each, integrating the three, shifting effortlessly. As circumstances change, the flexible therapist empathically changes style to serve their needs. This is easier with plenty of feedback so that each person can express opinions about how the system is functioning. Each of us has enough internal characters to integrate styles, and advance our job, our family, and our therapy.

A Classic Experiment in Leadership

Seventeen therapists representing various orientations (psychoanalytic, gestaltist, psychodramatic, and so on) each conducted a treatment group. The results were disheartening. Thirty-three of the 206 group members changed for the worse, and 17 of these were psychiatric casualties. In addition, 78 did not change and 27 dropped out. Only 108 improved; 40 only moderately.

In sharp contrast, the group led by Bob Goulding was most productive. Of the 12 persons who started, ten changed positively, one remained unchanged, and one dropped out. None changed for the worse and there were no psychiatric casualties.

Goulding's leadership style is revealing.* He made a contract for change with each member, and they took that contract seriously. The ten who improved accomplished what they agreed to accomplish. Several qualities of his style stood out:

- Took responsibility for what occurred in the group.
- Stimulated only moderate intensity of emotional involvement.
- Exhibited a moderate level of executive functioning and structure, such as limit setting, exercises, and managing the group.
- Offered explanations of what he observed, and information about how people learn and change.
- Helped members to gain insight, to understand their thinking and feeling, and to accept ideas on how to change.
- Aimed at members' taking charge of their personal growth.
- Provided high cognitive and conceptual input.
- Translated feelings and behavior into ideas.
- Did not confront members frequently.
- Expected that new consciousness would lead to a better lifestyle.
- Focused on both interpersonal and intrapsychic material.
- Provided high levels of support, caring, explanation, information, comparison, acceptance, and recapitulation.
- Maintained clear boundaries between leader and members.
- Encouraged, but did not push for, self-disclosure in the service of cognitive learning.
- Helped members make their own decisions about how much work they wanted to do.
- Shifted the focus onto another member without censure when a member had gone as far as she or he wanted at that moment.

---

*A description of Goulding's style of leadership can be found in Morton Lieberman, Irvin Yalom, and Matthew Miles, *Encounter Groups: First Facts,* Basic Books, 1973.

Shared Leadership

How much and with whom is leadership shared? An essential of the therapeutic community originated by Maxwell Jones[74] is the concept of multiple leadership. Various members lead at different times, using their different styles, for different purposes.

I learned this at Plum Grove, and adapted it to other groups. And as our children developed, they have shared more family leadership. These days, they usually take full responsibility for creating and carrying out a family project. Generational reversal is a great relief!

In therapy, I share a bit of leadership from the start and then more as presenting problems subside. I want people eventually to take equal responsibility for our direction and results. My experience is convincing. Multiple leadership, properly carried out, is far more creative, richer, and successful than flying solo.

Leadership by a pair of leaders has special features that deserve more space. When the two are the same sex, issues of homodependence must be worked out. When the pair are male–female, there are additional complexities and benefits. And when the pair are married, even more complexities and benefits ensue. This wife–husband combination can be most powerful when functioning well, and most dysfunctional when not.

An effective leader of others must be an effective leader of self, understanding, organizing, and using the internal cast of characters in a blend of the three styles. All need to be listened to and respected (egalitarian). All must have their needs taken care of (nurturant). And we orchestrate the whole cast so that we live the kind of life and practice the kind of therapy we aspire to (with authority).

Good leadership is exhilarating, a fulfillment that makes bumbling efforts worthwhile. Good leadership takes old-fashioned courage to let go of fear, create the right ambience, dare to step out, rise to the challenge, even a dollop of defiance. I highly recommend it!

Reflections

- Trace the evolution of your attitudes toward leadership. Who are the important people you looked up to as good leaders? What leadership did you dislike?
- How do you feel about being a leader of therapy? Are

you compatible with authority? Are you wary? Are you opposed to the idea?

- Spell out your way, perhaps assigning a percentage to each of the three styles discussed.
- How do the percentages change with different patients and at different stages of therapy?
- How flexible are you? How well do you share leadership?

21

The Accomplishment Triangle

Effective therapy goes beyond problem solving. The therapist-leader has the task of organizing the group (the therapist plus one or more) so that they accomplish something worthwhile—anything at all, from what we do in today's session to having fun on Saturday, to what my purpose is in life.

In August 1984, Jan and I attended a conference where Bob Shaw, contextual psychiatrist and family therapist, presented a framework for understanding accomplishment. I am indebted to him for the core of these ideas that I have applied to family therapy, to organizations, to my family, to life in general. Conceptually and experientially, he brought clarity and meaning to the integration of therapy and administration I had been seeking: Contextuality—Accomplishment—Mastery. Not the only way to get things done, but clear and practical.

Years of experience, especially on dissertation committees, convince me that the things that matter most—in therapy, in organizations, in life—cannot be logically explained or scientifically measured. They are beyond technique, beyond theory, beyond language. This is not to say that we should dispense with technique, theory, or language—we couldn't if we tried. But we foster a distorting illusion when we are satisfied with verbal descriptions of what we do and why. Therapists do not practice long before they produce, often inadvertently, extraordinary results beyond their known limits.

Bob's term "*mastery*" will do as a label for this surprise. Everyone knows that mastery exists, can sense its power when experienced, but—like love—we are hard put for consensus in defining it. Mastery has to do with using a full range of our internal resources, our entire cast of characters. It means removing the self-imposed limits that shackle us, limits that keep us in ordinary competence or even mediocrity. Opening up to our latent creativity means letting go of *attachment* to years of training in technique and theory. It means not being dominated by a relentless need to find and solve problems.

By "letting go," I mean not being preoccupied, not being committed to specific techniques and theories. Letting go means being fully present to what is, now, here, without preconceptions. It means being prepared for *whatever* presents itself, accepting results without rationalization, and without worrying whether the technique was "right" or fits a theory.

> *Therefore, the Master says:*
> *I let go of the law,*
> *and people become honest.*
> *I let go of economics,*
> *and people become prosperous.*
> *I let go of religion,*
> *and people become serene.*
> *I let go of all desire for the common good,*
> *and the good becomes common as grass.*
> Lao-tze

Letting go means correcting oneself without blame of self or other, then taking another committed action toward our vision, and improving that thrust with a minimum of comparing and judgment. This is a difficult, almost impossible, goal, yet worth striving toward. It also generates another paradox. Learn from those with mastery, then dismiss awe and resentment of the master. The ancients encapsulated this freedom: If you see the Buddha on the road, kill him! I add, "After learning from him."

We begin with *accomplishment*. The word stands for result, outcome, goal, achievement, transformation, or any term for success. In our case, it is how therapy—our lives and the lives of patients—turns

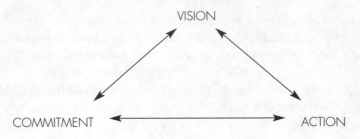

out. Accomplishment has three foundational elements: *Vision, Commitment*, and *Action* (see above diagram). These three are all of a piece, all-in-one. Any event that moves people toward their goals results from interaction among all three. The effective therapist-leader models creative integration through presence, confidence, patience— mastery. There is nothing in the diagram for reaction to the circumstances surrounding the group. The therapist-leader's power comes from understanding context and the ability to manage the context of therapy in such a way that new meanings arise and new connections are made.

Vision

Leading the patient or family to construct a vision for what will be accomplished in therapy is the therapist's most important job. William James[75] emphasized this many years ago, "The single most important fact about a person is his or her *vision*." This means exploring each member's unique vision of what she or he *ultimately* wants to accomplish. Some know immediately, others are vague, uncertain, or caught up in turmoil of the moment. When two or more come to the first session, their visions range from slightly different to incompatible.

I help each person shape the vision until it is clear to all of us. Time devoted to this task, which might take most of the first session, is well spent. A carefully constructed vision is already a huge step toward its achievement. While each is pondering over a vision, I listen with full, uncluttered attention to see if this is a vision I can accept. If it is legally or ethically questionable, I raise this at once. As the various visions are expressed, I make sure I fully understand them. Sometimes it helps to write them on a flip chart, a tool every therapist should keep handy.

I ask them to join me in evaluating whether they want to reach their vision *no matter what happens*. Some visions clash, so the sooner we know it, the better. The vision should be something that matters,

236

makes an impact, grabs everyone. "Make no little plans, they have no power to stir men's souls" is attributed to architect Daniel Burnham, principal designer of Chicago's magnificent, world-renowned lakefront.

A vision makes people uncomfortable when it calls for audacious changes that threaten the status quo. Getting to a vision means taking risks that call for courage to create dangerously. The Roman poet Terence advises, "Fortune favors the brave." Vision is an outcome that makes a difference, that transforms intention into actuality.

Vision is abstract, and thus encompasses the less abstract. It is inspirational, it alters situations and people. It is invented. It is *not* dependent on circumstances. Vision does not tell how to get there. Nor does it guarantee arrival. Vision is the source of leadership, the expansive dream state where everything begins and anything is possible. A lofty dream, not a pipe dream.

Words can only approximate vision. It is an expression of the personhoods of the people working toward it and of the therapist-leader. Having vision doesn't *make* it happen, it *allows* it to happen. There is no evidence the outcome will actually happen. But vision creates possibility. And from possibility can come anything.

When we construct images of outcomes, however vague, we have more to work toward, even though each person's image of the same outcome is different. The vision can be near or far, small or big—the immediate outcome of one session or the grand outcome of life far down the road. Vision determines the quality of life. Picasso said, "Everything you can imagine is real."

Vision is the "leading part." Like the rudder of a boat, it guides committed action toward accomplishment. Yet vision alone—without commitment and action—accomplishes nothing. How often we flit from vision to vision, hope to hope, wish to wish, yet taking little committed action—like adolescents in flux.

Commitment

Commitment is inspired by vision. It is derived from vision, not from circumstances. It is an internal reception and acceptance of vision. Commitment to vision creates a context within which the outcome can unfold. Like vision, it also does not tell how to get there.

The quality and intensity of their commitment keep people going. Asked to explain his good luck in tournaments, golfer Ben Hogan said, "I don't know. But the more I practice, the luckier I get." We are looking for voluntary commitment to goals and values by patients.

Family members have different goals and values. Part of the task is to help them respect these differences and work toward their own goals, even though they seem to conflict with each other. Strong commitment is necessary.

Therapists also make a commitment. Sharing the same values with patients may be helpful, but not obligatory. What *is* necessary is a willingness to commit to visions that emerge from patients.

> *I conducted a successful case (many therapists have) with these apparent incompatibilities: a 17-year-old clearly aware he is gay, with his vision of values and goals. A homophobic mother and father whose vision, values, and goals for him are in direct opposition to his. A heterosexual therapist who is neither gay nor homophobic and able to relate to both generations. It can be done.*

Once committed, unanticipated things happen to further a vision. Goethe[76] puts it movingly:

> *Until one is committed*
> *There is hesitancy, the chance to draw back,*
> *Always ineffectiveness . . .*
>
> *The moment one definitely commits oneself*
> *Then Providence moves too.*
>
> *All sorts of things occur to help one*
> *That would never otherwise have occurred . . .*
> *All manner of unforeseen incidents and meetings*
> *And material assistance*
> *Which no man could have dreamt*
> *Would have come his way.*
>
> *Whatever you can do or dream you can, begin it.*
> *Boldness has genius, power and magic in it.*

Commitment alters the raw materials of life so you can get to your vision—"whatever you can do or *dream* you can." Great power to surmount circumstances is generated through commitment to a vision. Power and accomplishment are compromised when commitment is *only* to circumstances, or to material things, or to ideologies, or to terminologies, or to thinking, or to feeling, or to action, or to—especially for therapists—problems, or to anything other than vision.

The commitment is to being yourself, with all your strengths and faults. Commitment welcomes, doesn't shrink from, failure. It makes dangerous creativity possible. It is a matter of pleasure, says author and writing teacher Natalie Goldberg,[77] urging us to let it be *deep* pleasure.

From time to time, both therapist and patient have their commitments tested. These are the times to renew them. Only after repeated failures should a well-designed vision be reassessed, altered, or replaced by a new, more relevant vision.

Yet commitment alone, without action guided by vision, is meaningless. And commitment to a vision without effective action results in the unfulfilled visions of enthusiastic idealists who talk and plan but never act. Similarly, vision and action without commitment waste energy, not accomplishing anything: the adolescent who flits from project to project.

Most therapists have had patients who were committed to coming without changing. When there is no vision, and no committed action toward a vision, treatment drags on, turning into a frustrating and destructive stalemate. This denouement is far more likely with individuals than with couples and families; sooner or later, someone in the family rebels loudly.

Action

The therapist coaches people to design whatever actions will get them to their visions. Right actions, *skillful means,* have an impact, move toward results. Actions are selected from possibility, beyond techniques and theories, and not only from circumstances.

A distinction is critical. *Possibility* is abstract, unlimited, open-ended to infinity. It does not have to exist anywhere to be invented. It is intuitive. The first law of creative accomplishment and of life: Learn to trust your gut. Possibility is easily confused with *possibilities,* which make up a list—however long—of discrete known actions, recipes, formulas, operations, and menus, and thus are valuable, but limited.

Technique-focused therapists work from a list of possibilities. Creative masters work from possibility.

Carl Whitaker tells of a regressed schizophrenic curled up on her bed. He had an image of an infant wanting her bottle. On a hunch, to the next session he brought a baby bottle with nipple and warm milk. She gulped it down, relaxed, and for the first time came into meaningful contact with him. Impressed and hoping he had found a new technique, he brought a baby bottle of warm milk to each of his schizophrenic patients. No others responded!

Whatever seems likely to get to the vision can be done. Imagine proposed actions, and estimate the likelihood that each could lead toward the vision. Conduct thought experiments, mental trial action, and imagine all the consequences. People mindlessly act for action's sake without a chance of reaching the vision. Yet some proposed actions that appear impossible may unexpectedly achieve your vision.

Randas Batista, a Brazilian surgeon in an isolated jungle hospital, invents a unique surgical treatment for severely damaged hearts. American and European surgeons are testing it out. An experimenter states, "This is one of the major contributions in the history of cardiac surgery." Dr. Batista explains, "In the jungle, I don't have much help. So, once you don't have the facilities, you always question, 'Is there any other way to treat this patient?' " He is creatively acting from possibility, not from a list of possibilities.

I keep asking, "How will the proposed action get you to your vision?" If there is doubt, or if the patient insists on action I think will not forward the vision, I say something like, "I don't see how this will get to your vision (giving reasons), but it's your life. However it turns out, we will learn something useful. And I certainly won't hold it against you for not 'obeying' me. I support your freedom to make mistakes and learn from consequences." Same thing my young adult kids taught me to say. Each action is evaluated to see if it *does, in fact,* forward the vision. If not, correct the action—go back to possibility with new information. Look for another action that is not seen right now. The less blame, the better.

Therapists and patients look for breakthroughs, hoping for something big and positive just around the corner, a great *aha!* Until you have done it a few times, it is hard to realize that Goethe was right—simply taking action *is* a breakthrough. If nothing more, it breaks through resistance to taking action. It is not only intellectual. It must *feel right* as well. Effective action is primarily determined by vision

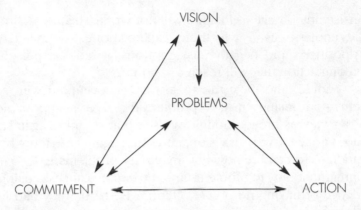

and intuitive feeling, secondarily by problems and circumstances. While action may be needed for certain problems or to deal with specific circumstances, such action should be guided by the vision.

Insist on enlivenment. Act, rather than react. Expect resistance to all action and change, then deal with the resistance. Action to further a vision challenges cherished presuppositions. Far better to drop our presuppositions than to change a meaningful vision.

As actions are taken that give evidence of getting to the vision, they become self-reinforcing. Vision becomes the guide. Puzzling over every move is less necessary. People say of an effective therapist-leader committed to action in the service of a vision, "She doesn't waste our time. She energizes us without straining. She keeps things moving. We're getting what we came for, even if it's different from—and better than—what we thought we wanted."

Action alone will not lead to effective accomplishment, only to wheel spinning, wrong directions, frustration, and no change. So will action driven by commitment if vision is lacking. All three are essential.

Problems

No worthwhile vision is reached without encountering problems, obstacles and difficult circumstances. Since any group of people seldom goes directly to its vision, there must also be a way to think about and handle problems. The question then becomes one of how to deal with obstacles. Are they stumbling blocks? Or steppingstones? So we add "problems" to the accomplishment triangle. (See above diagram.)

Many who come to us do not really believe in success. (Neither do some therapists!) An influential internal character, frequently a young part, insistently proclaims that life will not work. This "Yes, But" voice supplies endless reasons why things can't be done. Committed to false presuppositions and negative assumptions, it holds a person back from taking action that will reach a vision.

Most people, and most therapists, are preoccupied with solving problems—surprising since a problem-free life is impossible. Yet when our view is broad enough, we see that straining against problems does not get us to our vision, and often aggravates them by blind dedication to forceful removal of imaginary problems.

Commitment only to problems and the circumstances causing them is evidence of having no power. George Bernard Shaw had it right, "People are always blaming their circumstances for what they are. I don't believe in circumstances. The people who get on in this world are the people who get up and look for the circumstances they want, and if they can't find them, make them." Belief in the permanence of *what is* gives us reason to believe that we *cannot.* So we withhold energy and refrain from taking action, thus proving we cannot. The vicious self-fulfilling circle rolls on. Belief in what is necessary for results diminishes power.

> *Bob Shaw challenges the group to say what they absolutely need to do their jobs. A dentist says he could not fix caries without drills. He is stumped when Bob suggests he might invent a different way if unable to use his tools. A few months later, I read of a new treatment for dental caries using enzymes that obviates drilling!*

Careful exploration may be enough for simple problems of well-functioning people or for those seeking only symptom reduction, but rarely enough for the vast majority of problems brought to therapy. Further, resolving problems without a compelling vision invites more problems. A problem is only a problem when it is defined as a problem.

> *Medical students are making rounds with their instructor in the children's orthopedic hospital. The next patient has no hands or wrists; his forearms taper down to just below his elbows. The instructor says, "Tell us about your problem." The boy looks puzzled, "What problem?" Uncomfortable, the instructor points to his stumps. The boy says, "That's not a problem," and shows us how he feeds himself with his toes. He is there for appendicitis!*

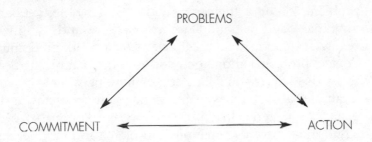

VISION

PROBLEMS

COMMITMENT ⟷ ACTION

E. F. Schumacher[66] says in his wry way, "Second-class people have problems. First-class people don't." They have "opportunities."

> *I diagram the accomplishment triangle for Tim who wants to figure out why his 12-lawyer staff works so hard and accomplishes so little. Before I finish explaining, he knows the answer. Jumping to his feet, he draws arrows showing their investment of energy. They are limited to the action–commitment–problem triangle with no awareness of a vision.*
>
> *Tim takes a weekend in seclusion to work out a vision for himself and the group, and presents it on Monday morning. Several years later, he and his group are international leaders in their new legal specialty. They still are excellent and committed problem solvers, only now their efforts are inspired and guided by a shared vision.*

The group had all the necessary elements except for an articulated, shared vision, which was only in Tim's head. It seems like magic, but it's not. The magic, à la Goethe, unexpectedly becomes available when committed action is taken toward a shared vision.

Commitment to action without a guiding vision is a misapplication of energy characteristic of our society, and evident in psychotherapy. Although occurring in all therapies, it is typical of those limited to problems, solutions, brevity, and managed care. Handling a problem and its circumstances is the therapist's validation and addiction. Beating against a problem wastes power and commits us to *it*, not to the vision. It increases the power of the problem.

Each patient needs two classes of healing: *psychological* problems and *situational (actual, material)* problems. The two are interactive, but distinct. Psychological problems are in the inner world, are subject to interpretation, and call for our full therapy armamentarium. Situational problems occur in the outer world, are tangible, verifiable in reality by others; and respond to common sense and using various resources. We can set up a complementary series with predominantly psychological problems at one end and predominantly situational at the other, with each person falling somewhere between.

For example, a battered wife has situational problems and may need legal aid, sheltered living, police protection, and so on. The battering husband also has situational problems and may need separation from the family, restraining orders, etc. In addition, they both need help for the psychological problems that got them into the actual ones. We must not confuse the two classes, No amount of psychologizing will provide the legal and situational help they need. And believing in the actuality of their psychological problems makes them harder to get rid of, not easier.

A psychological problem is only a problem in the thinking system in which it operates. When the thinking system changes and the problem has vanished or is transformed into an asset, the mental pain vanishes. Sometimes immediately. Our psychological distress is learned, and can be unlearned. That is what therapy is for.

Whether a thing is an obstacle or a breakthrough *depends on our interpretation.* Once we see it as a possibility for breakthrough, the outcome changes. Therapists whose thinking is outside of, not conditioned by, patients' beliefs make this shift far easier. This is a basic dynamic in supervision and consultation, and one of the reasons that peers with equal training and experience can be excellent consultants to each other.

When we solve problems and move into the domain of possibility, we come to new ways of being—of thinking, of feeling, of doing. Problems no longer are impediments but a route to vision. Someone has said that we destroy the devil by delicious recourse to the devil's own methods. Squeeze the lemons thrown at you into lemonade.

Reflections

- Explore a problem and imagine what life would be like without it. Is this vision, blocked by that problem, valuable and worth striving for, or is it trivial? How strong is your commitment? What are the best actions to take to reach your vision? Invent audacious, long-shot actions. How can the problem be used to reach it? Is there a further vision beyond that one?

- What is your ultimate life vision? How committed are you to it? How committed is your primary partner to it? Has your vision evolved over time?
- Which corner of the accomplishment triangle is the strongest for you? Which corner needs the most work?
- If you are primarily a problem-oriented therapist, consider adding vision to your conceptual thinking. It may help you do more effective and creative problem-solving and prevent an endless round of problem–solution, problem–solution.

22

Significance for Therapeutic Mastery

Once we grasp the essence of accomplishment through mastery, significant changes in the way we do therapy follow.

Changing a Belief System

At the Shaw conference I interview Amanda. I ask what she wants to accomplish right now. She wants help with a problem she has been trying to solve for many years with several therapists. When she meets new people, she is scared—her heart pounds, her mouth becomes dry, her hands are wet and shaky. As she feels taken over by these symptoms and struggles to control them, she becomes more anxious and her misery escalates. Therapy hasn't helped.

When she pauses for breath I say, "Sorry, I can't help you get rid of that. You have normal reactions to strangers." She looks puzzled and distressed. I describe stranger anxiety starting at eight months and continuing all our lives. "This is a built-in signal to alert us to possible dangerous situations. It happens in every new relationship. It's valuable. But fighting the feelings makes them worse. You need to accept them as normal and desirable. There's

246

no way I can help you get rid of them, and I wouldn't if I could. If your body didn't warn you, you wouldn't be psyched up for new people."

She listens, fascinated. When I stop, she looks stunned. A long golden moment of silence. Then with a peal of relieved laughter that rivets the conference, she shouts, "That's it! That's it!" Continuing to chuckle, she murmurs, "That's it. Thank you very much." Taken aback, I ask if there is anything else. She says, "No. Thank you very much," holds out her hand, shakes firmly, and says goodbye. Suspicious of fast results, and reluctant to let such a responsive subject go so quickly, I clutch her hand and implore once more, "Are you sure there isn't anything else?" "Nope. That's it. Goodbye." And she's gone. I didn't even get 15 minutes of fame.

New patients in a clinic waiting room were asked how many visits they thought it would take to get what they came for. The most common answer: One! In minutes, Amanda realizes that straining to solve a "problem" is bankrupt. So she lets it go and takes in a new, more life-enhancing belief in natural human reactions. She confirms Shakespeare's,[78] "There is nothing either good or bad, but thinking makes it so." She probably still has mild symptoms in new situations, but they no longer unhinge her. Snowballing anxiety is not set in motion. When meeting new people, she functions in spite of mild symptoms, and they subside when she welcomes them.

This vignette illustrates several points. I asked her to *tell me what she wants to accomplish right now.* I listened attentively, without bias, taking her at her word, her *literal* words. I noted what she did not say. Amanda said, "I want help with this problem." She did not ask to get rid of it. Sensitive to nuances, we may intuitively pick up on what we think is implied. But implications can lead us astray without verifying them. It's easy to misconceive a wrong assumption for an accurate one. Therapists tried to "resolve" her reactions. Had I not listened to exactly what she asked, I might have made the same assumption, with the same failure. I've made that mistake many times. The help she got was unexpected for both of us—help not in changing the "problem" but in changing her belief about the meaning of her symptoms.

I listened with no preconceptions, no agenda, an empty beginner's mind. This can be developed by meditation. To everything you hear, you count on an effortless flow of associations. You do not have to think. The unconscious resonates with what you hear and see; when the singer's voice matches the latent vibration of the glass, it shatters.

With little in the mind's forefront, the way is clear for spontaneity. Preconceived plans for what to do or say block creative responsivity. So do your personal problems. Be prepared by being ready for whatever.

Conventional neuropsychological theory says that memories come from storage areas in the brain. Rupert Sheldrake[79] has proposed an intriguing alternate theory of morphic resonance. Memories come from a part of the brain that tunes in, TV-like, to as-yet-unidentified waves in collective memory fields surrounding us. For our purposes, either theory works.

Let theories and techniques fade. They do not disappear. They come to the fore when you need them, not when you force them. Be a pure observer, as though delving into an engrossing new book, ready for anything. Let a picture emerge from the other. In seconds, your own inner picture will emerge. The two pictures are related. As the two pictures unfold, your task changes. Decide whether, when, how, and to what end you will put your picture into words so the two can be compared. Gaining experience, these choices take less pondering. Trust intuition to guide you. That was my state of mind with Amanda.

As her story unfolded, I checked as to which part of the accomplishment triangle she focused on. Action? Commitment? Problem? Vision? Devoted to therapy and volunteering to be interviewed before observers expressed commitment to action. But her commitment was to the circumstances of a problem, not to a vision—like Tim's team of problem-solving lawyers. And her therapists bought into fixing, not inspiring. Good intentions failed. Amanda did not have an "actual" problem. Once she changed her belief, she no longer had problem.

If she had given me a chance, I could have explained this and pressed her for a vision. What if you get rid of this problem? Then what? What is your image of who you would be, what you would do? We can only guess at what she might say. Be happy? Change to a more satisfying career? Marry her ideal man? Summon up courage to make a radical life change she has dreamed about? When people come for therapy without an explicit vision, I explain why they need one and help them define and refine one. It also must be one I will go along with.

Instead, I chose to bring forth a different reality, wherein her "problem" was interpreted as normal and an asset. I made this choice without stewing, responding spontaneously with the first thing that came to mind. Child psychiatry and six children probably helped.

This explanation is after analysis for teaching. It "explains" some aspects, but does not get to the heart of mastery. What happened more closely resembles magic, electricity, rarely-in-a-lifetime peak experience. The moment she realized her belief in needing therapy was a superstition, it no longer had a grip on her.

Mastery, like everything in life, has down sides. For example, when therapists truly "get" mastery, understand it in their bones, treatment is briefer. Their practices shrink, an economic concern for some successful therapists. Another negative is the high that comes with apparent magic. Bob Shaw's students brag how fast they cured someone, or how they teach subjects they knew nothing about. I had a taste of ego inflation after my stellar performance with Amanda. I became something of a workshop celebrity, the focus of admiring questioners.

> *I do a second interview with a psychiatrist. We go nowhere with his vision, which, significantly, I do not remember! The more I ask, the more we flounder. We are too much alike. I slip into psychiatric interviewing instead of spontaneity. Observers were told to raise their hands if nothing is happening. Hands pop up and we quit. I am grateful to be out of it. My heady omnipotence collapses.*

Briefer therapy occurs when patients have creative and open-to-possibility changes in thinking structure, not only by focusing on behavior or brevity. Behavior changes result from thinking changes. Our field is dominated by brief, quick-fix therapies—"psychotherapy lite"—whose main thrust is to get people out as soon as the presenting problem seems less a problem.

> *A consultee is frustrated with a problem/solution-oriented supervisor. After six weekly sessions, the family has resolved the original problem and comes in with new ones. The supervisor insists, "When the presenting problem is gone, therapy should be terminated. You should not take up other problems the family wants to work on." The consultee is torn between following his supervisor and going with what the family and he want.*

The instant-gratification mentality that pervades American culture has insinuated itself into psychotherapy. And "managed cost" abets addiction to therapeutic fast food to the point that life-enhancing depth psychotherapy is faced with extinction for all but the wealthy.

When mastery produces a brief result, brevity is a by-product, not the intention, à la Amanda. Many people, not satisfied with one startling insight and change in behavior, want further self-exploration. Mastery is like a football play, designed to make a touchdown every time. It usually does not, so a series of plays are needed to cross the goal line. Each play, if executed flawlessly, could be the one to score. The vision is to win the game at the end, not get it over quickly. When we work with the mind-set that therapy *must* be brief, the outcome is compromised. This presupposition blocks creativity, the very creativity that could produce results quickly when based on authentic and lasting change in belief.

> *For years, I was plagued by Amanda-like anxiety before giving a speech, leading a workshop, teaching a class, meeting new patients. But one time, walking to the podium to speak, I realize I am calm. I mentally congratulate myself on finally conquering this evidence that I'm not perfect. It's a terrible speech—flat, boring, no spark. I feel as though nothing significant happened. Friends in the audience feel the same way. I finally realize in my guts—intellect knew this—performance anxiety is nature's way of preparing for the unexpected, psyching up for success.*

Athletes learn this. My track coach asked, "How many of you guys have to pee just before you run?" Cautiously, hands went up. "Good! That means you're ready." Musicians learn it, actors, dancers. Therapists should, too. Now if I have not felt that welcome twinge in the belly before sticking my neck out, I create it. Another reflection I use in therapy that did not come to mind with Amanda:

> *I pace back and forth just before a speech to colleagues at Northwestern University Medical School, the first time in memory a faculty member is the Distinguished Lecturer in Psychiatry. (Out-of-towners are More Distinguished.) At Northwestern less than a year, I'm overly anxious to do well. Feeling as though I might burst, I ask John Schwartzman, Institute staff member, if anything in the anthropology literature might help. Yes. Parachute jumpers fall into two groups: Those whose hearts pound and hands sweat before jumping, and those without prejump symptoms. Injuries occur in the second group who panic during the*

jump. *The first group calms down as soon as they jump and have no injuries. Just as I calm down with no injuries after starting the speech. So it was easy to tell Amanda to welcome her anxiety. The sky diver story is another I tell patients and students. Amanda got away too soon.*

Refining a Vision

Time is well spent in the first interview creating a vision that satisfies all. We don't realize that when commitment is to problems, "Then what?" is likely to bring more problems. Solution of one leads to new problems in need of solution. The same is true of "solution-oriented" therapy, which is essentially problem based. But when commitment is to vision, vision is what we get in spite of, and sometimes because of, problems. As the vision becomes clear, the associations that come to therapist and patient provide possible guidelines for action.

You must be comfortable with the vision and willing to be a party to its accomplishment. If the vision is illegal, or unethical, or possibly not in a person's best interest, objection should be raised at once. Going along without comment would itself be unethical. If you think the vision is impossible or undesirable, say so. To string along with such a vision, hoping that during therapy the patient will catch on, is a common subterfuge I don't recommend. I do accept a patient's vision that is not my vision.

A young adult wants to come to terms with being gay and come out to his family and friends. That is his vision. He doesn't know how to go about it, but is committed to the idea of "coming to terms with," whatever that means. My vision is to help him reach his, and to deal with the consequences. I do not have to be homosexual to do that; he knows there is support from the gay community. From me he needs a neutral, open-to-possibility stance and comfort with my heterosexuality and his homosexuality. No doubt the vision of some of his family and friends will be for him to become heterosexual. In planning his strategy, those visions also have to be taken into account.

Couples may present a version of this: "I want a happier marriage." An okay start for creating a vision—abstract, worthwhile—but not enough. I don't accept this vision without knowing what it means. When the camouflage is swept away, commitment usually is conditional: I can reach my vision if only he would be more loving . . . if only her mother would leave us alone . . . If only my husband would get on his feet financially, "Vision language" conceals problem-oriented thinking based on "if-onlies." A problem (I don't like the way my partner is) is disguised as a vision (I want a better marriage). The problem belongs to someone else. It depends on another person, on circumstances that cannot be reliably controlled. This so-called vision has no power.

And the one who wants to change another does not realize this is impossible. When the complainer finally realizes that the task of changing another by demands is impossible unless the other is willing to change, the demands usually stop, at least temporarily. If they don't stop, the marriage is doomed. Self cannot force another to change to be the way self wants, unless other is willing. Change comes when the other sees that it is in his or her best interest to change—and changes. Often, when the defendant *does* change, the blamer still isn't satisfied. Projection is at work.

I begin at once to challenge the likelihood of getting another to change, if the other is not willing. The complainer's response provides an early hint, a rough prognosis, of how long it will take to get him or her to accept that futility. If the person gets the point, we are off and running. If we have to go over it with little self-awareness, insight-oriented therapy will be problematic. A quick strategic fix may be effective and the better part of valor.

At this stage, too confronting an attitude risks never seeing the couple again. But accepting a vision to change another is trying the impossible. So the idea has to be presented in a way the complainer sees as valid. Both must get beyond complaints about the other. (The defendant always has them, but may harbor blame silently and indirectly.) Both need to recognize their projections, a process that takes patiently reworking many interactions. Eventually, projections by both must be given up, if they are to reach a healthy mutuality.

Key questions are: What if he is never loving in the way you want him to be? What if your mother-in-law doesn't leave you alone? What if this recession never lifts? Each "if only" must be ruthlessly shown to be what it is: a copout, a no-win strategy.

The only vision worth commitment is *unconditional*: I want a fulfilling life *no matter what*, whether or not others change, whether or not circumstances improve, whether or not problems are solved. Robert Louis Stevenson had it right: "Life is not a matter of holding good cards, but of playing a poor hand well." Even this commitment is not enough when it comes to marriage, which requires *both* to make an unconditional commitment. It takes two to make a marriage work, only one for a divorce. Without a willing, committed partner, a fulfilling marriage is unattainable. And, of course, life without marriage can be fulfilling.

Some patients deliberately conceal their goals. Conscious concealment is hard to recognize. A variety of behavior experts, including therapists, were unable to tell consistently when subjects were lying. Only Secret Service agents, accustomed to dealing with phonies, could spot the liars. Therapists are notoriously gullible when they should be suspicious, skeptical when they should be accepting.

> *Jan and I worked with a conflictual couple once a week for a year. They reached a mutual decision to divorce. In many ways, both the therapy and the divorce were successful. When they returned posttermination questionnaires, Marvin left his blank and wrote across the top, "I never was in therapy. I brought my wife in for therapy so she could get strong enough for me to divorce her." We had suspected this motive and had suggested it, but he never owned up. Only from the safety of a completed divorce and a new marriage for each could he finally acknowledge his true, concealed motivation.*

Attitude and Strategy

Once I grasped the power of vision, I changed how I think about and do therapy. As I changed and had more success, conviction solidified—circular amplification of concept and practice augmenting each other. I start at the beginning of the first interview. After everyone has taken a seat—in itself worthy of study because this demonstration of family dynamics suggests therapeutic possibilities—I say in a trance-inducing monotone something like this.

> *"Meeting today is special, an opportunity to make good things happen. You each have hopes. I'd like you to quiet yourselves . . . let go of the turmoil of getting here . . . look inward . . . close your eyes, if that will help . . . focus on what you want to accomplish*

for yourself. What's the best thing that could happen as a result of coming here? Suppose you could get exactly what you want by the end of this session, something that would move you toward your goals in life. What would that be? Don't worry if it sounds crazy or impossible, just say the most important thing you want."

There is a moment of thoughtful silence. I wait. It took months to be comfortable with this silence. Meeting strangers makes me anxious to get on with it, and I used to talk to fill the gap. To talk now interferes with the thoughtful visions I am requesting. (I use a similar opening for group therapy, for supervision, and for all small classes.) Eventually, someone breaks the silence, most often the family spokesperson.

I am asking each to construct and focus on what might be a vision to guide our work. I am defining this time and space as important, *sacred* time and space. I want each to commit to a self-constructed vision of how things could be better for self. This goal usually brings forth more than one vision. How compatible these are is explored. Family therapy can succeed even when family members have apparently conflicting visions. The therapeutic process, whether one session or hundreds, will be tuned toward each reaching his or her vision. I avoid, if at all possible, getting into an either–or battle. Both–and is our goal.

Training in hypnotic techniques is useful for all therapists, including those who do not do formal hypnosis. Even without training, the quiet, enclosed space; low-key decor; comfortable chairs; and smoke-free air at the right temperature make this a sacred place for reflection. A calm, soothing, slightly boring voice and confidence to "make good things happen" build on their magical expectations, hopes, fears, and the placebo effects.

In a decade of starting this way, every new patient and family has cooperated by quieting down, relaxing, and reflecting—even the noisy foot-draggers and the eager beavers who can hardly wait to plunge in. Later, when they are again anxious, I remind them of this time and teach relaxation and simple meditation.

"Focus on what you want to accomplish for yourself" announces a theme for all our work. When they want someone else to change, I gently and firmly bring them back to how they could benefit themselves. If unwilling to do so, we begin work on dependency, control, vulnerability, and helplessness. I seek change that benefits all.

Change in presenting myself brings home the power of wording and phrasing to affect what follows. Many therapists, especially beginners, do not appreciate the power and choice they have at the beginning of the first interview. Once set on a wrong path, it will be hard to change, just as a wrong first bid in contract bridge is hard to correct. Here are openers I no longer use.

"How can I help?" I used this in medicine. It was appropriate and defined me as someone who helps, which I tried hard to do. But it didn't work in therapy. When the new relationship is defined as me helping them, and that mode continues, it promotes crippling dependency, failure to use inner resources, and perpetuation of the one-up-therapist/one-down-patient stereotype.

It's a fine art for physicians, therapists, teachers, and parents to support dependency early, then gradually, as a person recovers, learns, and grows, to encourage independence. All too often, I did not make that shift soon enough. I still hear of very long (20+ years) analyses. And pushing for independence before the person is ready reveals practitioners' insufficient empathy, impatience, and lack of support.

Fine-tuning dependency is needed in psychotherapy. When we ask why we became therapists, peeling off layers of rationalization, we find healthy self-interest and dependency. I still remember being shocked when I heard someone say that physicians are as dependent on patients as the converse. Conviction came when I became anxious if my practice fell off or during vacation. These two circumstances give us a glimpse into our unmet, dependency needs.

"Tell me about your problem." This opening statement will be followed by more problems with solutions that become problems. It is amazing how often people present an ordinary aspect of their life as though it is a problem, guessing—usually accurately—the therapist is vitally interested in problems.

Problems are obstacles to vision. If working on a problem is a declaration of what is wanted and its solution is defined as what is needed, the vision never comes into view. Like Tim and this 12 lawyers. Therapists who are content to address the presenting difficulty and end as soon as it appears solved, do not have the perspective to see emerging "problems." They sell themselves and their patients short.

If Marvin's secret goal of divorce had been made explicit, therapy could have been shorter and as effective. Misreading his wife as too fragile to survive a divorce without a year of therapy could have been challenged. She would have realized what she was up against, instead of trying in vain to make an unworkable marriage work. As it turned out, she wended herself and her children through a divorce and re-marriage quite well. This therapy occurred before we realized the importance of defining a vision. Today I would press harder for an honest vision from Marvin. And he might have faced up to his pro-jections. (But probably not!)

"What brings you here?" Or *"Tell me about your family."* These and similar apparently innocuous openers put emphasis in the wrong place. They announce that history is our greatest interest, and invite unleashing complaints about problems. While history plays a vital role in my therapy, I do not bog down in it. History in psychotherapy gains its relevance from the influence it has on the present, and on preven-tion. It is secondary to dealing with the here and now. Couples are adept at recounting the terrible things the partner has done, going back to before the first meeting. I may explore history in detail—we ignore it at our peril—but only to serve the vision we have agreed upon. Vision first, then history.

Focus on vision is valuable in consulting with therapists who are stuck. Typically, they are caught in a fruitless round of attempts at problem solving that prevents identification of a vision. To pause, to focus on what is really wanted in the long run, while anxiety provok-ing, is also refreshing and clarifying. The most important cards are on the table, revealing the defensive stories we may have bought into.

When we are stuck, we are usually telling ourself a story, an excuse, a life-inhibiting falsity that cuts down on possibility. Internally, two or more strong characters are in a standoff. Each brings conflicting and *true* stories from the past that are stubbornly defended but outdated. The deadlock drains energy and paralyzes action.

Occasionally during ongoing therapy, and during supervision, I re-fer to the original visions, checking to make sure they are still valid. As vision makers mature, visions change. When they are no longer held with conviction, it is time to reassess, no matter what the noisy distraction of current problems and circumstances may be. Besides, an unspoken change in vision may be responsible for an impasse.

When interviewing two or more people, a conflict between visions is unmistakable, even though they agree on many problems to be solved.

> Ralph phones for an appointment for himself and his wife. They are seeing individual therapists, but their marriage has not im-proved. (I hear this all the time.) Communication is poor, espe-cially about their seven-year-old son. (I hear this all the time.) I

start the first session with my monotonous monologue. Ralph has three goals: create a compatible work group, finish a doctorate, improve and stay in the marriage. He cares about Betty, still has a spark for her.

Betty says she wants to understand their relationship and improve communication. Their visions sound similar. But "understanding the relationship" and "improving communication" are only means to an end, not acceptable visions—passive, little action. I gently push for what she wants from understanding their relationship and communicating better. After much hesitation, she bursts out for the first time that she is not committed to Ralph, never has been in nine years of marriage, and never felt passion for him.

Ralph is thunderstruck and demands an explanation. She says before they married they had a plan to get Ph.D.s together, but she found out he didn't even have a college degree. The therapy group in which both worked pressured them to get married, and she obliged. She pretended to be in love and passionate until the last two years when she has been more open, but vague, about dissatisfaction. We finally pin down her vision: Get out of the marriage and make a new life. In the next few sessions, we test the possibility of living with their clashing visions, but they are unbending and their visions incompatible. They separate and divorce with only minor turmoil, cooperating well in coparenting their son.

Had Ralph and Betty come a few years earlier, I would have accepted their shared goals of improving communication and understanding their relationship. Isn't that what couples therapists do? I might have been preoccupied with helping them talk more congruently, strategizing more amiably about their son, and resolving sexual incompatibilities. These "problems," the bread-and-butter of many marital therapists, would frustrate all three of us. We would have put off the day when we finally realized the marriage—as well as problem-oriented therapy—was unworkable from the start.

Several years after this eight-session therapy, Betty, who insisted on divorce, is relieved to get on with her life in an honest way. Ralph, who did *not* want the divorce, is recovering from hurt, putting his life together, and recognizing his part in the marriage and its ending. Clarifying visions was the turning point for both.

Reflections

- Review several completed cases and identify belief changes. Were they a by-product of therapy, or was work done directly on changing? Were there ways these changes could come about more quickly? If so, see if something similar can be done with a new case. If there are no changes in beliefs, how come? Will improvement last?

- How successful are you at bringing out the vision of each patient? How do you screen proposed visions to avoid dead ends, false leads, problems disguised as visions—*pseudo*-visions?

- With someone in your practice, find a way to convert a presented problem into a way to advance on the path to that person's vision.

- What is your vision for yourself—as a therapist—as a person—with your family—with your friends?

- Study the first few minutes of several sessions. What are your typical openers? What effect do your comments have on the rest of the session? The rest of the therapy? Are there changes to make?

- What is your reaction to my opening monologue? Would you try it a few times and see what happens? (Legitimate use of "try"!) Your experience will be more convincing than anything you read. You may come up with another way that is more effective for you. Remember Buddha's praise of doubt. Just let the idea of eliciting a vision guide your beginning.

Epilogue

Becoming a more effective and creative therapist is a lifetime journey. Whether you are a practitioner, a student, or just dreaming about it, you are already on your way.

Therapy is the outcome of an intricate concatenation of factors, many intangible, a mystery. The one thing we can be certain of is the importance of the inner world of the therapist. Maturing as a person both inside and outside the consultation room, ultimately you will find that what you have to offer is not a technique, not a theory, but who you are.

Therapy is only a brief interlude in the span of an entire life, but if it is good therapy, it stays with you and enhances you forever. In the same way, I hope that the brief time you spend reading this book will serve as inspiration and motivation to move you ahead on your journey. May you never stop learning and growing.

References

1. Zehme, B. (1997). *The way you wear your hat: Frank Sinatra and the lost art of living.* New York: HarperCollins.
2. Emerson, R. W. (1929). *The complete writings of Ralph Waldo Emerson,* New York: Wise.
3. Jackson, P. (1995). *Sacred hoops: Spiritual lessons of a hardwood warrior.* Westport, CT: Hyperion Press.
4. Montaigne, M. de (1949). *Montaigne: Selected essays, book II.* New York: Modern Library.
5. Saddhatissa, H. (1997). Buddha, Gautama, The Kalamas Sutra. In *Buddhist ethics.* Boston: Wisdom Publications.
6. Cleary, T. (1995). *The Dhammapada: Sayings of Buddha.* New York: Bantam Books.
7. Thich Nhat Hanh (1991). *Peace is every step.* New York: Bantam Books.
8. Einstein, A. (1982). *Ideas and opinions.* New York: Crown.
9. cummings, e. e. (1953). *Six nonlectures.* Cambridge, MA: Harvard University Press.
10. Zinsser, W. (1990). *On writing well: An informal guide to writing nonfiction* (4th ed.). New York: Harper & Row.
11. Whitehead, A. N. (1967). *Dialogues (of Alfred North Whitehead): Recorded by Lucien Price.* See *Adventures of ideas.* New York: Free Press.

12. Fox, M. (1980). *Breakthrough: Meister Eckhart's creation, spirituality in new translation.* New York: Doubleday.
13. May, R. (1995). *The courage to create.* New York: Norton.
14. Kramer, C. H. (1968). *Psychoanalytically oriented family therapy: Ten year evolution in a private child psychiatry practice,* Kramer Foundation (may be obtained from the author: chuckramer@aol.com).
15. Suzuki, S. (1984). *Zen mind, beginner's mind.* New York: Weatherhill.
16. Michalko, M. (1998). The art of genius: Eight ways to think like Einstein. *Utne reader,* July–August.
17. Lao-tzu (1988). *Tao De Ching.* Translation by Stephen Mitchell. New York: Harper.
18. Kramer, C. H. (1980). *Becoming a family therapist: Developing an integrated approach to working with families.* New York: Human Sciences Press.
19. Maslow, A. (1968). *Toward a psychology of being.* (2nd ed.). New York: Van Nostrand Reinhold.
20. *The I Ching* (1985). Wilhelm/Baynes edition, Bollingen Series XIX, Princeton, NJ: Princeton University Press.
21. Watanabe-Hammond, S. (1988). Blueprints from the past: A character work perspective on siblings and personality formation. In *Siblings in therapy.* New York: Norton.
22. Watanabe-Hammond, S. (1987). The many faces of Paul and Dora. *The Family Therapy Networker,* January–February.
23. Watanabe-Hammond, S. (1986). Cast of character work: Systemically exploring the naturally organized personality. *Contemporary Family Therapy,* Spring.
24. Ornstein, R. (1986). *Multimind: A new way of looking at human behavior.* Boston: Houghton Miflin.
25. Berlin, I. (1978). The hedgehog and the fox. In *Russian thinkers.* New York: Viking.
26. Goulding, M., & Goulding, R. (1979). *Changing lives through redecision therapy.* New York: Brunner/Mazel.
27. Kadis, L. B. (Ed.) (1985). *Redecision therapy: Expanded horizons.* Western Institute for Group and Family Therapy.
28. Berne, E. (1964). *Games people play.* New York: Grove Press.
29. Joy, B. (1979). *Joy's way: A map for the transformational journey.* New York: Tarcher.
30. Berne, E. (1964). Consultation room games. In *Games people play.* New York: Grove Press.
31. Feldman, L. (1992). *Integrating individual and family therapy,* New York: Brunner/Mazel.

32. Wachtel & Wachtel (1986). *Family dynamics in individual therapy*. New York: Guilford.

33. Van Loon, H. W., (1925). *Tolerance*. Boni Liveright.

34. Peck, S. (1993). *Further along the road less traveled: The unending journey toward spiritual growth*. New York: Simon & Schuster.

35. Watts, A. (1975). *Tao: The watercourse way*. New York: Pantheon Books.

36. Scherman, T. (1996). The music of democracy: Wynton Marsalis puts jazz in its place. *Utne Reader*, March–April.

37. Lindamood, K. C. (1996). Second silence in the city. *Cresset*, Valparaiso University, February.

38. Ring, K. (1985). *Heading toward omega: In search of the meaning of the near-death experience*. New York: Morrow.

39. Tillich, P. *The courage to be*. New Haven CT: Yale University Press.

40. Rotheburg, A. & Hausman C. (Eds) (1976). *The creativity question*. Durham, NC: Duke University Press.

41. De Bono, E. (1992). *Serious creativity: Using the power of lateral thinking to create new ideas*. New York: Harper Business.

42. Ornstein, R. (1997). *The right mind: Making sense of the hemispheres*, New York: Harcourt Brace.

43. Freud, S. (1966). *The psychopathology of everyday life, Standard Edition*. London: Hogarth Press.

44. Davis, M. (1987). To share or not to share. In W. Dryden (Ed.), *Therapeutic dilemmas*. Bristol, PA: Hemisphere.

45. Pennebaker, J. (1998). *Opening up: The healing power of expressing emotions*. New York: Guilford.

46. Psychoneuroimmunology: Interactions between central nervous system and immune system (1987). *Journal of Neuroscience Research*, *18*, 1–9.

47. Vorse, M. H. (1995). *Autobiography of an elderly woman*. Wainscott, NY: Pushcart Press.

48. Schulz, M. L. (1998). *Awakening intuition: Using your mind–body network for insight and healing*. New York: Crown.

49. Goldberg, P. (1987). *The intuitive eye*. New York: Tarcher.

50. Peat, D. (1987). *Synchronicity: The bridge between mind and matter*. New York: Bantam Books.

51. Progoff, I. (1985). *The dynamics of hope*. New York: Dialogue House. Library.

52. Joy, B. (1990). *Avalanche: Heretical reflections on the dark and the light*. New York: Ballantine.

53. Kramer, J. R. (1985). *Family interfaces: Transgenerational patterns*. New York: Brunner/Mazel.

54. Bowen, M. (1978). *Family therapy in clinical practice.* Northvale, NJ: Jason Aronson.

55. Bly, R. (1996). *The sibling society: The culture of half-adults.* Reading, MA: Addison-Wesley.

56. Bridges, W. (1980). *Transitions: Making sense of life's changes.* Reading, MA: Addison-Wesley.

57. Ornish, D. (1998). *Love and survival: The scientific basis for the healing power of intimacy.* New York: HarperCollins.

58. De Mello, A. (1984). *The song of the bird.* New York: Doubleday.

59. Pearsall, P. (1998). *The heart's code: Tapping the wisdom and power of our heart energy.* New York: Broadway Books.

60. Grof, S. (1985). *Beyond the brain: Birth, death, and transcendence in psychotherapy.* State University of New York Press.

61. *The Second Letter of Paul to Timothy,* 4:7.

62. Alexander, F. & French, T. M. (1946). *Psychoanalytic therapy: Principles and application.* New York: Ronald Press.

63. Jourard, S. M. (1971). *The transparent self.* New York: Van Nostrand.

64. Chelune, G., et al. (Eds.) (1979). *Self-disclosure: Origins, patterns, and implications of openness in interpersonal relationships.* San Francisco: Jossey-Bass.

65. Kardener, S., Fuller, M., & Mensh, I. (1973). A survey of physician's attitudes and practices regarding erotic and nonerotic contact with patients. *American Journal of Psychiatry, 130,* 1077–1081.

66. Schumacher, E, F. (1973). *Small is beautiful.* New York: Harper.

67. Brunton, P. (1984) *The spiritual crisis of man.* York Beach, ME: Weiser.

68. Schwartz & Silva (1990). *Illness of the analyst.* New York: International Universities Press.

69. Paul, N., & Paul, B. (1975). *A marital puzzle: Transgenerational analysis in marriage counseling.* New York: Norton.

70. Osler, W. (1932). *Aequanimitas: With other addresses to medical students, nurses, and practitioners of medicine.* New York: McGraw-Hill.

71. Freud, S. (1966). *Recommendations to physicians practicing psychoanalysis. Standard Edition,* vol. XII. London: Hogarth.

72. Drucker, P. (1985). *Innovation and entrepreneurship: Practices and principles.* New York: Harper Business.

73. Liebowitz, B. (1970). Patriarchal, egalitarian, maternal—the best style combines all three. *Modern Nursing Home,* January.

74. Jones, M. (1953). *The therapeutic community.* New York: Basic Books.

75. James, W. (1985). *The varieties of religious experience.* Cambridge, MA: Harvard University Press.

76. Mann, T. (1948). *The permanent Goethe.* New York: Dial Press.

77. Goldberg, N. (1990). *Wild mind: Living the writer's life*. New York: Bantam Books.
78. Shakespeare, W. *Hamlet*, II, ii.
79. Sheldrake, R. (1988). *The presence of the past*. New York: Times Books.

Suggested Readings

Introduction and Part I

Aponte, H. L. (1994). *Bread and spirit*. New York: Norton. The foremost exponent of the mastery of both technical and personal aspects of therapy describes his training program, with verbatim examples.

Baldwin, M. & Satir V. (Eds.) (1987, rev. 1999). *The use of self in therapy*. New York: Haworth. Valuable collection of articles that emphasize the importance of the person of therapists in training.

Csikszentmihalyi, M. (1993). *The evolving self: A psychology for the third millennium*. New York: HarperCollins. Understanding evolution creates the possibility of transforming life into a unified flow experience by acquiring many abilities so that they harmonize and enhance each other.

Epstein, M. (1998). *Going to pieces without falling apart: Lessons from meditation and psychotherapy*. New York: Broadway Books. American psychiatrist calls Buddhism the most psychological of the world's religions and most spiritual of the world's psychologies.

Goldberg, C. (1986). *On being a psychotherapist.* New York: Gardner Press. A fine encyclopedic book by a seasoned therapist on many aspects of the therapist's journey.

Gray, J. D. (1987). *The personal life of the psychotherapist,* New York: Wiley. A compelling guide to the career of psychotherapy. Good sections on the therapist's family and on impairment of therapists.

Greben, S. (1984). *Love's labor.* New York: New American Library. Humanistic psychoanalyst describes the importance of the therapist's personal qualities, such as compassion and presence in the therapy relationship.

Kaslow, F. (Ed.) (1987). *The family life of psychotherapists.* New York: Haworth Press. Useful collection written by therapists, for therapists, about therapists' lives.

Kottler, J. (1986). *On being a therapist.* San Francisco: Jossey-Bass. Experienced therapist explores the risks, challenges, headaches, and satisfactions, emphasizing the reciprocal process by which patient and therapist change and grow.

Part II

Berne, E. (1964). *Games people play.* New York: Grove Press. The psychiatrist founder of Transactional Analysis is still relevant for therapists who want to understand and change consultation room games.

Bugental, J. F. T. (1987). *The art of the psychotherapist.* New York: Norton. An experienced and talented therapist spells out his humanistic and existential approach to empathy, subjectivity, self-disclosure, and more.

Carlson, R. & Shield, B. (Eds.) (1989). *Healers on healing.* New York: Tarcher. Some of the world's leading healers share their personal and professional experience to reveal the underlying principles of healing.

Ferrucci, P. (1982). *What we may be.* New York: Tarcher. In Chapter 4, the main exponent of psychosynthesis provides a useful approach to understanding and working with the subpersonalities who make up the whole person.

Peck, M. S. (1993). *Further along the road less traveled: The unending journey toward spiritual growth*. New York: Simon & Schuster. The most widely read psychiatrist addresses urgent questions of the stages of personal and spiritual growth, including blame and forgiveness, meaning of death, self-love and self-esteem, and sexuality.

Satir, V. (1978). *Your many faces*. Berkeley, CA: Celestial Arts. Pioneer of family therapy demonstrates the exciting possibilities created by recognizing, accepting, and constructively managing our various internal selves.

Schwartz, R. (1995). *Internal family systems therapy*. New York: Guilford. Applies the systems concept to the inner world, with guidelines for helping people bring balance and harmony to their subpersonalities.

Stone, H., & Winkelman, S. (1959). *Embracing our selves: The voice dialogue manual*. New York: New World Library. Complete description of working with the internal family using down-to-earth examples.

Watanabe-Hammond, S. (1986). Cast of character work: Systematically exploring the naturally organized personality. *Contemporary Family Therapy*, Spring. The basis for Chapter 6 in which the present author describes his internal personality.

Part III

Benson, H. (1996). *Timeless healing: The power and biology of belief*. New York: Scribner's. Latest in a series of books by the physician who researched the mind/body results of *The Meditation Response*.

Garfield, P. (1974). *Creative dreaming*. New York: Ballantine. Complete manual with guidance and exercises for developing creative use of dreams.

Harman, W., & Reingold, H. (1984). *Higher creativity: Liberating the unconscious for breakthrough insights*. New York: Tarcher. Comprehensive account of the creative power of the unconscious, with validated procedures for reprogramming it to create insightful breakthroughs.

Joy, B. (1979). *Joy's way: A map for the transformational journey*. New York: Tarcher. Introduction to the potential for healing with body energy. Led to further experiences with Dr. Joy that have profoundly changed my life.

Leonard, G., & Murphy, M. (1995). *The life we are given*. New York: Tarcher. Describes an effective program for transforming body, mind, heart, and spirit through balanced and comprehensive long-term practice.

LeShan, L. (1974). *How to meditate*. New York: Bantam Books. Not only covers the essentials, but describes 11 different methods from which to choose and suggestions for the integration of meditation with psychotherapy.

Maslow, A. H. (1968). *Toward a psychology of being*. New York: Van Nostrand Reinhold. The pioneer of humanistic dedication to personality growth, motivation, and creativity still has essential wisdom for the therapist of today.

Ornish, D. (1998). *Love and survival: The scientific basis for the healing power of intimacy*. New York: HarperCollins. The physician who proved heart disease can be reversed without surgery says love and intimacy are essential for physical, mental, and spiritual growth. Contrariwise, loneliness, isolation, and withholding self predispose to disease.

Ornstein, R. (1997). *The right mind: Making sense of the hemispheres*. New York: Harcourt Brace. Brings up to date the integration of the right and left hemispheres so necessary for creativity.

Thich Nhat Hanh (1991). *Peace is every step*. New York: Bantam Books. Compilation of his best guides to a more serene life by this gentle and wise Vietnamese Buddhist monk.

Part IV

Bridges, W. (1980). *Transitions: Making sense of life's changes*. Reading, MA: Addison-Wesley. Useful for anyone, no matter how sophisticated.

Dossey, L. (1996). *Prayer is good medicine: How to reap healing benefits of prayer*. San Francisco: Harper. How to use the remarkable results of healing at a distance is described by a physician who has opened the field of medicine to spiritual and religious insights.

Dryden, W. (Ed.) (1987). *Therapists' dilemmas*. Bristol, PA: Hemisphere. A collection of helpful clinical essays on the dilemmas of practice by British therapists, including giving love to clients, sex therapy, self-disclosure, boundaries, transference, morality, and more.

Freud, S. (1992/1966). Recommendations to physicians practicing psychoanalysis. *Standard Edition*, Vol. XII. London: Hogarth Press. Set a standard to this day recognized for professionalized withholding of self.

Jourard, S. M. (1971). *The transparent self.* New York: Van Nostrand, Every therapist who aspires to authenticity should read and reread this book, especially Part 5, "The Disclosing Therapist."

Kabat-Zinn, J. (1990). *Full catastrophe living: Using the wisdom of your body and mind to face stress, pain, and illness.* New York: Dell. Describes his structured program using meditation, visualization, and changes in lifestyle to accomplish healing and health.

Ornstein, R. & Sobel, D. (1989). *Healthy pleasures.* Reading, MA: Addison-Wesley. Discover the proven medical benefits of pleasure and live a longer, healthier life.

Paul, N. & Paul, B. (1975). *A marital puzzle: Transgenerational analysis in marriage counseling.* New York: Norton. We need more such books with verbatim accounts of an entire therapy by innovative and courageous therapists describing their personal reactions.

Pearsall, P. (1998). *The heart's code: Tapping the wisdom and power of our heart energy.* New York: Broadway Books. Most recent in a series of profound books on the power of love and relationships to heal serious diseases, by a psychologist who healed himself using these principles.

Schwartz & Silva (Eds.) (1990). *Illness in the analyst.* New York: International Universities Press. The sad results of Freud's "Recommendations."

Part V

Bennis, W., & Nanus, B. (1986). *Leaders: The strategies for taking charge.* New York: HarperCollins. Based on an analysis of 90 top leaders in many different fields, this classic is a fascinating and practical guide to becoming an effective *leader,* not just a manager.

Drucker, P. (1985). *Innovation and entrepreneurship: Practice and principles.* New York: Harper Business. The guru of organizational development talks about the essential role of leadership.

Fritz, R. (1989). *The path of least resistance: Learning to become the creative force in your own life.* New York: Ballantine. Offers a path to discovering and enhancing your creativity and leadership.

Jones, M. (1953). *The therapeutic community.* New York: Basic Books. Multiple leadership is a core concept in this classic by the psychiatrist who first established a therapeutic community.

Index